THE ULTIMATE HR GENERALIST HANDBOOK: 2024

A PRACTICAL WORKBOOK AND GUIDE FOR HUMAN RESOURCE MANAGEMENT PROFESSIONALS WITH 50 HRM INTERVIEW Q&A'S

MEGHANA B.N

Made with ♥ on the Notion Press Platform
www.notionpress.com

Contents

Foreword ix

Hire To Retire Or Employee Life Cycle

1. Employee Life Cycle Management Or Hire To Retire Process: Introduction 3
2. Employee Life Cycle: Introduction 5
3. HR Metrics Or HR KPI's : Introduction 8
4. Branding Or Attraction: Stage 1 In ELC 11
5. Employee Value Proposition(EVP) For Branding / Attraction Stage 13
6. Tools, Technologies & HR Metrics For Branding Stage 20
7. Recruitment: Stage 2 In ELC 23
8. Tools, Technologies & HR Metrics For Recruitment Stage 25
9. Onboarding: Stage 3 In ELC 28
10. Tools, Technologies & HR Metrics Of Onboarding Stage 36
11. Development: Stage 4 In ELC 38
12. Tools, Technologies & HR Metrics For Development Stage 41
13. Retention: Stage 5 In ELC 43
14. Separation: Stage 6 In ELC 45
15. Tools, Technologies & HR Metrics For Separation Stage 47
16. Case Study: ELC 49
17. HR Templates / Formats: Pre Joining To Onboarding 51

Modern HR, Technology And Recruitment Process

18. The HR Landscape: Evolution And Current Trends 65
19. Modern HR: Beyond Administration 68
20. Top 10 Trends In HR Management: 2024 71
21. Technology In HR: A Digital Revolution 74
22. Top 10 Technological Tools For HRM 77
23. The Globalization Of Human Resources 80

Contents

24. Recruitment & Selection: The Art Of Finding Talent 83

25. Crafting The Perfect Job Description: Incorporating Diversity, Equity & Inclusion In Your JD 87

26. Job Description Or JD : Sample Format 90

27. Sourcing Strategies: Where Talent Hides 92

28. X-Ray Search And Boolean Search In Candidate Sourcing 96

29. The Science Of Screening 104

30. Mastering The Art Of Interviewing: A Guide For HR Professionals In The Recruitment Process. 108

31. Candidate Evaluation Form: Sample 114

32. Case Study Exercise: Interviewing 116

HR Policies & Procedures

33. Introduction To HR Policies & HR Procedures 121

34. Types Of HR Policies 124

35. Case Study: HR Policies 128

36. HR Procedures 130

37. Case Study: HR Procedures 133

HR Manual Or Employee Handbook

38. HR Manual Or Employee Handbook 137

39. Sample HR Manual Or Employee Handbook Template 140

HR Metrics And HR Analytics

40. Introduction To HR Metrics 181

41. Key HR Metrics Or KPI's 184

42. Introduction To HR Analytics 204

43. HR Analytics Communication 207

44. Qualitative & Quantitative Data 209

45. Data Collection Methods And Tools (surveys, HRIS, Performance Management Systems) 212

Contents

46. Data Cleaning, Analysis, And Visualization Techniques 214
47. Types Of HR Analytics 216
48. Case Studies In HR Analytics 218
49. HR Analytics In Action: Example 220
50. HR Dashboards & Software Applications: Examples 222

Compensation, Benefits & Payroll Management

51. Compensation, Benefits & Reward System 231
52. Introduction To International Payroll Management 233
53. Intro To Indian Payroll Components 236
54. Compensation Structuring In India 239
55. Global Compensation Strategies 247
56. Case Study In Compensation & Payroll Management 249

HR Balanced Scorecard

57. HR Balanced Scorecard 253
58. Case Study: Balanced Scorecard 259

Performance Management System

59. Introduction To Performance Management Process 265
60. Methods In Performance Management: Traditional 268
61. Methods In Performance Management: Modern 271
62. Performance Appraisal Forms: Templates 276

Employee Experience Design (EX-Design)

63. A Guide On Employee Experience Design In HR 281
64. How Employee Experience Design Works 288
65. Candidate Experience Design: Case Study 292
66. Case Studies In Employee Experience Design 295
67. Real-Life Case Studies: Design Thinking 298

Employee Engagement

68. Introduction To Employee Engagement 303

Contents

69. HR Metrics In Engagement And Engagement Survey 308

70. Engagement Trends For 2024 312

71. How To Enhance Engagement 314

72. Employee Engagement Ideas 319

73. Case Studies: Improving Engagement 325

HRM Interview Questions & Answers: A Comprehensive Guide To Crack HRM Interviews

74. Preparing For HR Professional Interview 339

75. Recruitment: HR Manager / Generalist Interview Questions And Answers Guide: 342

76. Employee Engagement: HR Manager / Generalist Interview Questions & Answers 346

77. HR Administration: HR Manager / Generalist Interview Questions & Answers 349

78. Compensation, Benefits & Payroll (Indian): HR Manager / Generalist Interview Questions & Answers 351

79. Compensation, Benefits & Payroll (International): HR Manager / Generalist Interview Questions & Answers 354

80. Training & Development: HR Manager / Generalist Interview Questions & Answers 357

81. Performance Management System: HR Manager / Generalist Interview Questions & Answers 362

Diversity, Equity And Inclusion

82. Defining Diversity, Equity And Inclusion 369

83. Importance Of DE&I 373

84. Dimensions Of DE&I 375

85. Intersectionality At Work 377

86. Benefits Of A Diverse Workforce 381

Contents

87. Unconscious Bias: Making Fair Decisions At Work 384

88. Examples Of Unconscious Bias And How To Avoid Them 386

89. Case Study: Unconscious Bias At Work 388

90. Strategies For Mitigating Unconscious Bias 390

91. DE&I At Each Stage Of HRM 392

92. DEI: Creating Inclusive Policies And Practices 396

93. Psychological Safety & Belonging In The Workplace 398

94. Addressing DE&I Challenges & Conflicts 401

95. Handling Discrimination, Harassment, And Microaggressions 404

96. DE&I Best Practices From Corporates 407

NextGen HR Reviews 411

Key Take-Aways from Course 417

Foreword

Welcome Aboard!

Every year, lots of work conversations happen, each one a part of human resources. In this big picture, 65% of managers say they struggle with HR tasks, which are supposed to be done by experts. Why does this matter? Because a successful organization relies on its HR department, but this fact is often overlooked.

Welcome to the 'The Ultimate HR Generalist Handbook: 2024.' I am Meghana, the Founder and Head of Training at NextGen HR, an online training academy (nextgenhr.co.in). I have trained over 15,000 HR aspirants and professionals on various aspects of HR Management. I'll guide you through the complicated world of HR functions. This guide is like a map, showing you what and how things work, with real-life examples to make it all clearer.

Ever wonder how individual talents come together for corporate success? In the upcoming chapters, we'll uncover this mystery. But before we start, think about this: the next page has a secret that could change how you see HR. Will you turn the page?

In a world where 53% of employees feel disconnected at work, causing turnover, lost productivity, and a struggling company culture, a vital question arises: who fixes the discord? The underestimated answer is the HR Generalist.

This stat isn't just a number. It's a call to HR professionals who guard workplace engagement and culture. It's a reminder that the health of a company's human capital is in their hands, affecting countless individuals and businesses. HR isn't just administrative; it's the heartbeat, the architect, the guardian of its most precious asset—its people.

As we go deeper into HR, you'll see it's more complex than it seems. How do you navigate employment law, talent acquisition, benefits, and compensation while fostering diversity, equity, and inclusion? The upcoming chapters are your guide, leading you through uncharted HR territories, where every decision has a ripple effect.

Imagine holding paints in front of a canvas, with the power to create a masterpiece or chaos. The HR Generalist is the artist, shaping the organization's future with policies, conflict resolution, and programs. This book is your palette, full of knowledge, experience, and insight.

Do you feel the responsibility? The potential impact? The thrill of shaping the human side of business? Let this introduction be a bridge, taking you from what you know to what you can achieve. It's a journey of learning and transformation, for you and the organizations you guide.

With over 12 years in HR Management, I've seen the power of effective HR practices. Through NextGen HR, I've tried to capture what it means to excel in this field. In these pages, you won't find abstract theory; it's the real, vivid reality of HR work through stories and examples.

Are you ready for this discovery? To explore the hidden truths and new paths in HR? If so, get ready. Every policy, procedure, and cubicle has a story, and this book invites you to listen, learn, and lead. It's time to turn the page.

Meghana B.N
Founder & Head-Training
NextGen HR
Get in touch with me at: NextGenHR.co.in
or email me at: nextgenhr.training@gmail.com

Hire To Retire or Employee Life Cycle

CHAPTER ONE

Employee Life Cycle Management or Hire To Retire Process: Introduction

Section 1: Hire to Retire or Employee Life Cycle Management (ELC)

This section contains chapters on each stage of Employee Life Cycle, what are the Tools and Technologies you can use for each stage and the HR Metrics to use for each stage.

1. Attraction / Branding
2. Recruitment
3. Onboarding
4. Development
5. Retention
6. Separation

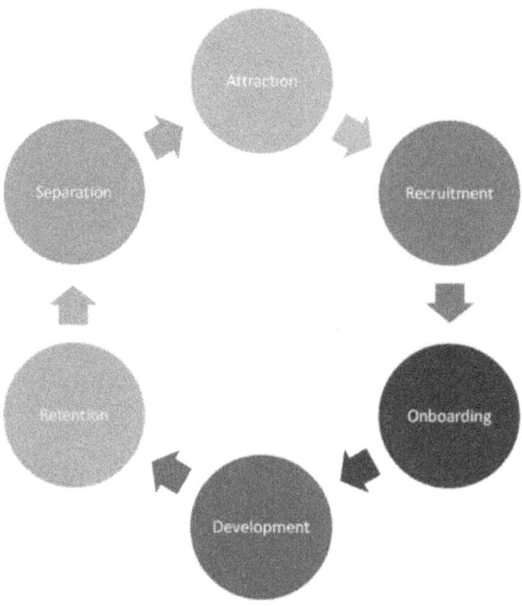

Employee Life Cycle Management

CHAPTER TWO

Employee Life Cycle: Introduction

Welcome to the chapter on **Employee Life Cycle Management.**

We will explore the fascinating topic of employee lifecycle management, which is at the forefront of HR management.

You will discover what is employee lifecycle management and why it is crucial for HR professionals to understand it.

We will delve into the various stages of employee lifecycle within an organization and explore how HR can create an optimal employee experience for each stage using the right tools and technologies.

Additionally, we will learn about measuring the effectiveness of each stage using relevant HR metrics.

So what exactly is the employee life cycle?

It's an HR model that identify the different stages an employee goes through in an organization. HR plays a vital role in optimizing employee progress and their overall experience throughout this cycle. Understanding the life cycle of employees is vital for HR professionals because employees needs and experiences change depending on the stage that they are in.

For example, during the onboarding stage, employees have different expectations, such as gettingacquainted with the company, understanding the culture, roles, responsibilities and receiving proper training.

On the other hand, employees who are in the quitting stage expect a smooth exit, clear handover and knowledge transfer.

As HR professionals, it's crucial to grasp each stage to cater to employees needs and provide a positive experience.

Now let's explore the six stages of the employee life cycle in more detail.

1. ATTRACTION: The first stage is attraction or branding, where the focus is on attracting potential employees through branding activities like advertisements, social media presence and referrals.

The more candidates applying, the better chances of attracting top talent. If you have very less number of candidates applying for a job, you don't have much chance of attracting the top talent.

2. RECRUITMENT: Next comes recruitment, where HR acquires the best available talent for the organization. This stage is all about finding the right fit.

3. ONBOARDING: Then we have onboarding where new joiners are warmly welcomed and equipped with the necessary knowledge about companies, culture processes and business operations through training and onboarding programs.

4. DEVELOPMENT: Development is the fourth stage, which emphasizes on providing opportunities for professional growth and skill development by offering development opportunities to employees.Organizations can retain their valuable employees.

5. RETENTION: Retention is the fifth stage, and it focuses on ensuring employees are satisfied and they're happy within the organization and encouraging them to stay and contribute to their best.

6. SEPARATION: Lastly, we have Separation which involves creating a positive exit experience for employees who are leaving the organization. Handling separations gracefully is essential to maintain a positive reputation of the organization throughout each cycle.

HR relies on various tools and technologies to optimize the employee experience, so it's crucial to measure the effectiveness of these stages using HR matrix. By understanding the detailed aspects of each cycle, as well as the HR tools and technologies which are utilized in each stage, you as an HR professional can make informed decisions and you can ensure best outcomes for both employees and your organization.

So let's dive into the details of each stage of employee lifecycle and explore how HR can enhance employee experience.

Join me in this journey as we uncover the exciting world of employee lifecycle management.

Activity for you:

Write down the list of activities involved in hire to retire process, from your own experience. Recall your current or previous employment and list the activities that were involved from HR point of view in your hire to

retire(or resign) process:

....

....

CHAPTER THREE

HR Metrics or HR KPI's : Introduction

What is a Metric?

A metric is a quantifiable measure used to track, assess, and evaluate performance, progress, or effectiveness of a particular process, activity, or system. In the context of Human Resources (HR), metrics are specific measurements used to analyze various aspects of the workforce, HR processes, and organizational performance. These metrics provide valuable insights that enable HR professionals and organizational leaders to make data-driven decisions, improve efficiency, and achieve strategic goals.

Understanding HR Metrics: Enhancing Human Resource Management

In today's competitive business landscape, organizations rely on data-driven insights to make informed decisions across all departments, and Human Resources (HR) is no exception. HR metrics, also known as HR analytics or HR Key Performance Indicators (KPIs), are quantitative measures used to assess various aspects of the workforce. These metrics provide valuable insights into employee performance, engagement, satisfaction, and other critical areas, enabling HR professionals to optimize strategies and processes for better organizational outcomes.

Usage of HR Metrics in HR Management - Some commonly used HR Metrics:

Talent Acquisition and Recruitment:

Time-to-Hire: This metric measures the time it takes to fill a vacant position from the moment it is approved to the moment a candidate accepts the offer. A shorter time-to-hire indicates an efficient recruitment process, ensuring the organization attracts top talent promptly.

Sourcing Channel Effectiveness: Assessing which recruitment channels (e.g., job boards, employee referrals, social media) yield the highest-quality candidates and the lowest cost per hire helps optimize recruitment budgets and strategies.

Employee Performance and Productivity:

Employee Turnover Rate: Calculating the percentage of employees who leave the organization within a given period helps identify trends and underlying issues affecting retention. High turnover rates may indicate dissatisfaction or problems within the workplace environment.

Absenteeism Rate: Monitoring the frequency and duration of employee absences can reveal patterns that may indicate underlying issues such as low morale, health concerns, or workload issues.

Employee Engagement and Satisfaction:

Employee Net Promoter Score (eNPS): Similar to the customer Net Promoter Score, eNPS measures the likelihood of employees recommending their organization as a place to work. High eNPS scores correlate with higher employee satisfaction and engagement levels.

Employee Satisfaction Surveys: Regular surveys measuring various aspects of job satisfaction, work-life balance, and organizational culture provide insights into employee perceptions and areas for improvement.

Training and Development:

Training ROI: Calculating the return on investment (ROI) of training programs helps assess their effectiveness in enhancing employee skills and performance. It involves comparing the cost of training to the resulting improvements in productivity, revenue, or other relevant metrics.

Skills Gap Analysis: Identifying gaps between the skills employees possess and those required for their roles enables HR to design targeted training and development initiatives to bridge these gaps and ensure a skilled workforce.

Diversity and Inclusion:

Diversity Index: This metric quantifies the diversity of the workforce based on factors such as gender, ethnicity, age, and more. Tracking diversity metrics helps organizations assess their progress toward building a more inclusive workplace culture.

Inclusion Survey Results: Surveys measuring employees' perceptions of inclusivity and belongingness within the organization provide valuable feedback for diversity and inclusion initiatives.

Conclusion:

HR metrics serve as powerful tools for HR professionals to assess, analyze, and improve various aspects of the workforce. By leveraging data-driven insights, organizations can make informed decisions, optimize HR processes, and ultimately enhance employee satisfaction, productivity, and organizational performance. However, it's essential to select metrics aligned with organizational goals and values and interpret them in context to drive meaningful change and improvement within the workforce.

In the upcoming chapters, we will be looking at some of the key HR Metrics used in relation to each stage of Employee Life Cycle Management (Hire to Retire process).

CHAPTER FOUR

Branding or Attraction: Stage 1 in ELC

Let's kick off with the first stage of the employee life cycle, known as "attraction," or more commonly, **employer branding.**

This stage is all about showcasing your organization as an amazing place to work, not just to your current employees but also to folks outside your company who could potentially join your team.

In simpler terms, the employee life cycle begins even before you've met your potential hires. Imagine it as laying the groundwork before you've even built the house!

Attraction might seem easier for big-name brands or well-known companies, but regardless of size, getting people interested in working for you is crucial. Whether it's through job postings, word of mouth, or other means, potential employees need to know about your company and what it stands for before they'll consider joining.

So, attraction is essentially about spreading the word about your company, generating interest, and encouraging people to apply for your job openings.

Now, to succeed in attracting talent, there are a few key things you need to nail down:

Firstly, your company's mission, vision, and challenges should be crystal clear, both internally among your team and externally to potential hires.

Secondly, you need fantastic people already on board and a solid presence on social media platforms.

Lastly, you've got to offer opportunities for personal growth and development to your employees.

But here's the thing: all these efforts need to be shouted from the rooftops, or at least posted on social media and other platforms, so that more and more people know what your company is all about. Otherwise, your branding efforts won't be very effective.

That's where your **Employee Value Proposition (EVP)** comes into play. Your EVP is essentially the unique package of benefits and perks that employees receive in exchange for their skills and experience.

It's not just about the salary and benefits; it's also about the career prospects, well-being programs, and the overall purpose of your organization.

In essence, your EVP is what sets you apart from other companies and makes you an attractive choice for potential hires.

Let's illustrate this with an example: Imagine you have a job offer from a lesser-known company, let's call it "New Enterprises," and another from the tech giant Google. Which one would you choose?

Chances are, you'd lean towards Google because of its strong brand reputation, awesome perks, and innovative culture that fosters employee creativity and growth.

So, as you can see, branding plays a huge role in attracting talent, and it's not just about the money. It's about creating an environment where employees feel valued, inspired, and excited to come to work every day.

Activity for you:

Take a moment to think about how you got attracted to your current employer or how you heard about your employer? (if you are working) or list the branding strategies used by some of the well-known companies:

....

....

CHAPTER FIVE

Employee Value Proposition(EVP) for Branding / Attraction Stage

What is EVP?

An employee value proposition (EVP) is a set of benefits that a company offers to employees in exchange for their skills, capabilities, and experience. EVPs can include monetary and non-monetary benefits.

In other words, An employee value proposition is the unique value you offer as an employer to your employees in return for their skills, experience, and commitment to your company.

Here are some elements of an EVP: Compensation, Work-life balance, Stability, Location, Respect.

EVP of Apple company

Here are some examples of EVPs:

- Student loan paydown program
- Gym memberships
- Inclusive culture
- Healthcare benefits
- Excellent working environment
- Unlimited vacation
- Child care support

Here are some steps you can take to create an EVP:

- Scope out what your company currently offers
- Collate feedback from employees
- Identify and define the key points to include in the EVP
- Draft your EVP
- Compare and evaluate your EVP
- Communicate your EVP via relevant channels
- Assess responses to your EVP
- Keep it current

How to craft your organization's EVP?!

Curious about crafting an **employer value proposition (EVP)** that stands out in 2024?

Securing top talent has become both crucial and challenging. McKinsey reports that 87% of companies are grappling with a skills gap or anticipate doing so soon. Furthermore, according to a survey by West Monroe Partners, C-level executives identify hiring and retention as primary threats to U.S. businesses.

In this competitive job market, it's essential to rethink how you attract and keep exceptional employees. The first step? Evaluating your employer value proposition. In this article, we'll delve into the five key pillars you should consider to distinguish your company from the competition.

1. Compensation: While compensation is undoubtedly important to candidates and employees, it's not the sole factor driving their employment decisions. Studies indicate that satisfaction among employees isn't solely determined by paychecks. In today's tight talent landscape, offering more than just competitive wages is imperative. It's about providing opportunities for career advancement and increasing earnings over time. Consider Target, for example. They raised their starting wages and even provided recognition bonuses to frontline workers during the pandemic. But they didn't stop there. Target also introduced a reskilling program, demonstrating a commitment to employee growth.

2. Total Rewards Package: There's a growing recognition of the significance of total rewards packages. As Tamla Oates-Forney, former Chief People Officer at Waste Management, puts it, "Any company can provide money—it has to be the total package." A whopping 94% of employers, according to Willis Towers Watson, see voluntary benefits as crucial components of their total rewards strategies for the next few years. But what exactly constitutes a comprehensive total rewards package?

Besides essential benefits like healthcare and paid time off, it's crucial to address the diverse needs of your workforce, such as mental health support, childcare, and educational opportunities.

For instance, Waste Management's Your Tomorrow education and upskilling benefits program offers nearly 36,000 US employees access to over 170 fully funded programs, including undergraduate and graduate degrees, short-term technology and business certificate programs, and high school completion.

Moreover, as of January 2022, the program has extended its benefits to include employees' dependents, including children and spouses.

Statistics show that employees who participate in Waste Management's education benefits program are 60% more likely to remain with the company, underscoring its value in retention.

The program's investment will pay off by reducing employee turnover and attracting top talent. Additionally, offering educational benefits for dependents can establish a natural talent pipeline for young individuals into the company.

3. Career advancement opportunities: Career advancement opportunities have become a critical consideration for today's job seekers, who seek clear pathways for growth and development.

According to insights from Harvard Business Review, workplace satisfaction is heavily influenced by the organizational culture and values, closely followed by the caliber of senior leadership and the potential for career progression within the company.

In light of the prevailing labor shortages, the demand for opportunities for advancement has become more urgent – prompting a response from employers.

For instance, recent analyses of employer job postings for roles not mandating a four-year degree reveal a significant uptick in the inclusion of the phrase "career advancement," indicating a heightened emphasis on growth prospects within organizations compared to two years ago.

Moreover, there has been a notable increase in the occurrence of the term "training" in such postings, suggesting a renewed focus on skill development and enhancement within the workforce.

As exemplified by certain companies, such as one major retailer, initiatives have been introduced to address these demands. In an impressive move, this retailer not only raised wages during the pandemic but also augmented its offerings by providing avenues for career growth.

Notably, all employees of this retailer – totaling 340,000 individuals – now have access to tuition-free education through a strategic partnership.

Experts in the field suggest that the most forward-thinking organizations are recognizing that differentiation as an employer hinges on offering not only competitive wages but also opportunities for economic mobility, reskilling, and professional advancement within the company.

4. Contribution to the World: In today's workforce, employees are increasingly seeking roles that allow them to make a meaningful impact on the world around them. This desire for purposeful work is so strong that nine out of ten individuals are willing to forgo higher salaries in exchange for more fulfilling occupations.

This sentiment is particularly pronounced among younger generations in the workforce, who place a significant emphasis on aligning their professional endeavors with their personal values. Millennials, in particular, are willing to make sacrifices to support causes they believe in, whether it's paying more for ethically sourced products, opting for sharing economies, or accepting lower salaries to work for socially responsible companies.

According to insights from Deloitte, winning over the hearts of Generation Z requires companies to showcase their commitment to being responsible global citizens. This entails more than mere rhetoric; companies must take tangible actions to address pressing societal issues such as sustainability, climate change, and hunger.

In essence, employees across all generations are increasingly prioritizing work that allows them to contribute positively to the world. For companies looking to attract and retain top talent, demonstrating a genuine commitment to social and environmental responsibility is no longer optional – it's essential.

5. Culture:

Creating a compelling employer value proposition goes beyond just attracting talent.

It's essential to recognize that any new hires you bring onboard are unlikely to stay if they don't feel welcomed and included in their work environment.

"Our EVP starts with culture," states a Chief People Officer at a major corporation. "Someone can make a lot of money, but if they're not happy with where they're working, they're not going to stick around."

Indeed, the culture of your company plays a significant role in retaining employees, with nearly a third of departures attributed to dissatisfaction with company culture.

Moreover, if diversity, equity, and inclusion (DE&I) are prioritized within your organization, your company's culture can either bolster or hinder these efforts.

Research published in Harvard Business Review suggests that companies fostering learning-oriented cultures tend to be more diverse and inclusive. By prioritizing qualities like flexibility, open-mindedness, and a spirit of exploration, companies create environments where employees from diverse backgrounds can thrive.

"I started at my current workplace as a summer job. I never anticipated it would lead to where I am today," shares an individual who has advanced to the role of General Manager. This individual is currently pursuing a BA program through their workplace's partnership with an educational institution. The flexibility offered by the online program allows them to balance work and studies at their own pace.

They firmly believe that such opportunities are only feasible due to their workplace's growth-oriented culture.

"It speaks volumes about our company that they're willing to invest in their employees because fostering a better world goes beyond just our industry. It also involves nurturing individuals, and they truly prioritize that," they affirm.

EVP Examples from Real-Life

Let us see some of the examples of employee value proposition for from well-known company.

These examples will give you a better idea on how EVP is used for branding purpose.

Apple has a tagline or EVP of "Join US Be You".

So it is saying that join us and be yourself and make a difference kind of a thing, which is great.

Deloitte has a question. "What impact will you make?"

Google is saying "how we care for Googlers" and **Sodexo** saying "looking for a diverse and rewarding career".

Now let us go through this quick activity that you will be finding out the employee value proposition of your organization or any other organization in case if you're not working, yet. So you need to find out the EVP of an industry leading company and compare it with your company.

Or if you're not working in a particular company, you can compare two different companies employee value propositions and see how they're different, which is adding more value.

And just a hint for you is that you can find the EVP statements below the job advertisements or on the portals, the career pages of the companies. Or the job descriptions. Usually it might be mentioned under why you work for a column. And few companies may not have a well-defined EVP or they might have not defined EVP at all, and they might be using their mission, vision and value statements in their advertisements.

However, you can just have a look at the overall features of the advertisment, which shows the candidates what the company has to offer apart from the compensation that they're giving. So that gives you a great idea on the EVP.

Activity for you:

List the EVP's of 3 well-known companies or your own organization (if you are working). If you were asked to re-write the EVP, what will be the EVP that you will suggest?

....

....

CHAPTER SIX

Tools, Technologies & HR Metrics for Branding Stage

Tools and Technologies for Branding Stage:

Some of the tools that can be used to make a great employee experience and create great employee engagement are

- Pathmotion
- Social Seeder
- Ontame.io
- Vercida

and you could use the common and well-known social media platforms such as Twitter, LinkedIn, Facebook, YouTube and so on, to share relevant content related to your brand and even the employer employee engagement activities and other highlights of the company, including CSR activities.

Canva, which can be used for content creation. That is basically to design your properties or any brochures or advertisements, job advertisements and so on.

Glassdoor, which can be used to review employee reviews, it does single mindedly for your employees to leave their reviews on these sites.

Of course, you should be able to get both the positive and negative ones here, but you should be aiming for more positive ones on the Glassdoor.

HR Metrics to measure and evaluate Branding Effectiveness

Let us talk about the measurement of effectiveness, how the effectiveness of the attraction or blinding stage can be measured. So which are metrics we can use?

Net Promoter Score:-

Employer net promoter score is basically a scoring system which measures how employees measure the employee satisfaction and loyalty within their organization.

It's an index or a number from -100 to 100 generally. So it is calculated by asking survey participants to rate how likely they are to recommend the company or brand to a friend or colleague. So this is your Net Promoter Scores.

How to calculate NPS?

Subtract the percentage of detractors (those who have negative opnion about employer) from the percentage of promoters (those who are positive about the employer). (The percentage of passives is not used in the Net Promoter Score formula.)

For example, if 10% of the total responses are from detractors, 20% are passives and 70% are promoters, your NPS score would be 70-10 = 60.

Social media engagement score and Brand Awareness Score.

You are going to see how engaged the employees and the potential candidates or the general public regarding your brand, how interested they are. So this can give you a good idea on how people are well aware of your brand, and you could always work on more advertising in different media to create more awareness. Employer review rankings on Glassdoor, Google and so on.

These review rankings can be used to measure how effective is your brand. So the past employees or any candidates who came for interview, they might be leaving their reviews and rankings on these portals. You can use these to gauge how you are doing and how you can do better.

How to calculate Social Media Engagement Score?

- **Engagement rate by reach (ERR): most common:-**

  This formula is the most common way to calculate engagement with social media content. ERR measures the percentage of people who chose to interact with your content after seeing it. Use the first formula for a single post, and the second one to calculate the average rate across multiple posts.

ERR = total number of engagements per post / reach per post * 100

To determine the average, add up the all the ERRs from the posts you want to average, and divide by number of posts:

Average ERR = Total ERR / Total posts

In other words: Post 1 (3.4%) + Post 2 (3.5%) / 2 = 3.45%

- **Brand Awareness: Brand Search Volume**

  A good method of evaluating the general public's awareness of a particular brand is to evaluate branded search volume, or how many people search for your company name and associated keywords.

  For example, using Ahrefs‘ (ahref.com) Keyword Explorer, we can see that the monthly estimated average search volume for "Zapier" is 83,000 and that the majority of searches are coming from users based in the United States.
- Brand Awareness: Social Share of Voice :- Calculate your social SOV using this formula: Number of mentions of your brand/total number of brand mentions (yours + your competitors') x 100.

Activity for you:

Do a quick research on Google to find NPS (Net Promoter Score) of some well-known companies and list them here. List the branding strategies used by these companies.

....

....

CHAPTER SEVEN

Recruitment: Stage 2 in ELC

Recruitment is the second stage of the employee lifecycle.

So this is the stage that is focused on bringing in talent to the company after the candidates have been attracted to your company. Your company needs to have a bright recruitment plan. You need to ask yourself, what kind of employees are you looking forward to recruit? And how you're going to recruit them, what channels you're going to use, which are the relevant channels or forums to grab their attention and get them recruited and so on.

Ultimately, recruiting should be one of the company's biggest focus because recruiting brings in more talent and employees, and you should be ideally involving your existing employees for more referrals. To get successful in the Recruitment, you need to have a diverse recruitment channel mix.

So instead of relying on only one particular employment portal or any one particular channel of recruitment, you could go for a diverse mix to get a diversity of talent and you need to be clear in your job descriptions as to what you are looking for, what is the desiredcandidate profile, and what the company offers the roles and responsibilities and so on. You need to provide a great interview experience to the candidate.

Candidate Interview Experience Case Study

For example, let's say there are two companies: company A and company B. What kind of interview experience these companies had is providing company? There is no comprehensive details on the Company A website careers page. So there is not much of the relevant details that can be grabbed from here. There are a lot of negative reviews on glassdoor's and other websites.

Job description not very clear with the details of the job. Candidates are made to wait for more than 60 minutes for the interview. No answer after the interview. Candidates need to call several times to get the answer.

Talking of Company B. All the details, all the relevant details are there on the careers page of the website of the company. Great rankings on glassdoor's. Interview wait time, less than 10 minutes. Recruiters usually call back the candidate on either selection or rejection status.

So it is always good to give a callback whether that candidate is selected or rejected and not to make them wait or keep guessing for a long time. So obviously with these two comparisons, which company you would go for or which company you would recommend?

Obviously Company B, so company B is giving a great interview experience to the candidate. So the candidate is more likely to recommend this company to his friends and also leave positive reviews on the social media and other forums.

Activity for you:

List 5 Do's and Dont's of a great candidate interview experience:-

....

....

CHAPTER EIGHT

Tools, Technologies & HR Metrics for Recruitment Stage

What are some of the recruitment tools and technologies that can be used for a smooth employee engagement and employee experience?

Talent acquisition softwares and portals such as

- Indeed
- Zoho Recruiter
- Sum Total
- Greytip
- Ramco
- Ideal, etc. to help the process.

So these are all the different portals that can be used to get the candidates on board. And also you will be able to use some of these off this, both the joining of the employees as well.

So those are the apps or websites that can be used are pre-employment screening and background verification processes. These processes are very important in getting the right candidates with the right qualities. Pre-employment screening is very important to ensure that the background of the employees are very much clear that there are no there is no negative review of any of the candidates from the previous employers.

Applicant Tracking Systems (ATS) is a software tool which can be used to maintain the complete record of when the candidates were interviewed, who were the interviewers and what was the outcome, and so on. You could use apps or sites such as Zoho, recruit job, Viva Talent, Recruit, Bamboo, Voyager, Workable and so on.

So these are the recruitment tools and technologies that are used today.

Measurement of Recruitment Effectiveness

Talking about the measurement of effectiveness of recruitment process. So how to measure? Well, as any process you are doing in terms of the recruitment, it can be measured through some of the metrics, such as Time to Heart.

Time to Hire Metric

Time to Hire: This Metric measures the speed at which a candidate is processed, assessed, interviewed and accepted for a job done. So the longer the time or the number of days to hire the candidate shows a slow and inefficient process with unnecessary processes. Candidate experience can also be determined with the help of time to hire metric. It indicates the level of candidate experience as well.

Offer acceptanc: it shows What percentage of candidates are accepting your job offer? So this metric indicates how attractive and competitive your job offers are. If at all this metric is declining, then your team will not be able to have a lot of candidates that they want to have.

Quality of hire: This measures the value that your new hire brings to an organization. In other words, this recruiting metric is used to evaluate how much a new hire contributes to the organization's long term success based on their experience, performance and tenure at the company.

Cost per hire: This is a metric that measures the costs associated with the process of hiring new employees so they can include both internal and external expenses, including advertising costs, onboarding costs, referral bonus programs and so on. Your cost per hire should not be too high and it has to be balanced so as to not incur too much of costs towards hiring activities while still getting the best of talent.

Activity for you:

Find the average Time to Hire and average Offer Acceptance rate of few well-known companies by Googling. Calculate all the listed metrics on this chapter, using your own data:-

....

....

CHAPTER NINE

Onboarding: Stage 3 in ELC

CASE STUDY - 1

Riya has newly joined as HR at a big Multinational company in IT Sector.

The employee turnover is huge and there are new hires every now and then.

The management has informed her that the currently existing On boarding plan has failed in retaining and motivating new hires.

Riya is thrown with the challenge of coming up with a robust On boarding plan for first few months of new hire to avoid new-hire attrition and to keep them motivated.

How Riya can draft a robust on-boarding plan that complies with **4 C's of effective on boarding:**

1. **Compliance**
2. **Clarification**
3. **Culture**
4. **Connection**

Effective Onboarding

A SOLUTION FOR EFFECTIVE ONBOARDING: 4 C's of On boarding

Compliance

Covers key policies

Examples:

- Anti-harassment
- Personal conduct standards
- Progressive disciplinary actions
- Security

Clarification

Covers job-specific details

Examples:

- Team and project details
- Project training plan
- Performance expectation and plan
- Administrative policies: Payroll, Timesheets, Shipping, Business cards, Expense reports, Supplies

Culture

Helps in understanding company norms

Example activities:

- Attend weekly lunch with executives
- Review course on company values
- Meet your business unit head to hear about goals and culture alignment

Connection

Establish relationships and networks

Example activities:

- Assign a peer mentor
- Work with cross-functional teams
- 1:1s with people they'll work closely with
- Functional training

4 C's of Onboarding

4 C's of Onboarding: Following the 4 C's of Onboarding:

1. Compliance
2. Clarification
3. Culture and
4. Connection

These 4 C's ensure that your new joiner onboarding is a hit.

Riya Onboarding her employees

3-LevelBuddy Program: -

- **Leader Buddy: Level 3** - Leadership Buddy: The third level of the buddy program involves assigning a leadership buddy to the new employee. This buddy is typically a member of the leadership team or someone in a senior position within the company. The leadership buddy offers strategic guidance, helps the new joiner understand the company's vision and goals, and provides opportunities for career advancement. They may also serve as a sponsor, advocating for the new employee within the organization and helping them build important connections.

- **Culture Buddy: Level 2** - Mentor Buddy: In addition to the immediate buddy, the new employee is also assigned a mentor buddy. This mentor buddy is usually someone more experienced in the company or in a similar role. Their role is to provide deeper guidance and support on career development, navigating company politics, setting long-term goals, and offering insights into the industry. The mentor buddy acts as a mentor, offering advice and encouragement to help the new joiner grow professionally.

- **Role Buddy:Level 1** - Immediate Buddy: When a new employee joins the company, they are assigned an immediate buddy. This buddy is typically someone from the same team or department who can provide day-to-day support and guidance. The immediate buddy helps the new joiner with basic tasks, introduces them to colleagues, shows them around the office, and answers any initial questions they might have.

Having a Checklist & Welcome mail

The new hire checklist helps employers prepare for a new employee's first day at work.

The checklist includes key tasks to complete and documents to prepare before their arrival.

Riya needs to have a pre on boarding checklist as well,

covering most important things to be completed before new employee joins. It includes some of the important points like..

1. Asking new hire to send her personal data to enter company HRIS, i.e., ID proofs, Contact details, Passport, Tax details, Bank, Family details, Nominations, Certificate copies, etc. Asking new hire to come with any particular documents on the day of joining.

2. Send a welcome mail before arrival of new joiner, which includes *Arrival time of first day, *Copy of office map, office dress code, a first day agenda.

Send a joining announcement mail to new hire's reporting manager, his department and other stakeholders.

3. Before arrival of new hire, collect and send new hire's banking details to accounts dept to setup Payroll, id creation details to IT dept, Office Admin who can setup workstation.

All these before arrival of employee ensures, new hire does not waste time waiting for configurations to happen.

What are things a new hire expects on First Day?

Things to prepare..

- Most new hires prefer to have basic facilities set for them before they arrive and they are least likely to accept any surprises, issues or downtime on their first day. Waiting a lot is a big NO.
- Hence, Prepare your new hire's Desk and Tech, including :Laptop, Monitor, Phone, Mouse, Keyboard, Headset, etc.
- Arrange for new hire's ID card, building access fob and personal locker.
- Order new employee's business cards and/or name plates.

Ask for new hire's T-shirt size and place an order for a work uniform and/or a company T-shirt as a welcome gift.

Day of Joining: On boarding Kit

Prepare and handout an on boarding kit, what you can include in the kit :

- Employée handbook
- A welcome letter from their manager or CEO
- Computer setup instructions
- Stationery (e.g. notebook, pens, stickers)

- A company t-shirt
- A company mug
- A copy of your organizational chart
- A copy of a book relevant to your company or its culture
- A guide of local points of interest (e.g. nearby cafes and restaurants)

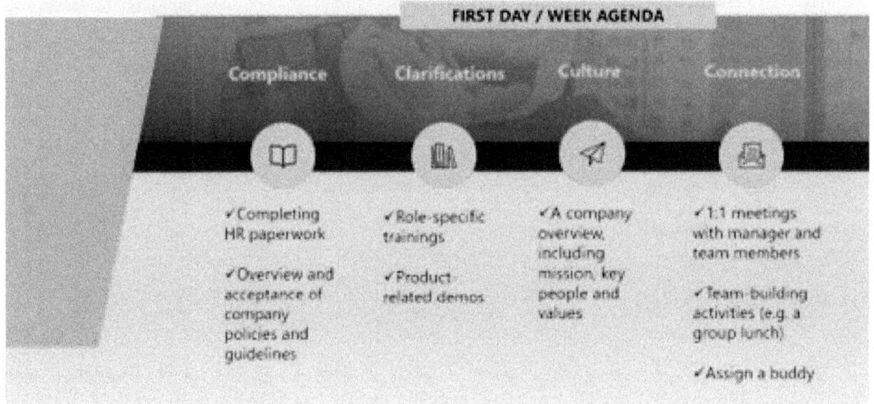

First Day & First week with 4C's

Activity for you:

If you are a new joiner in a company, what would you expect from your employer on the first day and first week at work?

....

....

Having a Checklist & Welcome mail

The new hire checklist helps employers prepare for a new employee's first day at work.

The checklist includes key tasks to complete and documents to prepare before their arrival.

Riya needs to have a pre on boarding checklist as well,

covering most important things to be completed before new employee joins. It includes some of the important points like..

1. Asking new hire to send her personal data to enter company HRIS, i.e., ID proofs, Contact details, Passport, Tax details, Bank, Family details, Nominations, Certificate copies, etc. Asking new hire to come with any particular documents on the day of joining.

2. Send a welcome mail before arrival of new joiner, which includes *Arrival time of first day, *Copy of office map, office dress code, a first day agenda.

Send a joining announcement mail to new hire's reporting manager, his department and other stakeholders.

3. Before arrival of new hire, collect and send new hire's banking details to accounts dept to setup Payroll, id creation details to IT dept, Office Admin who can setup workstation.

All these before arrival of employee ensures, new hire does not waste time waiting for configurations to happen.

What are things a new hire expects on First Day?

Things to prepare..

- Most new hires prefer to have basic facilities set for them before they arrive and they are least likely to accept any surprises, issues or downtime on their first day. Waiting a lot is a big NO.

- Hence, Prepare your new hire's Desk and Tech, including :Laptop, Monitor, Phone, Mouse, Keyboard, Headset, etc.

- Arrange for new hire's ID card, building access fob and personal locker.

- Order new employee's business cards and/or name plates.

Ask for new hire's T-shirt size and place an order for a work uniform and/or a company T-shirt as a welcome gift.

Day of Joining: On boarding Kit

Prepare and handout an on boarding kit, what you can include in the kit :

- Employée handbook
- A welcome letter from their manager or CEO

- Computer setup instructions
- Stationery (e.g. notebook, pens, stickers)
- A company t-shirt
- A company mug
- A copy of your organizational chart
- A copy of a book relevant to your company or its culture
- A guide of local points of interest (e.g. nearby cafes and restaurants)

CHAPTER TEN

Tools, Technologies & HR Metrics of Onboarding Stage

Tools & Technologies:

Some of the tools that can be used for success in this particular stage are using i

Identity and access management system for attendance and identification, such as biometric or swipe card system.

Providing Intranet access on the first day itself, providing welcome kit, job orientation and training modules to be used, which has to be updated and accurate.

Providing online benefits enrollment as soon as possible immediately off to the joining.

List of who is who: The contact details within the company to be provided on the day of joining.

Measurement with HR Metrics:

Measurement of effectiveness of onboarding: It can be done with the help of metrics such as Ramp Time.

Ramp Time means the number of days or the time taken between being hired to be productive on the job. It will be based on the average performance rating of the new high.

New her engagement level: This can be measured with the help of the absenteeism rate, employee net promoter score, reach and other key engagement drivers such as performance and on the job effectiveness and involvement.

Training effectiveness metrics: For example, you could take the learner engagement level or training return on investment or training experience satisfaction level or operational efficiency level.

So all these data will give you a measurement on how effective the employee's training has been.

These metrics can show you how effectively the onboarding process and the training process have been for the employee.

Activity for you:

Ramp Time metric: Define the parameters or methods you would use to know if the new hire is productive on the job or not? What is the ideal Ramp Time (in the number of days) according to you?

....

....

CHAPTER ELEVEN

Development: Stage 4 in ELC

The **Development** stage of the employee lifecycle includes everything that helps your employees mature within your organization from advancing in their career to learning new skills.

So this is the part of employee lifecycle that you can take your organization to new heights. Professional development is a win win scenario, empowering your team members to achieve things that they never thought possible while fostering a workplace that delivers for your customers, great service every time. So developing your workforce affects every other part of the employee lifecycle as well.

The development stage in the employee life cycle typically involves various tasks and activities aimed at enhancing the skills, knowledge, and capabilities of employees. These activities may include:

- Training and Onboarding: Providing new employees with orientation, training, and resources necessary to perform their job effectively.
- Skill Development: Offering opportunities for employees to learn new skills relevant to their roles through workshops, courses, seminars, or online training programs.
- Performance Management: Setting goals, providing feedback, and conducting performance evaluations to help employees understand their strengths and areas for improvement.
- Career Development: Supporting employees in setting career goals, identifying development opportunities, and creating plans for advancement within the organization.
- Mentoring and Coaching: Pairing employees with mentors or coaches who can provide guidance, advice, and support for their professional growth.

- Leadership Development: Providing training and experiences to employees who show potential for leadership roles within the organization.
- Cross-Training: Offering opportunities for employees to gain experience in different roles or departments to broaden their skills and perspectives.
- Continuous Learning: Encouraging a culture of lifelong learning and self-improvement through access to resources, development programs, and opportunities for personal growth.
- Succession Planning: Identifying and preparing employees for key positions within the organization to ensure continuity and smooth transitions during periods of change or leadership turnover.
- Feedback and Recognition: Providing regular feedback on performance and recognizing employees for their achievements and contributions to foster motivation and engagement.

Your employees are far more likely to remain within your company if it tangibly demonstrates, what are the investments that your company is making for your employees?

Every employee wants to join an organization that supports their growth.

Very few employees want to be in the same position for a long time without any learning or without any growth.

So as HR department, you should set a clear plan for your employees on their career development planand the progress. While some development might come from an employee's own self-motivation, the company should offer enough opportunities for development.

In order to be successful in development stage, professional development, training and classes can be conducted both from internal trainers and from external trainers.

Reimbursement of continuing education or courses can be done to motivate the employees to keep learning. The company should set a clear path of career opportunities for each and every employee so that the employees know what to look forward to in future and how to grow and reach their potential.

Let us now look at an example of Case-Study of Infosys.

So Infosys have been known as the world's best in employee training and development, and it greatly emphasizes on training and development activity. The organization has educational and training activities focused on the own job tasks in the forms of classroom training, on the job training and competitions within Infosys.

So the organization provides books and self-learning courses. Employees can choose to learn during work time or at weekends, so the flexibility of learning at their own pace and during the selected time is given by Infosys. Development activities such as the new hire orientation program, which needs to be attended by every new heart within first three months. This trains them on corporate culture policies, dress code, and other processes of the organization.

Management development programs, personal development programs are imparted at the later stage for the new hire.

ILI The Infosys Leadership System, which builds leadership in employees. This is one of the greatest programs that gives a lot of leadership skills and provides the relevant training to the employees. There are frequent quality process trainings which are imparted by Infosys.

So these are the different developmental activities being done by Infosys, which makes them one of the leaders in training and development as an organization.

Activity for you:

Ramp Time metric: Define the parameters or methods you would use to know if the new hire is productive on the job or not? What is the ideal Ramp Time (in the number of days) according to you?

....

....

CHAPTER TWELVE

Tools, Technologies & HR Metrics for Development Stage

Tools & Technologies

So what developmental tools can be used in this stage?

List of Tools and Technologies for performance management system and people development activities:-

People works, HR mantra, HR one, Pocket HRMS, Oracle, Office Timer, Zoho people, Great tip, ADP, SMP, Ascent PMS, etc.

So these all will support the performance development of the employees.

Technologies for Learning Management Software:

My class campus, Mintbook, Sum Total, Edapp, Udemy for Business, etc.

These can be used by the training and development functions of your organization to develop relevant learning materials for the employee. Companies can provide subscription to leading online learning platforms for the employee's continuous learning such as Udemy. This can be a great tool without much of an investment.

External trainers can be used for classroom trainings and workshops. Subject matter expert sessions within the company can be useful to develop the employees subject matter expertise.

HR Metrics for Development Stage:

Talking about the measurement of effectiveness. What are the metrics that can be used to measure the success of development training:

- Cost per employee
- Training return on investment

These metrics will measure what is the cost invested or cost spent for the employee and what is the return on investment.

That is basically the level of skill enhancement in the employee and the level of commitment and the productivity of the employee. These will be compared.

Talking about **360 degree feedback.** So 360 degree feedback can be a great tool to know how employee's doing in terms of his work from his subordinate, superior, from the person works under the employee and also from any external vendors or customers.

Training participants satisfaction tool, Learning outcomes measurement. That is basically what would be learning outcomes of particular training program. Then operational efficiency of the employee and learner engagement level scores.

These can be used to measure the effectiveness of development programs.

CHAPTER THIRTEEN

Retention: Stage 5 in ELC

The fifth seed in the employee lifecycle is retention.

You need to focus your energies on keeping the top performing employees with the company and ensuring that they are happy and sufficiently challenged in their respective roles within the team.

The influence of company cultures goes a long way in this speech. So if the culture of your organization is poor, it inevitably leads to higher employee turnover rate.

That means you will have to face replacement costs regularly. So improving the retention storage is a great way to counteract the risk and promote longevity and satisfaction among your team's career path.

I start with hiring the right person for each position and encourage open communication between employees and employers.

If you are successful in attracting, recruiting, onboarding and developing talent, then retaining talent becomes easier.

That means you need to emphasize and you need to put a lot of attention to the different stages that is attracting, recruiting, onboarding and developing your employees.

Exit interviews will be very much useful in understanding what employees want, why they're quitting the company. It is very vital to mark out few reasons or important reasons for exit and work on them in order to make sure people stick to the company.

Focus on overall retention strategy, including great P benefits, company culture and career opportunities.

A bucket of all the tools can make a great retention tool. Some of the tools technologies that can be used for retention are talent management, software, succession planning, return to work or state work programs and services. Work from home and flexible schedules. A Return to work program is something that is designed to get employees who have been out of work due to injury or illness or such reasons to come back to the work sooner by giving them easier jobs until they regain their full capacity.

But as a stay at work program, is a financial incentive program that encourages employers to bring their injured workers quickly and safely back to light duty or transitional work by reimbursing them for some of their costs.

You can provide work from home and flexible schedules to ensure employee engagement and a maximum employee experience during the retention stage. And also, it's good to have open door policies, executive officers and frequent company all hands meetings in order to keep your employees engaged.

Mentorship programs and buddy programs, rewards and recognitions programs, wellness programs, compensation benchmarking and ideal benefit programs can help retain the best people within your company.

So how do you measure the effectiveness of retention stage?

Some of the major metrics that you could use are e**mployee engagement level** through **employee surveys, and employee engagement survey or employee satisfaction survey** can be very much helpful in identifying what are the consistent initial issues of the employees, what they actually think and feel about the company, having direct feedback from employees instead of guessing how they feel. It can be used to get positive stats in recruiting materials.

Next measurement tool is attrition rate.

Basically the number of employees leaving the organization. This business metric helps you understand how well you're retaining your team members. It's also called as churn rate.

Attrition rate metric can also give insight to the causes of attrition, such as relocation, medical emergencies, family reasons, retirement termination transfers and so on. So this rate can be very much helpful in hiring and retention decisions and also helps in improvingproductivity.

CHAPTER FOURTEEN

Separation: Stage 6 in ELC

The final stage of the employee lifecycle is the **employee's separation stage**. For most of the employees, there comes a point where their employment lifecycle will reach its conclusion.

Either for retirement, new employment or for personal reasons. So treating the separation process with equal importance is very much necessary. Just like onboarding process, separation is important. How strategically you approach the separation of an employee matters a lot.

When a team member leaves, it has effect on the other members as well. So HR plays a vital role in ensuring each employee leaves without any major disruptions. Separation done in good terms means the employee and the company part without any hazzles.

In order to ensure hassle free separation. Some of the tips that you could follow are:-

Exit interview:

Understanding the reason behind the resignation and to be positive and to ask for honest feedback during the exit interviews.

So exit interviews are very important interviews held with the employee who's about to leave an organization, typically in order to discuss and assess employee's reasons for leaving and the experience of working for the organization. This serves as a great tool for your future planning of your retention tool as well.

All managers to be adequately trained on managing employee exit, because it's not only the HR who will be handling the employees, but the managers will be handling or dealing with the employees to a great extent.

So all the managers need to be adequately trained, knowledgeable about the exit process.

Succession planning:

What next?

Usually when one of the team member leaves the team, there can be some demoralizing among the other members and there can be a little bit of down or a dull moment among the team.

So it is very important as managers and our teams, to be able to guide them and keep them motivated at all times and to ensure that they look forward to future assignments and not just be stuck with the separated employees.

CHAPTER FIFTEEN

Tools, Technologies & HR Metrics for Separation Stage

What are the tools that can be used during the separation stage to ensure maximum employee experience and employee engagement?

30, 60 and 90 days feedback survey:

This is a great tool when used properly. All the employees who have joined your organization should be given a 30 days, 60 days and 90 days feedback. New employees get to tell you what they are going through and if there are any issues, how they feel about the company, are they really in line with the company's culture and goals, etc. So this can be a great tool that can be helpful for retaining as well as helps your separation as.

Exit interview:

Exit Interview and feedback are very important. Exit Clearance forms can be useful in ensuring that all the necessary documents and equipments and other accessories are handed over from the employee and there is a clearance from all the departments and associated people within the organization for the employee who is going away from the organization.

HR Metrics for Separation Stage

What are some of the other metrics that can be used for the measurement of this particular stage?

Separation rate voluntary and involuntary:

This is very important to note that how many are voluntary leaving and how many the company is making them to leave for some of the reasons which could be related to performance and so on.

Turnover rate

Turnover Rateis basically the number of employees left and replaced.

These metrics can be very much useful in measuring what are the costs involved and how effectively is the HR intervention in the separation stage. Also it helps to see how happy the employees are with the exit process of the company.

Activity for you:

List 5 important questions that need to be part of an Exit Interview Form.

....

....

CHAPTER SIXTEEN

Case Study: ELC

Elaborating on Adobe's Employee Life Cycle Management Case

Source: https://helpx.adobe.com/sign/how-to/adobe-workday-integration.html

The Case

Adobe realized that a significant portion of their new hires weren't lasting past the first year. This high turnover rate was costing the company money and impacting team morale. To address this challenge, Adobe implemented a focus on the employee life cycle, specifically targeting the onboarding and development stages.

Challenges Addressed:

High Turnover Rate: New hires leaving within the first year resulted in wasted recruitment costs, lost productivity, and potentially a demoralized existing workforce.

Solutions Implemented:

Improved Onboarding: Here's how Adobe might have addressed the onboarding issues:

Structured program: Move beyond basic company information to include role-specific training, team introductions, and clear expectations.

Mentorship: Pair new hires with experienced colleagues who can provide guidance and answer questions.

Socialization activities: Facilitate interaction with colleagues through team lunches, workshops, or social events to foster a sense of belonging.

Development Opportunities: By providing clear career paths and ongoing learning, Adobe likely addressed issues like:

Skill stagnation: Employees feel stagnant if they don't see opportunities to learn and grow in their roles.

Limited career mobility: A lack of clear career paths can lead to employees feeling stuck and looking for opportunities elsewhere.

Potential Outcomes:

Increased Retention: By feeling valued, supported, and having a clear path for growth, new hires are more likely to stay with the company.

Improved Morale: A positive onboarding experience and development opportunities can boost employee morale and create a more engaged workforce.

Enhanced Productivity: When employees feel supported and have the skills they need, they can be more productive in their roles.

Additional Considerations:

Metrics Tracked: It's important to note that Adobe likely tracked metrics such as time-to-productivity, employee engagement scores, and turnover rates to measure the success of their initiatives.

Customization: The specific onboarding and development programs might differ depending on the role and department within Adobe.

Overall, **Adobe's case study** demonstrates the positive impact that effective employee life cycle management can have on a company. By investing in all stages of the employee journey, from recruitment to development, companies can create a more positive work environment, reduce turnover, and ultimately build a stronger and more successful workforce.

CHAPTER SEVENTEEN

HR Templates / Formats: Pre Joining to Onboarding

Candidate Application Form: Template

APPLICATION FORM

PLEASE NOTE: ANY FALSE OR MISLEADING INFORMATION GIVEN IN THIS APPLICATION OR OMISSIONS OF INFORMATION MAY RESULT IN NON-SELECTION OR TERMINATION OF EMPLOYMENT.

PERSONAL DETAILS					
Post Applied For					
Where did you hear of this vacancy?					
Last Name			**First Name** ☐ **Mr** ☐ **Ms** ☐ **Mrs** ☐ **Miss**		
Present Address			**Permanent Address** (if different)		
Post Code:			Post Code:		
Phone Number			**May we contact you at work?**		
Home:	Work:	Mobile:	E-mail:	Yes ○	No ○

ACADEMIC RECORD		
Provide details of educational qualifications completed or in progress		
Name of University, College(s), Further Education	**Dates**	**Full details of qualification obtained** (Including Classification, if relevant)

OTHER RELEVANT INFORMATION	
Please detail additional information such as other qualifications, technical skills, experience, language, projects completed relevant to the position or other.	**Dates**
Membership of Professional Bodies	**Dates**

Application Form: Page 1

Current Employment				
Name & address of present/last employer	Dates From	Dates To	Job title	Reason for leaving
Brief summary of responsibilities				

Employment history			
Names and Address of Previous Employers	Period of Employment From / to dates	Position & responsibilities	Reason for leaving
ADDITIONAL INFORMATION			

Application Form: Page 2

Please indicate why you are applying for this post and what particular skills and qualities you would bring to the job. You may refer to skills gained from activities outside of the workplace if they are relevant to the role.
REFERENCES
Please give names and addresses of three referees (who should not be related to you) who may be approached in connection with your application. The first must be your current or most recent employer.
Name: **Address:** **Phone Number:** **E-mail Address:**
Name: **Address:** **Phone Number:** **E-mail Address:**
Name: **Address:**

Application Form: Page 3

Interview Evaluation Form: Template

(To be used by Interviewing Manager & HR)

INTERVIEW EVALUATION SHEET

NAME: **DEPARTMENT:**

POSITION: **LOCATION:**

Score in %:

S No.	Attributes	Excellent	Good	Average	Below Avg
1.	JOB KNOWLEDGE				
2.	EXPERIENCE (Relevance, Quality etc.)				
3.	PAST ACHIEVEMENTS				
4.	ACADEMICS (Division,%,Consistency,Scholarships)				
5.	CLARITY OF THOUGHT				
6.	COMMUNICATION				
7.	MOTIVATION / ATTITUDES				
8.	LIKELY STABILITY				
9.	COMPUTER SKILLS				
10.	Any other attributes relevant to the role:				
	OVERALL RATING				

FAMILY BACKGROUND:

OVERALL COMMENTS:

FINAL RECOMMENDATIONS:

[ ] Selected ------------------------------------

[ ] Not suitable for the role but suitable for: ------------------------------------

[ ] Rejected

[ ] Hold for future reference

Interview Evaluation Form: Page 1

SALARY RECOMMENDTIONS:

1 **CTC (p.a):**

2 **Assured Bonus:**

3 **Total CTC (1+2):**

4 Designation: **Grade: -------------------**

5 Notice period from prior company **--**

6 To be taken on our payroll: **Yes [ ]** **No (Contractual) [ ]**

7 Any other comments: ---

	PANEL MEMBERS		
	NAME	**SIGNATURE**	**DATE**
1			
2			
3			

Interview Evaluation Form: Page 2

Offer Letter Format

Date

Private & Confidential

[First and Last Name]
[Address]
[City]
[Zip Code]

Dear ,

We are pleased to offer you the position of (*Full-Time/ Part-Time*) in the (*department or unit*) at (*Company Name*) .

Your first date of employment will be (*Start Date*) . You will report directly to (*Person Name*) .

Compensation
Your rate will be ______________$, subject to applicable statutory deductions and paid by direct deposit to your bank account on a bi-weekly schedule.

Vacation
All employees are required to wait until their three-month probationary period is complete before being eligible to take vacation time. In each calendar year, you will be entitled to (*Number of Week*) week's vacation. This year your entitlement will be (*Number of Days*) days, which is pro-rated to your start date. All vacation time-off must be approved in writing in advance by your manager.

Paid Personal Holiday
After (*Number of Months*) of continuous service, you will be eligible for (*Number of Days*) paid personal holiday in each calendar year.

Hours of Work
As a full-time or part-time employee, your normal work week will consist (*Number of hours*) hours.

Page 1 of 3

Offer Letter Format: Page 1

Probationary Period
Your employment will be probationary for a period of three (3) months, during which time (*Company Name*) will assess your suitability for the position. Following the successful completion of your probationary period, your performance and salary will be reviewed in conjunction with (*Company Name*) annual time lines.

Short Term Disability Days
(*Company Name*) provides a short-term disability days of (Number of Days) days for non-work related illness or injury.

Group Insurance Benefits
After (*Number of Months*) of service, you will be eligible to participate (*Company Name*) group insurance benefit plan. This plan includes the following coverage: (*health care and dental care insurance, Life care*) available to you on a cost-sharing basis. Please refer to the attached summary for details.

(Company Name) reserves the right to change the carriers and/or level of coverage or eliminate any benefit in its entirety at any time upon 30 days written notice to you.

Pension Plan / Retirement Plan
As a (*Full-Time or Part-Time*) employee, you are eligible to join (*Company Name*) ______________ (*Pension Plan or Retirement Plan*) on (*Date*) .

Privacy/Confidentiality
"I shall safeguard the confidential and personal information of (*Company Name*) . I shall conform to all practices, procedures, standards and guidelines, which may be established from time to time by (*Company Name*) including but not limited to confidential, personal and proprietary information as well as privacy.

I shall protect (*Company Name*) confidential and/or proprietary information from any unauthorized access, disclosure, reproduction, alteration and/or use, both during and after my employment with (*Company Name*) . I shall not use confidential, personal or proprietary information gained by virtue of employment for personal gain or for any other purpose, which is not directly related to my employment.

Page 2 of 3

Offer Letter Format : Page 2

Upon the end of my employment (*Company Name*) , I shall immediately return to (*Company Name*) all personal, private and/or proprietary information (including any clientele books) and I will not disclose or make any use of personal, private and/or proprietary information of (*Company Name*) after my employment with (*Company Name*) ."

If the above terms are acceptable to you, please sign and date both copies of this letter and return one copy to (*Company Name*)__________ by (*Date*) .

(*First Name*)__________, we are delighted that you have considered joining the (*Company Name*) team. Should you have any questions, please feel free to contact (*Person Name*) at (*Phone Number*) .

Sincerely,

____

Hiring Person Name
Title

Accepted and agreed to the above terms and conditions this

____________________ day of____________________, (*Year*)____________.

____

Signature

Page 3 of 3

Offer Letter Format: Page 3

New Joiner Kit

Name of organization **Mr.**
NEW JOINERS KIT **Desig.:-**
A - To be given at 8.00 am on the day of joining. **DOJ.:-**

SR. NO	DETAILS		REMARKS
1	Welcome	- Bouquet presentation	
		- Letter	
		- Meeting with GM-HR & HOD	
2	Appointment Letter		
3	Job Description		
4	Induction Programme Schedule		
5	Punching Card		
6	I-Card		
7	Code of Conduct (If Applicable)		
8	Shift Timing Chart		
9	Monthly Pocket Diary		
10	Residence Proof Certificate (For salary account opening)		
11	Residence Proof Certificate (Gas Connection)		
12	Safety Helmet, Mask, Ear Plugs		
13	List of Paid Holidays		
14	Leave Entitlement		
15	Online - Leave procedure demo		
16	In house Magazine		
17	HR slide show run - Briefing about group / process etc.		

B- Kept ready at 8.00 am on the day of joining

SR. NO	DETAILS	REMARKS
1	Sitting Arrangement	
2	Computer / Email-ID arrangement, If applicable	
3	Quarter Arrangement, If applicable	
4	Stationary	

Jr. Officer - Personnel **Asst. Manager - P & HR** **New Employee**

Sample Joining Kit

Joining Format: Sample

JOINING REPORT

Dear Sir
I .... have joined duties in your Organization as

per details given bellow:-

Date & Time.................................
Unit ....
....
....
Designation ....
I ensure to abide by all rules & regulation/ standing orders of organization.

Yours Faithfully

Signature of Employee

Name ....
Date.............................

Verified by ....

Employee' Code.................................

Father's Name ....

Complete Local Address ....
....
....
Mobile No. ....

Gross Salary ....per month

Signature of Employees ....

Joining Format: To be filled by new joiner

Sample Welcome Mail to New Joiner: Template

Welcome Mail to New Joiner: Format

Dear Mr. Kumar,

We welcome you to please note the following:

1) Your employee code is:
2) Your E-mail ID is:
3) While sending emails please ensure that the following details are captured in the Signature' portion of your emails:

Name	:	
Designation	:	
Business Line / Support	:	
Company Name	:	
Company Address	:	
Landline Phone number(s)	:	
Fax number	:	
Mobile number	:	
Website	:	
Email ID	:	

Thanks & Regards
Human Resources
Website:
Email:

Welcome Mail to New Joiner from HR

Modern HR, Technology and Recruitment Process

CHAPTER EIGHTEEN

The HR Landscape: Evolution and Current Trends

The Genesis of HR Management

As the sun rises in the old industrial city of the 1800s, the air is filled with the noise of machines, steam, and workers shouting. This is the time of the Industrial Revolution, a big change in how people work and relate to their bosses. In the midst of the dirty factories, a new idea starts to form—one that will set the foundation for today's Human Resource Management.

HRM Trends

In these busy factories, workers work hard for long hours in tough conditions, often without much care for their well-being or rights.

This leads to discontent and social problems, sparking the rise of labor unions fighting for workers‘ rights. In this chaotic situation, the need for a more organized way of managing people becomes clear.

Over time, societies progress, and people realize that taking care of workers is not just the right thing to do, but also good for business. The healthier and happier the worker, the better the work. This realization gives birth to Personnel Management, which comes before Human Resource Management.

Jump to the mid-1900s, and another big change happens. The world has just come out of two devastating world wars, economies are being rebuilt, and businesses are growing a lot. It becomes clear that managing people well is not just about taking care of them—it's about making sure they work well with the goals of the organization. The term "Human Resources" starts to be used, showing a broader view of workers as assets that can be developed.

Now, look at the present. Today's HR Generalists face new challenges like globalization, technology changes, demographic shifts, and a focus on diversity and inclusion. These aren't just passing trends; they are the realities that shape today's workplaces.

So, why does history matter? To understand today's HR challenges, we need to know the journey that brought us here. The past teaches us lessons that help us deal with today's problems and predict future ones.

Doesn't the HR Generalist today benefit from those who fought for workers' rights and recognized the value of aligning employee goals with business objectives? This book is your guide in this ever-changing landscape. By understanding the origins of HR Management, we get a clearer picture of its importance today. HR principles and practices aren't fixed—they change as society changes, adapting to new challenges and opportunities.

As we move from the past to the present exploration of HR, remember that the role of the HR Generalist is just as important now as in the early days. It requires insight, empathy, and strategic thinking. We need to understand where we've been to navigate where we're going.

In the upcoming chapters, we'll break down the core functions of HR, look at employee engagement, and see how technology and data analytics are changing the field. We'll meet HR pioneers, learn from their successes and mistakes, and use those lessons in our work.

Imagine the vast field of Human Resources as a powerful river. From its small beginnings in the Industrial Revolution to today's complex system, it continues to flow. As HR Generalists, we guide and protect this river. Our job is to plan its route wisely, making sure it helps and enriches the organizations and lives it touches.

Are you ready for this important journey? To create new paths in HR, armed with the wisdom of the past and a vision for the future? If your answer is a strong yes, then let's go on this journey together. Turn the page, and let the story of Human Resource Management keep unfolding.

CHAPTER NINETEEN

Modern HR: Beyond Administration

Today's Human Resources (HR) is more than just paperwork. In the changing story of HR Management, we find ourselves at a crucial point where the role of the HR Generalist goes beyond traditional tasks. Let's explore what this means.

In the past, HR professionals were seen as rule enforcers, record keepers, and form managers. While these tasks are still important, today's HR Generalist has a bigger role. They need to understand business strategy, how organizations work, and even human behaviour.

Modern HR

Why has this change happened? The business world is more complicated now with fast technology, diverse cultures, and tough competition. The HR Generalist is like a key player, connecting how people work with the big goals of the company.

But before we dive into this change, let's set some clear standards for comparison. We'll look at how much influence HR has, how they help employees grow, how they manage the company's culture, and how they support innovation.

Even though both traditional and modern HR care about employees and follow the rules, there are clear differences. Modern HR isn't separate from the big picture of the company. They're part of decision-making and planning for the future.

Pictures like Venn diagrams or flowcharts could help show the differences between old and new HR roles, but you can still see the contrast without them.

Going deeper, we see that the change in the HR Generalist's role is not just about different tasks but a big change in thinking. Today's HR professional is like a guide, a coach, a person who makes positive changes, and a supporter of both employees and the organization.

What do these comparisons tell us? They show that HR is a key part of any successful business. Businesses that understand and support their HR function tend to be stronger, more flexible, and more innovative.

Think about a big company with employees all over the world. The modern HR Generalist is super important here. They have to create a culture where everyone feels included, find and grow talent across borders, and make sure the company's values fit in different cultures.

Imagine walking into an office full of energy and teamwork.

The HR Generalist is there, not just watching but helping create this environment. They plan things that bring teams together, support policies for a good work-life balance, and use technology to make work smoother and encourage learning.

As an HR professional, can you do this for your company? The answer depends on how well you understand the strategic part of your role and if you can see beyond just doing administrative tasks.

So, let me ask you directly: Are you ready to use strategy and empathy in your role? Can you be the keeper of your company's culture and bring in new ideas?

In the next chapters, we'll look at real examples where HR Generalists made big changes in their companies. We'll explore how to manage talent in a time where job roles change as quickly as the technology around them.

Think of yourself as an HR Generalist like a gardener in a big, thriving space. Every decision you make—from what you start to how you help it grow—shapes the health of the garden. Your role is both strategic and caring, making sure the garden grows and adapts to different seasons.

In our journey through the world of HR, simplicity is our guide, and clarity is our map.

Let's move forward with confidence, understanding the past and building a future that values the human element in every business.

Turn the page, and let's keep exploring modern HR, a field that combines tradition and innovation, guided by the wisdom of experience and the light of progress.

CHAPTER TWENTY

Top 10 Trends in HR Management: 2024

Get Ready to Reimagine HR: Top 10 Trends Shaping the Future of Work in 2024

The world of work is in constant flux, and HR professionals are at the forefront of navigating these changes. As we step into 2024, exciting trends are emerging that will reshape how we attract, develop, and retain top talent. Here's a glimpse into the top 10 trends that HR leaders should be aware of:

1. The Hybrid Hustle: Finding Harmony Between Remote and In-Office Work

Gone are the days of rigid work schedules. With technology enabling seamless remote work, organizations are embracing hybrid models. The key lies in finding the right balance that fosters collaboration, engagement, and productivity for both in-office and remote employees.

2. Employee Experience Takes Center Stage: It's All About You

In today's competitive landscape, attracting and retaining talent requires a focus on the employee experience. This goes beyond just pay and benefits. It encompasses everything from onboarding and development opportunities to fostering a positive and inclusive work environment.

3. Lifelong Learning: Equipping Your Workforce for the Future

The pace of change is relentless, and the skills needed to succeed are constantly evolving. HR is taking the lead in creating a culture of continuous learning, offering programs and resources that help employees adapt and thrive in the changing world of work.

4. AI Enters the HR Arena: Friend or Foe?

The rise of artificial intelligence (AI) is making waves in HR. While some may fear AI replacing human jobs, the reality is that it can be a powerful tool for streamlining HR processes, automating tasks, and providing valuable data insights. The key is to leverage AI responsibly, focusing on human-centric approaches that complement the unique strengths of both humans and machines.

5. Prioritizing Well-being: It's Not Just About Work, It's About Life

Organizations are recognizing the importance of employee well-being and are investing in programs that promote physical, mental, and emotional health. This can range from offering flexible work arrangements to providing access to wellness resources like mindfulness training and stress management programs.

6. Data-Driven Decisions: Numbers Don't Lie

HR is becoming increasingly data-driven. By leveraging people analytics, HR professionals can gain valuable insights into employee engagement, performance, and sentiment, allowing them to make informed decisions that drive positive outcomes for both the organization and its employees.

7. Diversity, Equity, and Inclusion (DE&I): More Than Just a Buzzword

Creating a truly diverse, equitable, and inclusive workplace is no longer optional. HR is taking the lead in fostering inclusive cultures that value and respect all employees, regardless of their background or identity.

8. Reskilling and Upskilling: Unlocking the Potential of Your People

Instead of solely relying on external talent acquisition, organizations are increasingly focusing on internal mobility. This involves reskilling and upskilling existing employees to equip them with the skills and knowledge needed to take on new roles and responsibilities within the company.

9. The Rise of the Gig Economy: Redefining the Traditional Workforce

The gig economy is on the rise, and HR needs to adapt to this changing landscape. This involves developing strategies to attract and manage talent in a flexible and contingent manner.

10. Reimagining Leadership: Putting the "Human" Back in Human Resources

Effective leadership is critical for employee engagement and organizational success. HR is playing a crucial role in developing leaders who are empathetic, adaptable, and capable of inspiring and motivating their teams in the ever-changing world of work.

These are just a few of the exciting trends shaping the future of HR. By embracing these changes and staying ahead of the curve, HR professionals can play a vital role in creating thriving workplaces that attract, retain, and empower a diverse and talented workforce.

CHAPTER TWENTY-ONE

Technology in HR: A Digital Revolution

Technology has changed how human resource (HR) works a lot. It's like a big change, almost like when a strong wave washes over a sandcastle. To understand how big this change is, we need to look back at where it all started and see how we got to where we are now.

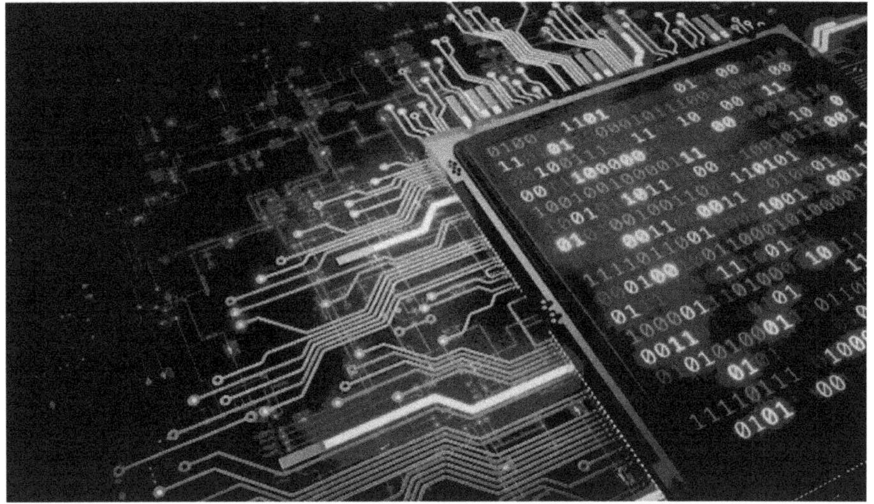

Technology in HRM

The story of technology in HR is not about a sudden big change but more about a slow but really important transformation. At first, simple computers in the 1940s and 1950s helped HR with administrative tasks, making things easier.

As time went on, we hit some important points. In the 1970s, we got HR Information Systems (HRIS) that organized employee data and made it easier to find. Then, in the 1980s, personal computers came into offices, making digital tools available to more people.

The 1990s brought the internet, changing everything in life, including HR. Online job boards like Monster.com and networking sites like LinkedIn in the early 2000s changed how we find and connect with people for jobs.

Later on, in the late 2000s, cloud computing and Software as a Service (SaaS) made HR work even smoother. It meant HR could use solutions that worked from anywhere, making things flexible and letting people work together from different places.

Think of a flowchart showing the path of technology in HR. From big computers in the 1950s to the small smartphones and tablets we use now, each jump in technology has opened up new possibilities for HR.

But this digital change didn't happen the same way everywhere. Western countries started using HR technology early, but other places like Japan first focused on making organizations centered around people before adding technology. On the other hand, countries like India skipped some steps and went straight to mobile and cloud-based solutions because lots of people there use smartphones.

Today, HR looks really different from before. Algorithms and artificial intelligence help with hiring, big data analytics give real-time feedback, and tools for employee engagement use games to make work better.

But with all these changes, there are also problems. Using AI in hiring makes some worry about biases in the algorithms and the risk of losing human judgment. And as technology is everywhere, there are debates about privacy and finding the right balance between keeping an eye on employees and trusting them.

ChatGPT, since 2022, is taking the world on storm! You cant be left behind in this AI journey. HR professionals and all management professionals are using ChatGPT to maximize their productivity.

Now, HR professionals have an important choice to make: How do they use technology's power while still keeping the human side of the job? How do they balance being efficient with being understanding?

If you work in HR, do you feel the weight of these questions? Are you ready to use technology's abilities while still understanding how people work?

In the next chapters, we'll look at examples where HR blended digital tools with the special understanding of humans. We'll see the role of an HR professional as both a tech expert and someone who cares about people at work.

Imagine a future where technology helps HR but doesn't replace the human part—it makes it even better. Picture HR professionals not just doing paperwork but also making smart plans, using data, and caring about people.

Get ready for the next part of this story with the goal of being at the front of this digital change. Use what you know, learn from wisdom, and get inspired by the exciting possibilities of a future where technology and humanity come together to make work better.

CHAPTER TWENTY-TWO

Top 10 Technological Tools for HRM

Here are the top 10 technological tools used by HR professionals and employers:

Human Resource Information Systems (HRIS): This is a central system that stores and manages all employee data, from basic information like contact details to payroll and benefits information.

Applicant Tracking Systems (ATS): These systems help manage the recruitment process by streamlining applications, scheduling interviews, and keeping track of candidate information.

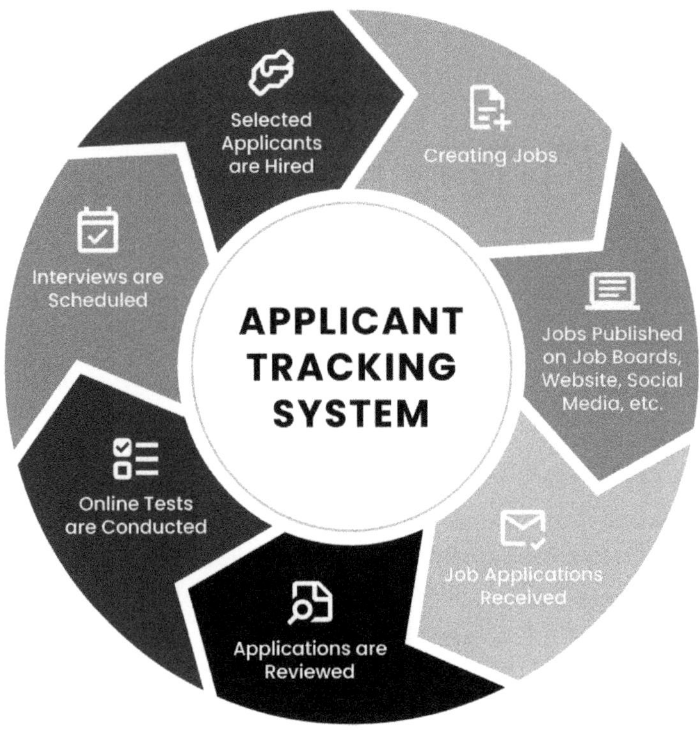

ATS

Learning Management Systems (LMS): These platforms deliver and track employee training and development programs. They can be used for onboarding new hires, providing ongoing training, and tracking compliance with regulations.

Performance Management Software: These tools help automate and streamline the performance management process, including setting goals, providing feedback, and conducting performance reviews.

Talent Management Software: This software goes beyond just recruitment and helps manage the entire employee lifecycle, from onboarding to development to retirement.

Employee Engagement Platforms: These platforms provide various features to improve employee engagement, such as communication tools, recognition programs, and surveys.

Workforce Management Systems: These systems help manage scheduling, timekeeping, and attendance for employees.

Social Media Platforms: Social media is no longer just for personal use. HR professionals use social media platforms like LinkedIn to connect with potential candidates, promote their employer brand, and share company news and updates.

Video Conferencing and Collaboration Tools: These tools allow HR professionals to connect with employees and candidates remotely, which is especially important in a hybrid work environment.

Artificial Intelligence (AI): AI is increasingly being used in HR for tasks such as screening resumes, identifying top candidates, and providing chatbot support to employees.

These are just a few of the many technological tools that HR professionals and employers use to manage their workforce. By using the right tools, HR can improve efficiency, streamline processes, and create a more positive experience for employees.

Activity for you:

Research and List down popular tools or softwares in each of the above 10 categories:

....

....

CHAPTER TWENTY-THREE

The Globalization of Human Resources

Emerging HR Paradigms

Have you ever wondered how things at work are changing? Well, let me spill the beans on something exciting – it's all about the way Human Resources (HR) is going global. Buckle up for a ride into the world of HR and the cool new things happening!

Picture this: You're part of a company, and suddenly, things aren't just about the folks in your office or town. Nope, we're talking about a bigger game – a worldwide game! That's what we call the globalization of Human Resources. It's like HR is spreading its wings and connecting with people all around the globe.

Global HRM

Now, let's break it down without getting too tangled up in fancy words. HR used to be about managing things in one place, like making sure everyone gets paid and has the right forms. But guess what? Now, it's like HR has upgraded to the world stage.

Think about it like this – you might be in a company based in New York, but your team members could be in Tokyo, Sydney, or Mumbai. How cool is that? It's like having work buddies from all corners of the world.

But, you might be thinking, "What's in it for me?" Well, my friend, that's where the Emerging HR Paradigms come into play. Paradigms might sound like a mouthful, but all it means is new and exciting ways of doing things. Let's dive into the juicy details!

1. **Tech Magic**: Thanks to technology, HR can now connect with employees no matter where they are. It's not just about sending emails; we're talking video calls, instant messaging, and all the cool tech stuff. So, if you're sipping coffee in Paris while your boss is having tea in London, you can still catch up in a blink.
2. **Culture Mix and Match**: With teams spanning the globe, you get this awesome mix of cultures. It's like a global potluck! Imagine celebrating different festivals, learning new languages, and understanding that not everyone loves the same kind of pizza – mind-blowing, right?
3. **Flexibility Rocks**: Global HR brings in a whole new level of flexibility. Work doesn't have to be a 9-to-5 cubicle gig anymore. You might find yourself working in your PJs or joining a meeting at the crack of dawn. It's all about getting the job done while juggling life's adventures.
4. **Career Passport**: Now, here's the big one – the chance to grow your career on a global scale. You might start as a whiz-kid in your local team and end up leading projects that involve people from all over. It's like having a passport to career adventures around the world.

So, what's the bottom line? The globalization of HR is like giving work a global makeover. It's not just about where you live; it's about being part of a big, diverse family where everyone brings something unique to the table.

As you flip through the pages of this book, get ready to explore these new horizons in HR. It's not just about the usual office stuff; it's about how

HR is making work more exciting, connected, and full of possibilities. So, fasten your seatbelt – the HR adventure is about to take you places you've never been!

CHAPTER TWENTY-FOUR

Recruitment & Selection: The Art of Finding Talent

Recruitment and Selection: The Art of Finding Talent

The recruitment process in Human Resource Management (HRM) typically involves several stages, each designed to identify, attract, and select the right candidates for job vacancies. Let's break down the key stages with their corresponding HRM terminologies:

1. **Identifying the Need:**

    - **Definition:** Recognizing the need for a new employee based on organizational requirements.
    - **Terminology:** Workforce planning, demand forecasting, or job requisition.

Recruitment

1. **Job Analysis and Description:**

   - **Definition:** Conducting a thorough analysis of the job and creating a detailed description, including responsibilities, qualifications, and other relevant details.
   - **Terminology:** Job analysis, job description, and job specification.

3. **Posting the Job:**

   - **Definition:** Announcing the job opening through various channels to attract potential candidates.
   - **Terminology:** Job posting, job advertisement, or job announcement.

4. **Receiving and Screening Applications:**

   - **Definition:** Collecting and reviewing applications to shortlist candidates who meet the specified criteria.

- **Terminology:** Application screening or resume shortlisting.

5. **Conducting Initial Assessments:**

    - **Definition:** Evaluating candidates through initial assessments, such as skills tests or preliminary interviews.
    - **Terminology:** Initial screening, pre-employment assessments, or competency tests.

6. **Interviewing Candidates:**

    - **Definition:** Engaging candidates in one or more interview sessions to assess their suitability for the position.
    - **Terminology:** Job interview, structured interview, or behavioural interview.

7. **Conducting Background Checks:**

    - **Definition:** Verifying a candidate's background, including their education, work experience, and other relevant details.
    - **Terminology:** Background screening or reference checks.

8. **Making the Job Offer:**

    - **Definition:** Extending a formal offer of employment to the selected candidate.
    - **Terminology:** Job offer or offer of employment.

9. **Negotiating and Finalizing Terms:**

    - **Definition:** Discussing and finalizing details such as salary, benefits, and other terms of employment.
    - **Terminology:** Salary negotiation or offer acceptance.

10. **Onboarding:**

    - **Definition:** Integrating the new employee into the organization and providing necessary orientation and training.

- **Terminology:** Employee onboarding or orientation.

Throughout these stages, HR professionals use various HRM tools and techniques to ensure a smooth and effective recruitment process. These stages collectively contribute to acquiring and retaining talented individuals who align with the organization's goals and culture.

CHAPTER TWENTY-FIVE

Crafting the Perfect Job Description: Incorporating Diversity, Equity & Inclusion in your JD

Navigating Inclusive Excellence: Crafting the Perfect Job Description"

In the ever-evolving landscape of hiring, the job description serves as the compass, guiding organizations toward a diverse and inclusive workforce. Let's delve into the essential elements of a job description and explore how strategic crafting can attract a broad spectrum of talents.

Understanding the Job Description:

A job description is more than just a list of tasks and requirements; it's a powerful tool that shapes the narrative of your workplace and signals your commitment to diversity and inclusion. It's the first impression candidates have of your organization, setting the tone for an inclusive and welcoming environment.

Job Description

1. Inclusive Language:

The words we choose matter. Crafting an inclusive job description begins with using language that appeals to a diverse audience. Avoid gendered pronouns and stereotypes. Instead, opt for neutral language that welcomes candidates regardless of their background, age, or gender identity. For instance, replace "salesman" with "sales representative."

2. Clear Responsibilities and Duties:

Present a transparent and detailed breakdown of the role's responsibilities. However, be mindful not to overemphasize unnecessary qualifications. Prioritize the core skills and responsibilities, allowing candidates from diverse backgrounds to envision themselves succeeding in the role.

3. Qualifications and Requirements:

Distinguish between "must-haves" and "nice-to-haves." Highlight the essential skills necessary for success in the role, avoiding unnecessarily restrictive criteria. Encourage candidates to apply based on their unique skills and experiences, fostering a diverse pool of applicants.

4. Company Culture and Values:

Integrate statements that reflect your organization's commitment to diversity and inclusion. Showcase success stories of individuals from diverse backgrounds within your company, emphasizing that everyone has a place at the table. This fosters a sense of belonging and illustrates that diversity is not just a goal but a reality within your organization.

5. Commitment to Flexibility and Accessibility:

Acknowledge the diverse needs and work styles of your potential candidates. Consider incorporating statements about workplace flexibility, accommodation for different abilities, and support for various working arrangements. This demonstrates an understanding of the diverse challenges individuals may face and emphasizes your commitment to accommodating those needs.

Conclusion:

Crafting an inclusive job description is not just about finding the right candidate; it's about creating an environment where everyone feels valued and empowered. By choosing your words carefully, outlining responsibilities transparently, embracing diverse qualifications, showcasing your inclusive culture, and committing to flexibility, your job description becomes a beacon attracting a spectrum of talents. Remember, the journey to an inclusive workplace starts with the first job description.

Activity for you:

Refer to the Job Description format on the next page and write a Job Description for HR Generalist for NextGen HR.

....

....

CHAPTER TWENTY-SIX

Job Description or JD : Sample Format

Job Description Template: HR Manager

Company: EXAMPLE CompanyLocation: Bangalore, India

Position: HR Manager

Job Overview:

As an HR Manager at EXAMPLE Company, you will play a pivotal role in shaping and implementing human resources strategies to support our organizational goals. This position requires a strategic thinker with a passion for fostering a positive workplace culture, talent management, and employee engagement.

Responsibilities:

1. Recruitment and Talent Acquisition:

- Lead end-to-end recruitment processes, from job posting to onboarding.
- Develop and maintain effective sourcing strategies to attract top-tier talent.
- Collaborate with hiring managers to define job requirements and expectations.

2. Employee Relations:

- Foster positive employee relations by addressing concerns and promoting open communication.
- Conduct investigations and provide resolutions for employee relations issues.
- Develop and implement employee engagement initiatives.

3. Training and Development:

- Identify training needs and develop programs to enhance employee skills.
- Coordinate with external trainers and oversee in-house training sessions.
- Implement career development initiatives to support employee growth.

4. Performance Management:

- Oversee the performance management process, including goal setting and performance appraisals.
- Provide guidance to managers on performance improvement plans.
- Implement a fair and transparent performance evaluation system.

5. Compliance and Policies:

- Ensure compliance with labor laws and regulations.
- Update and communicate company policies and procedures.
- Conduct regular audits to ensure adherence to compliance standards.

Qualifications:

- Bachelor's degree in Human Resources or related field; Master's degree preferred.
- Proven experience as an HR Manager or similar role.
- In-depth knowledge of labor law and HR best practices.
- Excellent communication and interpersonal skills.

Experience: Minimum of 5 years of HR management experience, with a track record of implementing successful HR initiatives.

How to Apply:

Please submit your resume and cover letter to HR@examplecompany.com with the subject line "Application: HR Manager - Bangalore." Applications will be accepted until [Insert Deadline].

Last Date: Applications will be accepted until February 28, 2023.

CHAPTER TWENTY-SEVEN

Sourcing Strategies: Where Talent Hides

In the dynamic landscape of recruitment, finding the right talent is akin to a treasure hunt. The best candidates aren't always in plain sight; they often lurk in unexpected corners. This article unravels the mystery of sourcing strategies, guiding recruiters on how to unearth the hidden gems of talent acquisition.

Understanding the Hunt: Where Talent Hides

1. **Online Platforms and Job Boards:**

- **The Gold Mine of Resumes:**
    - Platforms like LinkedIn, Indeed, and specialized job boards are the initial hunting grounds.
    - Use advanced filters to zero in on candidates with specific skills, experience, and geographical preferences.
- **Example:** A financial analyst with a knack for data visualization might be hiding in the profiles of finance professionals on LinkedIn.

Sourcing Candidates

2. **Social Media Sourcing:**

- **Beyond the Resume:**
    - Platforms like Facebook, Twitter, and Instagram provide insights into a candidate's personality, interests, and values.
    - Engage with potential candidates through professional networking groups.
- **Example:** A software developer with a passion for open-source projects might be active in relevant Twitter communities.

3. **Referrals and Networking:**

- **The Power of Connections:**
    - Leverage your existing network and encourage employees to refer qualified candidates.

- Attend industry events, conferences, and meet-ups to expand your professional circle.

- **Example:** Your next top sales executive might be a recommendation from a current high-performing team member.

4. **University and Alumni Networks:**

- **Nurturing Future Talent:**
    - Partner with universities and tap into alumni networks for entry-level and experienced hires.
    - Attend career fairs and establish relationships with academic institutions.
- **Example:** A promising marketing graduate might be waiting to shine in your next internship program.

5. **Professional Associations and Communities:**

- **Specialized Talent Pools:**
    - Join industry-specific forums, associations, and online communities.
    - Engage with professionals sharing insights and participate in relevant discussions.
- **Example:** An experienced project manager could be an active contributor in project management forums.

Crafting Effective Sourcing Strategies:

1. **Define Your Ideal Candidate Profile:**

- Clearly outline the skills, experience, and cultural fit you're seeking.
- Tailor your sourcing strategy to align with the unique requirements of each role.

2. **Leverage Technology:**

- Utilize AI-powered tools to automate candidate sourcing and identify potential matches.
- Implement applicant tracking systems (ATS) to streamline the sourcing and recruitment process.

3. **Build and Nurture Talent Pools:**

- Create and maintain a talent pool for future needs.
- Regularly engage with potential candidates through newsletters, webinars, and relevant content.

4. **Measure and Optimize:**

- Track the success of your sourcing strategies using key performance indicators (KPIs).
- Continuously refine your approach based on performance data and feedback.

Conclusion: Unveiling the Hidden Talents

In the ever-evolving realm of recruitment, sourcing strategies are the compass guiding talent acquisition professionals. By diversifying your approach and exploring unconventional avenues, you open doors to a wealth of untapped potential. Remember, the best talents aren't always in plain sight; sometimes, they're waiting to be discovered in the unexplored corners of the talent landscape. Embrace the thrill of the hunt, and let your sourcing strategies uncover the hidden gems that will shape the future of your organization.

Activity for you:

Search for suitable candidates for HR Manager role for a company at Delhi, India (with minimum 5 years experience in manufacturing sector) using LinkedIn.

....

....

CHAPTER TWENTY-EIGHT

X-Ray Search and Boolean Search in Candidate Sourcing

Mastering Candidate Sourcing with X-Ray Search and Boolean Strings

Introduction

We will explore how to master candidate sourcing with X-Ray Search and Boolean Strings in this chapter. In today's competitive talent market, finding the right people for your team requires efficient and targeted strategies. X-Ray Search and Boolean Strings are powerful tools that can help you achieve just that.

What is X-Ray Search?

Simply put, X-Ray Search leverages Google's search capabilities to uncover relevant profiles on specific websites. It's like using Google as an X-ray machine, peering through a website's structure to find what you need.

The Power of Boolean Strings

Boolean Strings are the secret sauce of X-Ray Search. These are special commands like AND, OR, and NOT that allow you to refine your search queries significantly. By combining keywords and operators, you can create highly targeted searches that pinpoint the ideal candidates.

What are Strings?

In X-ray search and Boolean search, a string refers to a sequence of characters that defines your search criteria. It's like a mini-sentence you build to tell the search engine exactly what you're looking for.

In simple terms, a string in X-ray or Boolean search is just a bunch of text characters put together that tells the search engine what to look for. Imagine it like a mini instruction written in words and symbols.

These strings can include keywords related to the job title, skills, experience, or any other relevant information you want to find in candidate profiles.

Here's a breakdown of how strings work in each technique:

X-ray Search Strings: When searching on a specific website like LinkedIn, your X-ray search string will typically include:

Site Identifier: This tells the search engine which website to focus on, like "site:linkedin.com".

Keywords: These are the core terms related to the job you're trying to fill, like "Java Developer" or "Marketing Manager".

Boolean Operators (Optional): You can incorporate AND, OR, and NOT to refine your search further. For example, "Java Developer" AND "machine learning" to find developers with both skillsets.

Boolean Search Strings: These are used on general search engines and focus on combining keywords with Boolean operators to achieve high precision. They typically consist of:

Keywords: Similar to X-ray search, these are the terms associated with the skills or experience you need.

Boolean Operators (AND, OR, NOT): These operators are essential for crafting effective Boolean search strings. They allow you to broaden your search (OR), narrow it down (AND), or exclude irrelevant results (NOT).

By combining these elements strategically, you can create powerful search strings that pinpoint the ideal candidates for your job openings.

X-Ray Search Examples for Candidate Sourcing

Let's dive into some practical X-Ray Search examples using a popular platform like LinkedIn:

Finding Social Media Managers in a Specific Location:

Search String: site:linkedin.com ("Social Media Manager") (Gurgaon OR Delhi OR Noida) -inurl:jobs

This search focuses on LinkedIn profiles containing "Social Media Manager" in the title or description, located in Gurgaon, Delhi, or Noida, and excludes job postings (indicated by "-inurl:jobs").

Targeting Python Developers with Experience in Machine Learning:

Search String: site:linkedin.com ("Python Developer" OR "Software Engineer") (Machine Learning) AND NOT "React"

This broader search includes both "Python Developer" and "Software Engineer" titles, filters for "Machine Learning" experience, and excludes profiles mentioning "React" to focus on pure Python expertise.

Boolean Search Examples

Beyond X-Ray Search, mastering Boolean operators directly on search engines can further enhance your sourcing. Here are some examples:

Identifying Marketing Professionals with Campaign Management Skills:

Search String: "marketing" (campaign* OR lead generation) experience

This search uses the asterisk (*) as a wildcard, capturing terms like "campaign management" or "campaign planning."

Finding Data Analysts with Experience in SQL and Tableau:

Search String: "data analyst" (SQL OR Tableau) NOT "Excel"

This targets data analysts with SQL or Tableau proficiency while excluding those focused solely on Excel.

Remember: These are just a few examples. The key is to understand your specific needs and tailor your search strings accordingly.

Tips for Success

Start broad, then refine: Begin with a general search and gradually add keywords and operators to narrow down your results.

Use quotes for exact phrases: Enclose specific phrases in quotes to ensure they appear together in the search results.

Experiment and iterate: Don't be afraid to experiment with different Boolean operators and keywords to find the most effective combinations.

Stay updated: Keep pace with evolving job titles and industry jargon to adapt your search strings.

By mastering X-Ray Search and Boolean Strings, you can unlock a world of efficient candidate sourcing. These techniques allow you to target the most qualified individuals, saving time and effort in your talent acquisition process. So, put these powerful tools to work and build your dream team!

X-ray Search:

While X-ray search leverages some functionalities similar to Boolean search, it primarily relies on a few key elements:

Site Identifier: This specifies the website to search within, like "site:linkedin.com".

Keywords: These are the core terms related to the job title, skills, or experience (e.g., "Software Engineer", "Machine Learning").

Exclusion Terms (Optional): Some platforms might allow excluding terms with a minus sign (-) before them (e.g., "Data Analyst" -Excel). However, this functionality isn't universally supported in X-ray search.

Boolean Search:

Boolean search offers a wider range of operators for refined searches. Here are some commonly used ones (note that the top 20 might not be a definitive list):

Logical Operators:

AND: Narrows results by requiring all specified terms to be present (e.g., "marketing AND social media").

OR: Broadens results by finding instances with any of the listed terms (e.g., "Java OR Python developer").

NOT: Excludes results containing the following term (e.g., "data analyst" NOT "entry level").

Grouping Operators:

Parentheses: Define the order of operations within your search string (e.g., "(Java OR Python) AND developer").

Proximity Operators:

NEAR: Finds terms within a specific word distance (e.g., "artificial intelligence" NEAR "machine learning").

WITHIN: Similar to NEAR but defines a broader range (e.g., "cloud computing" WITHIN 5 "security").

Wildcard Operators:

Asterisk (*): Represents one or more characters (e.g., "data scientist*"). Useful for finding variations of a term (e.g., "data scientist" or "data science").

Remember, the specific operators supported by a search engine or platform might vary. It's always a good idea to consult their documentation for the most up-to-date information.

Where to use Boolean Search?

On job boards (job portals), Google and other search engines.

Examples of Boolean Search Strings used in Recruitment:

Google: ("software engineer" OR "developer") AND ("Python" OR "Java") site:linkedin.com

This search string instructs Google to find profiles containing either "software engineer" or "developer" and either "Python" or "Java" on the website LinkedIn.

While Google may not offer all the advanced search functionalities of dedicated job boards or professional networking sites, it remains a valuable tool for recruiters to supplement their candidate sourcing efforts and discover potential candidates across a wide range of online platforms.

Job Portals where you can use Boolean Search or Advanced Search:

- **LinkedIn:** LinkedIn is one of the largest professional networking sites where recruiters can search for candidates based on job titles, skills, experience, and location.
- **Indeed:** Indeed is a popular job board where recruiters can post job openings and search for resumes using boolean search strings to find suitable candidates.
- **Monster:** Monster is another well-known job board where recruiters can search for resumes and job postings using advanced search options, including boolean operators.
- **CareerBuilder:** CareerBuilder offers a wide range of job postings and resume search functionalities, allowing recruiters to use boolean search strings to find qualified candidates.
- **Dice:** Dice specializes in technology and engineering jobs, making it a go-to platform for IT recruiters who often use boolean search strings to identify candidates with specific technical skills.
- **Glassdoor:** Glassdoor not only provides job postings but also allows employers to search for candidates based on their resumes and profiles, using boolean search techniques.
- **ZipRecruiter:** ZipRecruiter is known for its user-friendly interface and extensive job listings. Recruiters can use boolean search strings to refine their candidate searches on this platform.
- **AngelList:** AngelList is a platform specifically designed for startups and tech companies. Recruiters can use boolean search strings to find candidates interested in joining early-stage companies.
- **Stack Overflow Careers:** Stack Overflow is popular among software developers and IT professionals. Recruiters can search for candidates with specific programming skills using boolean search strings.
- **Xing:** Xing is a professional networking site similar to LinkedIn, primarily used in European countries. Recruiters can utilize boolean search strings to find candidates with desired qualifications and experience.

These websites typically provide advanced search options that allow recruiters to input boolean search strings to refine their candidate searches and find the most suitable candidates for their job openings.

Top 10 Boolean Search Strings used in Recruitment by Recruiters or HR professionals:

1. ("software engineer" OR "developer") AND ("Python" OR "Java")

This string is used to find candidates who are either software engineers or developers proficient in Python or Java.

2. ("marketing manager" OR "marketing director") AND ("social media" OR "digital marketing")

This string targets candidates with experience in marketing management roles, specifically in social media or digital marketing.

3. (engineer OR developer) AND (C++ OR "C#") AND ("machine learning" OR AI)

This string is designed to find engineers or developers with skills in C++ or C#, particularly in the field of machine learning or artificial intelligence.

4. (nurse OR RN) AND (ICU OR "intensive care unit") AND (BLS OR ACLS)

Used to identify nurses or registered nurses specialized in ICU with certifications in Basic Life Support (BLS) or Advanced Cardiovascular Life Support (ACLS).

5. ("financial analyst" OR "investment analyst") AND (Excel OR "financial modeling")

Targets candidates for financial analyst or investment analyst positions with proficiency in Excel and financial modeling.

6. ("UX designer" OR "UI designer") AND (Sketch OR Figma) AND (prototyping OR wireframing)

Aims to find UX/UI designers skilled in either Sketch or Figma, with experience in prototyping or wireframing.

7. (project manager OR "PM") AND (PMP OR "Project Management Professional") AND (Agile OR Scrum)

Searches for project managers or PMs certified as Project Management Professionals (PMP) with experience in Agile or Scrum methodologies.

8. (sales OR "business development") AND ("account executive" OR "account manager") AND (B2B OR "business to business")

Targets candidates in sales or business development roles, specifically for account executive or account manager positions in the B2B sector.

9. (HR OR "human resources") AND ("talent acquisition" OR "recruitment") AND (ATS OR "applicant tracking system")

Used to find HR professionals specializing in talent acquisition or recruitment with experience in using Applicant Tracking Systems (ATS).

10. ("data scientist" OR "data analyst") AND (SQL OR Python) AND ("machine learning" OR statistics)

Targets candidates for data scientist or data analyst roles proficient in SQL or Python, with expertise in machine learning or statistics.

These boolean search strings can be adjusted and combined based on specific job requirements to effectively narrow down candidate searches.

X-Ray Search Examples

X-ray searching is a technique used by recruiters to search within a specific website, typically social networks like LinkedIn, using Google's advanced search operators. This method allows recruiters to access profiles and information that may not be readily available through the site's own search interface. Here's a step-by-step explanation of how to conduct an X-ray search in recruitment:

Step 1: Determine the Website to X-Ray Search

Identify the website you want to search within. In recruitment, common websites for X-ray searching include **LinkedIn, GitHub, Stack Overflow, and others.**

Step 2: Construct the X-Ray Search String

Use **Google's advanced search operators** to specify the website you want to search and the criteria for your search. The basic syntax for an X-ray search is:

site:website.com [search terms]

Replace "website.com" with the actual website domain and specify your search terms within the square brackets.

Step 3: Add Boolean Operators and Keywords

Include boolean operators (AND, OR, NOT) and relevant keywords to narrow down your search to specific criteria such as job titles, skills, or locations.

Step 4: Review Search Results

Evaluate the search results to find potential candidates or information that matches your criteria. Refine your search string as needed to improve the relevance of results.

Example 1: X-Ray Search on LinkedIn for Software Engineers in New York

site:linkedin.com/in software engineer New York

This search string targets LinkedIn profiles containing the term "software engineer" located in New York.

Example 2: X-Ray Search on GitHub for Frontend Developers with React Experience

site:github.com frontend developer React

This search string looks for GitHub profiles mentioning "frontend developer" with experience in React.

Example 3: X-Ray Search on Stack Overflow for Data Scientists proficient in Python

site:stackoverflow.com/users data scientist Python

This search string focuses on Stack Overflow user profiles associated with the term "data scientist" and proficiency in Python.

Example 4: X-Ray Search on AngelList for Startup Founders in San Francisco

site:angel.co/people startup founder San Francisco

This search string targets AngelList profiles containing the term "startup founder" based in San Francisco.

By using X-ray searching, recruiters can effectively explore specific websites to identify potential candidates or gather valuable information relevant to their recruitment needs.

CHAPTER TWENTY-NINE

The Science of Screening

In the intricate dance of recruitment, the screening process emerges as a critical act, akin to a meticulous sieve separating the grains of talent from the vast pool of applicants. This article delves into the science of screening, unraveling the intricacies that transform this process into a strategic art within the broader recruitment landscape.

Understanding the Screening Process: A Symphony of Selection

1. Resume Parsing and Keyword Matching:

- **Digital Vigilance:**
  - Applicant Tracking Systems (ATS) employ algorithms to parse resumes and match keywords.
  - Strategic use of keywords ensures alignment with job descriptions.
- **Example:** A software developer's resume should highlight relevant programming languages and technical skills to pass through the digital gates.

Screening Candidates

2. **Skill and Aptitude Assessments:**

- **Objective Evaluation:**
  - Administer tests and assessments to objectively measure specific skills and competencies.
  - Customize assessments to align with the role's requirements.
- **Example:** A graphic designer might undergo a design challenge to showcase their creativity and technical proficiency.

3. **Behavioral and Situational Interviews:**

- **Probing for Fit:**
  - Conduct interviews that explore past behaviors and responses to hypothetical scenarios.

    - Evaluate how candidates handle challenges and align with organizational values.

- **Example:** An aspiring team leader might be asked to share experiences in resolving conflicts within a team.

4. **Cultural Fit Assessment:**

- **Harmony with Values:**
    - Assess candidates for alignment with the company's culture, values, and mission.
    - Gauge interpersonal skills and compatibility with the existing team.

- **Example:** A candidate emphasizing collaboration and adaptability may align with a company prioritizing teamwork and innovation.

5. **Reference Checks:**

- **Validation Stage:**
    - Reach out to previous employers or professional references to verify qualifications and performance.
    - Gain insights into the candidate's work ethic, reliability, and interpersonal skills.

- **Example:** Confirming a candidate's track record of meeting deadlines and collaborating effectively with colleagues.

Crafting an Effective Screening Strategy:

1. **Define Screening Criteria:**

- Clearly outline the key skills, competencies, and cultural attributes required for success in the role.
- Tailor screening criteria based on the unique demands of each position.

2. **Leverage Technology:**

- Incorporate advanced analytics and machine learning to enhance the screening process.
- Utilize video interviewing platforms to evaluate non-verbal cues and communication skills.

3. **Structured Screening Protocols:**

- Develop a standardized screening process to ensure consistency.
- Train hiring managers and interviewers on objective evaluation techniques.

4. **Feedback Mechanisms:**

- Establish clear channels for feedback between recruiters, hiring managers, and other stakeholders.
- Regularly review and refine screening protocols based on feedback and performance data.

Conclusion: The Art and Science of Selection

Screening is not a one-size-fits-all process; rather, it's a carefully orchestrated symphony of methodologies designed to unearth the best-fit candidates. By understanding the nuances of resume parsing, skill assessments, interviews, and reference checks, recruiters can elevate the screening process from a routine task to a strategic endeavour.

Embracing the science of screening enables organizations to make informed decisions, ensuring that the talents selected not only possess the required skills but also align with the company's values and culture. In this dynamic dance of selection, the artistry lies in balancing objectivity with intuition, creating a harmonious blend that leads to the discovery of the perfect candidate for the role.

CHAPTER THIRTY

Mastering the Art of Interviewing: A Guide for HR Professionals in the Recruitment Process.

In the realm of recruitment, the interview is a pivotal moment—a delicate dance where HR professionals engage with potential candidates to unveil the qualities that transcend a resume. This article explores the nuances of interviewing skills, offering a comprehensive guide for HR professionals to conduct interviews that are not just conversations but strategic assessments.

Art of Interviewing

Understanding the Significance of Effective Interviewing:

Interviews are the bridge between a candidate's credentials on paper and their potential contributions to an organization. As an HR professional, your interviewing skills shape the narrative, providing insights into a candidate's personality, skills, and cultural fit within the company. Here's how to master this art:

1. **Preparation is Key:**

- **Study the Candidate:**

- Thoroughly review the candidate's resume, cover letter, and any submitted assessments.
- Understand the candidate's background, experiences, and potential areas of interest or concern.

2. **Creating a Welcoming Environment:**

- **Set the Tone:**
    - Begin the interview with a warm greeting and an overview of the session.
    - Explain the interview format, ensuring the candidate feels at ease.
- **Example:** "Welcome! Today, we'll discuss your experiences and how they align with our team. Feel free to ask questions at any point."

3. **Behavioral Interviewing Techniques:**

- **Focus on Past Behaviors:**
    - Use the STAR method (Situation, Task, Action, Result) to elicit detailed responses.
    - Ask about specific situations where the candidate demonstrated key competencies.
- **Example:** "Can you share an example of a challenging project you worked on and how you overcame obstacles?"

4. **Probing for Cultural Fit:**

- **Explore Values and Work Environment Preferences:**
    - Ask questions that unveil a candidate's alignment with the company culture.
    - Gauge their values, communication style, and preferred work environment.

- **Example:** "How do you approach collaboration and teamwork in a professional setting?"

Crafting Strategic Interview Questions:

1. **Open-Ended Questions:**

- **Encourage Thoughtful Responses:**

    - Use questions that prompt candidates to share insights and elaborate on their experiences.
    - Avoid yes/no questions to encourage in-depth responses.

- **Example:** "Tell us about a project where you had to think creatively to overcome a challenge."

2. **Situational Questions:**

- **Assess Problem-Solving Skills:**

    - Pose hypothetical scenarios relevant to the role to assess a candidate's approach.
    - Evaluate their thought process and decision-making abilities.

- **Example:** "How would you handle a situation where you disagreed with a team member's approach?"

3. **Role-Specific Inquiries:**

- **Tailor Questions to the Job Requirements:**

    - Align questions with the key competencies and skills essential for the role.
    - Assess the candidate's technical proficiency and industry knowledge.

- **Example:** "Can you provide an example of a successful project where you utilized [specific skill]?"

Active Listening and Non-Verbal Cues:

1. **Focused Listening:**

- **Stay Attentive Throughout:**
    - Demonstrate active listening by nodding, making eye contact, and offering verbal cues.
    - Avoid interrupting and allow the candidate to complete their thoughts.
- **Example:** "I appreciate your insights. Could you elaborate further on that point?"

2. **Non-Verbal Communication:**

- **Convey Positivity and Openness:**
    - Smile, maintain good posture, and usc gestures to express engagement.
    - Be mindful of your own non-verbal cues to create a comfortable atmosphere.
- **Example:** "Your enthusiasm about your previous project is evident. Can you share more details?"

Assessment and Decision-Making:

1. **Scoring and Evaluation:**

- **Create a Scoring System:**
    - Develop a structured scoring system to evaluate responses objectively.
    - Focus on key competencies and align scores with the job requirements.

- **Example:** Assign scores on a scale of 1 to 5 for each competency, considering depth of response and alignment with company values.

2. **Post-Interview Debrief:**

- **Collaborate with Hiring Team:**
  - Conduct a post-interview debrief with the hiring team to discuss candidate evaluations.
  - Gather diverse perspectives to make informed decisions.
- **Example:** "What were your impressions of the candidate's problem-solving skills during the interview?"

Conclusion: Elevating the Interview Experience

Mastering the art of interviewing is a continual journey of refinement and adaptation. As an HR professional, your skills in conducting effective interviews not only impact the hiring process but also contribute to shaping the future of your organization. By embracing strategic questioning, active listening skills, you can elevate the interviewing experience.

Activity for you:

List 5 technical, experience related, behavioral and culture fit related questions to ask a Software Engineer with 10 years of experience.

....

....

CHAPTER THIRTY-ONE

Candidate Evaluation Form: Sample

Interviewer: ....

Candidate Name: ....

Interview evaluation forms are to be completed by the interviewer to rank the candidate's overall qualifications for the position for which they have applied. Under each heading, the interviewer should give the candidate a numerical rating and write specific job-related comments in the space provided. The numerical rating system is based on the scale below.

Scale:

5 – Exceptional

4 - Good

3 - Average

2 - Poor

Educational Background – Does the candidate have the appropriate educational qualifications or training for this position? **Rating:** ....

Comments: ....

Prior Work Experience – Has the candidate acquired similar skills or qualifications through past work experiences? **Rating:** ....

Comments: ....

Technical Qualifications/Experience – Does the candidate have the technical skills necessary for this position? **Rating:** ....

Comments: ....

Verbal Communication – How were the candidate's communication skills during the interview? **Rating:** ....

Comments: ....

Candidate Interest – How much interest did the candidate show in the position and the organization? **Rating:** ....

Comments: ....

Knowledge of Organization – Did the candidate research the organization prior to the interview? **Rating:** ....

Comments: ....

Teambuilding/Interpersonal Skills – Did the candidate demonstrate, through their answers, good teambuilding/interpersonal skills? **Rating:** ....

Comments: ....

Initiative – Did the candidate demonstrate, through their answers, a high degree of initiative? **Rating:** ....

Comments: ....

Time Management – Did the candidate demonstrate, through their answers, good time management skills? **Rating:** ....

Comments: ....

Customer Service – Did the candidate demonstrate, through their answers, a high level of customer service skills/abilities? **Rating:** ....

Comments: ....

Overall Impression and Recommendation – Rating: ....

Summary of your perceptions of the candidate's strengths/weaknesses. Final comments and recommendations for proceeding with the candidate.

Comments:

Interviewer's Decision: ....

Proceed

Hold

Do not Proceed

CHAPTER THIRTY-TWO

Case Study Exercise: Interviewing

Here's a real-life case study related to job interviewing from Unilever, a consumer goods giant:

Source: https://hbswk.hbs.edu/item/unilevera-case-study

Job Interview: The Case

In 2009, Unilever was looking to fill a Marketing Manager position for their laundry soap brand, Omo, in Nigeria. The Nigeria market presented a unique challenge - while Omo was the leading brand, a competitor, Proctor & Gamble's Ariel, was gaining significant traction. Unilever needed a strong candidate who could develop a marketing strategy to solidify Omo's position.

The case study details the interview process for three shortlisted candidates:

- **Aisha Johnson: A highly experienced Marketing Manager with a proven track record in the Nigerian market.**
- **Kwame Kwaw: A recent MBA graduate with limited practical experience but strong analytical skills.**
- **Molade Adenrele: A Marketing Manager with experience in a different industry but a deep understanding of consumer behavior.**

The case challenges you to analyze the strengths and weaknesses of each candidate and decide who would be the best fit for the role. It also prompts you to consider factors like cultural awareness, leadership potential, and strategic thinking.

Why it's valuable:

This case study provides valuable insights into Unilever's recruitment process and the specific qualities they look for in marketing candidates. It also highlights the importance of tailoring your skills and experience to the specific needs of the company and the position.

By analyzing the case and making your selection, you can gain a better understanding of how to approach job interviews and showcase your qualifications effectively.

Do write your answers:

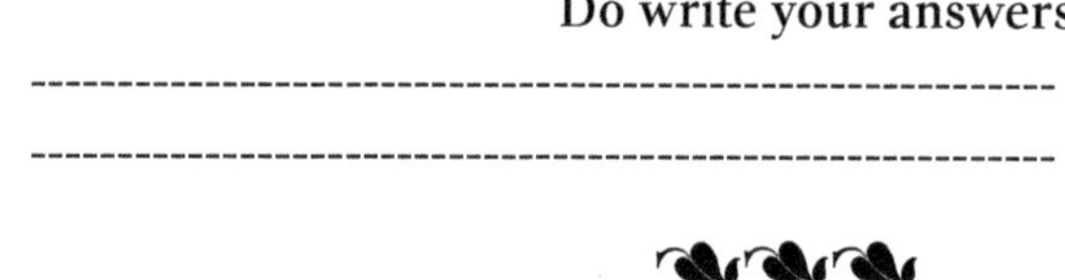

Possible Solutions for the Case:

The best candidate depends on Unilever's specific needs at that time. However, the candidates can be analyzed as below.

- **Aisha Johnson:** Strengths: Extensive experience, proven track record. Weaknesses: Might lack fresh ideas to combat a new competitor.
- **Kwame Kwaw:** Strengths: Strong analytical skills, potentially good for strategic planning. Weaknesses: Limited practical experience, might need significant mentoring.
- **Molade Adenrele:** Strengths: Deep understanding of consumer behavior, valuable for market research and targeting. Weaknesses: Experience in a different industry, might require some learning curve for FMCG (Fast Moving Consumer Goods) specifics.

Here's the suggestion for approaching the case:

Prioritize Unilever's needs: Is Unilever looking for someone to hit the ground running with experience (Aisha), a strategic mind for long-term planning (Kwame), or a consumer behavior expert to understand the market shift (Molade)?

Consider the Nigerian market: Cultural awareness and understanding of local consumer preferences are crucial. Analyze which candidate demonstrates this best.

Evaluate leadership potential: Who seems like they can lead and motivate a marketing team?

Based on this analysis, you might choose:

- **Aisha:** If immediate results and leveraging existing experience is the priority.
- **Kwame:** If strategic planning and a fresh perspective are most important.
- **Molade:** If understanding the evolving consumer behavior and adapting the marketing strategy is key.

Remember, there’s no single "correct" answer. The best choice depends on Unilever’s specific situation and priorities.

HR Policies & Procedures

CHAPTER THIRTY-THREE

Introduction to HR Policies & HR Procedures

Introduction:

Human Resources policies and procedures are integral components of any organization's human resources management framework. They provide guidelines and instructions for managing various aspects of employee relations, organizational behavior, and compliance with legal and ethical standards. Understanding the distinction between HR policies and procedures is crucial for maintaining organizational efficiency and fostering a positive work environment.

Definition:

HR Policies: HR policies are formal statements that outline an organization's approach and stance on specific employment-related matters. These policies establish the principles, values, and expectations governing the behavior and conduct of employees within the organization. They serve as a framework for decision-making and guide employees and managers in understanding the organization's stance on various issues.

HR Procedures: HR procedures, on the other hand, are detailed, step-by-step instructions that outline the specific actions and processes to be followed in various HR-related activities. These procedures provide a structured approach to implementing HR policies and ensure consistency and fairness in decision-making and actions across the organization.

Difference:

HR Policies: Example 1: Equal Employment Opportunity Policy - This policy outlines the organization's commitment to providing equal employment opportunities to all individuals regardless of race, gender, age, or disability. Example 2: Code of Conduct Policy - This policy establishes the ethical standards and behavioral expectations for employees, including guidelines on professional conduct, conflicts of interest, and confidentiality.

HR Procedures: Example 1: Recruitment and Selection Procedure - This procedure outlines the steps to be followed in the recruitment process, including job posting, applicant screening, interviews, and selection criteria. Example 2: Performance Appraisal Procedure - This procedure details the process for evaluating employee performance, setting performance goals, conducting performance reviews, and providing feedback and development opportunities.

Contents of HR Policies:

Statement of Purpose: Clearly articulates the rationale and objectives of the policy.

Scope: Defines the employees, situations, or activities to which the policy applies.

Responsibilities: Identifies the roles and responsibilities of employees, managers, and HR personnel in adhering to and enforcing the policy.

Compliance: Outlines the legal and regulatory requirements associated with the policy.

Consequences: Specifies the consequences of non-compliance with the policy, including disciplinary actions or sanctions.

Contents of HR Procedures:

Objectives: Clearly defines the goals and objectives of the procedure.

Sequential Steps: Provides a detailed, step-by-step sequence of actions to be followed in executing the procedure.

Roles and Responsibilities: Identifies the individuals or departments responsible for performing each step of the procedure.

Timeframes: Specifies the timeframes and deadlines associated with each step of the procedure.

Documentation: Outlines the documentation requirements and record-keeping practices associated with the procedure.

In summary, while HR policies set forth the overarching principles and values guiding employee behavior and organizational decisions, HR procedures provide the specific guidelines and steps for implementing those policies in day-to-day HR operations. Both policies and procedures play a vital role in promoting consistency, fairness, and compliance within the organization.

CHAPTER THIRTY-FOUR

Types of HR Policies

Employment Policies: These policies govern the relationship between the organization and its employees from recruitment to termination. Examples include:

- Recruitment and Selection Policy
- Equal Employment Opportunity Policy
- Anti-Discrimination and Anti-Harassment Policy
- Employment Classification Policy (e.g., full-time, part-time, temporary)
- Probationary Period Policy

Compensation and Benefits Policies: These policies outline the organization's approach to employee compensation, rewards, and benefits. Examples include:

- Compensation Policy (salary structure, pay scales, bonuses)
- Benefits Policy (healthcare, retirement plans, leave policies)
- Overtime Policy
- Expense Reimbursement Policy
- Flexible Work Arrangements Policy

Workplace Policies: These policies govern the conduct of employees within the workplace and ensure a safe, respectful, and productive work environment. Examples include:

- Code of Conduct Policy
- Workplace Health and Safety Policy
- Drug and Alcohol Policy
- Social Media and Electronic Communications Policy

- Dress Code Policy

Performance Management Policies: These policies outline the organization's approach to managing and evaluating employee performance. Examples include:

- Performance Appraisal Policy
- Performance Improvement Plan (PIP) Policy
- Goal Setting and Performance Planning Policy
- Feedback and Coaching Policy

Training and Development Policies: These policies address employee training, development opportunities, and continuous learning initiatives. Examples include:

- Training and Development Policy
- Tuition Reimbursement Policy
- Professional Development Policy
- Succession Planning Policy

Leave and Time Off Policies: These policies outline employees' rights and obligations regarding various types of leave and time off from work. Examples include:

- Vacation and Paid Time Off (PTO) Policy
- Sick Leave Policy
- Family and Medical Leave Act (FMLA) Policy
- Bereavement Leave Policy
- Jury Duty Policy

Information Technology (IT) and Data Security Policies: These policies address the use of technology resources and the protection of sensitive information. Examples include:

- Acceptable Use of IT Resources Policy
- Data Security and Confidentiality Policy
- Bring Your Own Device (BYOD) Policy
- Email and Internet Usage Policy

These are just a few examples of the types of HR policies that organizations may implement. The specific policies adopted by each organization depend on factors such as industry regulations, organizational culture, size, and workforce composition. These policies also keep getting added from time-to-time according to situation such as Work From Home Policies, Hybrid Work Policies, etc.

New HR Policies Introduced post Covid-19 pandemic:

The COVID-19 pandemic has significantly impacted workplaces worldwide, leading organizations to implement new HR policies and adapt existing ones to address the challenges and changes brought about by the crisis. Some of the recently added HR policies in response to the COVID-19 situation include:

Remote Work Policy: With the shift to remote work becoming more prevalent during the pandemic, organizations have implemented or updated remote work policies to provide guidelines on expectations, communication protocols, technology requirements, and performance evaluation for employees working remotely.

Flexible Work Hours Policy: To accommodate employees' diverse needs and circumstances during the pandemic, organizations have introduced flexible work hours policies that allow employees to adjust their work schedules to better balance work and personal responsibilities, such as caregiving or homeschooling.

Health and Safety Protocols: Given the importance of ensuring employee health and safety in the workplace, organizations have implemented comprehensive health and safety protocols aligned with guidelines from health authorities. These protocols may include measures such as physical distancing, enhanced cleaning procedures, provision of personal protective equipment (PPE), and guidelines for COVID-19 testing and vaccination.

Sick Leave and Quarantine Policies: Organizations have updated their sick leave and quarantine policies to provide additional support to employees who contract COVID-19 or are required to quarantine due to exposure. These policies may include provisions for extended paid sick leave, flexible use of paid time off (PTO), and remote work options during quarantine periods.

Mental Health and Well-being Initiatives: Recognizing the impact of the pandemic on employees‘ mental health and well-being, organizations have implemented new policies and initiatives to support employees' mental health needs. These may include access to counseling services, mental health resources and training, flexible work arrangements, and promoting a culture of psychological safety and support.

Travel Restrictions and Guidelines: To minimize the risk of COVID-19 transmission, organizations have introduced travel restrictions and guidelines that limit non-essential business travel and provide protocols for essential travel. These policies may include requirements for pre-travel health screenings, quarantine upon return from travel, and approval processes for travel requests.

Crisis Communication Protocols: Given the rapidly evolving nature of the pandemic, organizations have developed crisis communication protocols to ensure timely and transparent communication with employees regarding COVID-19-related updates, developments, and organizational responses. These protocols may include designated communication channels, frequency of updates, and procedures for addressing employee concerns and questions.

Overall, the COVID-19 pandemic has prompted organizations to rethink and adapt their HR policies to address the unique challenges and uncertainties presented by the crisis while prioritizing employee health, safety, and well-being. These newly implemented policies reflect a proactive approach to managing the impact of the pandemic on the workforce and ensuring organizational resilience in the face of ongoing challenges.

CHAPTER THIRTY-FIVE

Case Study: HR Policies

Case Study: Overtime Blues at Baker's Delight

Company: Baker's Delight, a regional bakery chain known for its fresh bread and pastries.

Problem: Low employee morale, burnout, and increasing absenteeism due to a poorly defined overtime policy.

Background: Baker's Delight prides itself on its fresh-baked goods, requiring early morning starts and occasional weekend work. However, their overtime policy was a vague document outlining minimum overtime pay but lacking specifics on approval processes, workload expectations, and time-off compensation.

Consequences of Unclear Overtime Policy:

Employee Morale: Employees felt pressured to work long hours without clear guidelines or compensation for their extra time. This led to resentment towards management and a feeling of being taken advantage of.

Burnout and Absenteeism: The constant overtime demands resulted in employee burnout. Exhausted staff called in sick more frequently, further straining operations and creating a vicious cycle.

Inconsistent Application: With no clear approval process for overtime, managers inconsistently assigned extra hours, causing resentment among employees who felt unfairly burdened.

Impact on the Business:

Reduced Productivity: Burned-out employees became less productive, leading to decreased quality and efficiency.

Increased Costs: High absenteeism and low morale translated into increased recruitment and training costs.

Reputational Damage: Unhappy employees may share their experiences online or with potential hires, harming the company's employer brand.

The Overtime Policy Overhaul:

Recognizing the negative impact of their overtime policy, Baker's Delight implemented the following changes:

Clearly Defined Policy: Developed a comprehensive overtime policy outlining approval procedures, workload expectations, compensation rates, and time-off options in exchange for overtime hours.

Employee Input: Incorporated employee feedback during the policy development process, fostering a sense of ownership and fairness.

Manager Training: Trained managers on the new policy, ensuring consistent application and clear communication with employees.

Focus on Work-Life Balance: Introduced alternative solutions like temporary staff or schedule adjustments to minimize reliance on excessive overtime whenever possible.

Results:

The revised overtime policy led to significant improvements:

Improved Morale: Clear expectations and fair compensation practices boosted employee morale and trust in management.

Reduced Absenteeism: With a focus on work-life balance, burnout decreased, resulting in fewer absences.

Increased Productivity: A happier and healthier workforce led to improved productivity and overall efficiency.

Conclusion:

Baker's Delight's experience highlights the importance of a well-defined overtime policy. By taking the time to develop a clear, fair, and employee-centric policy, companies can foster a positive work environment, reduce costs, and improve overall business performance.

CHAPTER THIRTY-SIX

HR Procedures

Transactional & Development HR Procedures

Transactional HR procedures are those that focus on the day-to-day administrative tasks of HR, such as recruitment, onboarding, payroll, and benefits administration. These procedures are typically well-defined and step-by-step, ensuring consistency and compliance with legal requirements.

Developmental HR procedures are those that focus on improving employee performance and development. These procedures may be more flexible and adaptable, as they are tailored to the specific needs of the organization and its employees.

HR procedures encompass a wide range of processes and activities related to human resources management. Below are some common types of HR procedures along with examples of policies that may fall under each type:

Recruitment and Selection Procedures:

Job Posting Procedure: Guidelines for posting job vacancies internally or externally, including the required information and channels for advertisement.

Candidate Screening Procedure: Steps for screening job applications, including criteria for shortlisting candidates and conducting initial assessments.

Interviewing Procedure: Procedures for conducting interviews, including interview formats, question guidelines, and panel composition.

Reference Checking Procedure: Steps for verifying candidate credentials and conducting reference checks with previous employers or references.

Employee Onboarding Procedures:

Orientation Procedure: Steps for welcoming and orienting new employees to the organization, including introductions to company culture, policies, and procedures.

New Hire Paperwork Procedure: Guidelines for completing necessary paperwork, such as employment contracts, tax forms, and employee handbooks.

Training and Development Procedure: Procedures for providing initial training and ongoing development opportunities to new employees to support their integration into the organization.

Performance Management Procedures:

Goal Setting Procedure: Steps for setting performance goals and objectives aligned with organizational priorities and individual roles.

Performance Appraisal Procedure: Procedures for evaluating employee performance through formal appraisal processes, including performance reviews, feedback sessions, and performance improvement plans.

Recognition and Rewards Procedure: Guidelines for acknowledging and rewarding employee contributions and achievements, including incentives, awards, and recognition programs.

Employee Relations Procedures:

Grievance Handling Procedure: Steps for addressing employee grievances and complaints in a fair and timely manner, including channels for reporting grievances and resolution mechanisms.

Disciplinary Procedure: Procedures for addressing employee misconduct or performance issues, including investigation, disciplinary action, and appeal processes.

Conflict Resolution Procedure: Guidelines for resolving conflicts and disputes among employees or between employees and management through mediation, negotiation, or other conflict resolution techniques.

Compensation and Benefits Procedures:

Salary Administration Procedure: Procedures for administering employee salaries, including salary structures, pay scales, and salary adjustments.

Benefits Enrollment Procedure: Steps for enrolling employees in company benefits programs, such as health insurance, retirement plans, and other fringe benefits.

Leave Management Procedure: Guidelines for managing employee leave, including procedures for requesting, approving, and tracking various types of leave, such as vacation, sick leave, and parental leave.

Separation and Offboarding Procedures:

Resignation Procedure: Steps for managing employee resignations, including notification requirements, exit interviews, and processing final payments.

Termination Procedure: Procedures for terminating employee employment, including termination notice periods, exit interviews, and handling company property and access.

Retirement Procedure: Guidelines for managing employee retirement transitions, including retirement planning, benefits eligibility, and retirement ceremonies.

These are just a few examples of HR procedures and the associated policies that organizations may implement to effectively manage various aspects of human resources management. The specific procedures and policies adopted by an organization will depend on its size, industry, culture, and regulatory requirements.

CHAPTER THIRTY-SEVEN

Case Study: HR Procedures

Case Study: The Missing Piece: How a Flawed HR Procedure Led to Lost Talent

Company: Streamline Solutions, a fast-growing marketing agency.

Employee: Sarah Jones, a recent graduate hired for the Content Marketing Specialist role.

Problem: Sarah left the company after 45 days of inactivity due to a lack of a formal onboarding and orientation procedure within the HR department.

The Onboarding Flaw:

Streamline Solutions, despite its rapid growth, lacked a standardized onboarding and orientation procedure within its HR department. This critical lapse left Sarah in limbo from the very beginning.

HR Disconnect: Sarah's HR contact wasn't informed about her start date, leading to delays in essential tasks like equipment setup and account creation.

No Roadmap: Without an onboarding plan, Sarah had no clear path to integrate into the team or understand her role and responsibilities.

Managerial Uncertainty: Her designated manager, unsure of the onboarding process due to a lack of HR guidance, was unable to provide direction or training resources.

Social Isolation: With no official HR onboarding steps for team introductions or buddy assignments, Sarah felt isolated and without a support system.

Consequences of Missing HR Procedure:

Employee Disengagement: Left without guidance or resources, Sarah became disengaged and unsure of her value to the company.

Wasted Potential: Streamline lost 45 days of potential productivity while Sarah waited to be integrated into the team.

Diminished Morale: The lack of a structured onboarding process sent a message of disorganization and a disregard for Sarah's well-being, leading to low morale.

Increased Turnover: Sarah's negative experience ultimately resulted in her resignation, adding to Streamline's recruitment and training costs.

The Power of a Strong HR Procedure:

A well-defined HR onboarding and orientation procedure could have prevented Sarah's departure:

Pre-boarding Checklist: A standardized HR checklist would have ensured timely equipment setup, account creation, and pre-reading materials to prepare Sarah for her first day.

Structured Onboarding Plan: An HR-designed onboarding plan would have outlined a clear roadmap for Sarah, including training sessions, team introductions, and goal setting.

Managerial Onboarding Training: HR could have provided training for managers on their role in onboarding, ensuring they understood the process and could actively support new hires.

Buddy System Facilitation: The HR department could have facilitated a buddy system, pairing Sarah with a colleague for mentorship and social integration.

Conclusion:

Streamline Solutions' case study highlights the critical role of a well-defined HR onboarding and orientation procedure. Its absence led to a chaotic and unproductive experience for Sarah, ultimately resulting in her leaving the company. Investing in a standardized onboarding program managed by HR fosters a smooth transition for new hires, improves retention, and maximizes their contribution to the organization's success.

HR Manual or Employee Handbook

CHAPTER THIRTY-EIGHT

HR Manual or Employee Handbook

What is HR Manual or Employee Handbook?

An HR manual, also sometimes called an employee handbook, is a comprehensive document outlining an organization's policies and procedures related to employees. It serves as a guide for both employers and employees regarding expectations and guidelines in the workplace.

The contents of an HR (Human Resources) manual can vary depending on the organization's size, industry, and specific policies. However, here are some common sections that you might find in an HR manual:

Welcome Message or Introduction: This section typically provides an overview of the company's values, mission, and commitment to its employees.

Company Policies and Procedures: This section outlines various policies and procedures that govern employee conduct, including but not limited to:

- Equal Employment Opportunity (EEO)
- Anti-discrimination and harassment policies
- Code of Conduct/Ethics
- Attendance and punctuality
- Dress code
- Use of company property and resources (e.g., computers, vehicles)
- Workplace safety and security
- Drug and alcohol policies
- Social media and electronic communication guidelines
- Confidentiality and data protection policies

Employment Information:

- Employment classifications (full-time, part-time, temporary, etc.)
- Work schedules and hours
- Payroll information (pay periods, deductions, overtime)
- Benefits information (healthcare, retirement plans, vacation, sick leave)

Employee Relations:

- Grievance procedures
- Conflict resolution processes
- Employee discipline and termination policies
- Whistleblower protection policies

Training and Development: This section may include information about:

- Orientation and onboarding processes
- Training opportunities
- Performance management and appraisal procedures

Leaves of Absence: Information regarding various types of leaves available to employees, such as:

- Vacation leave
- Sick leave
- Family and medical leave (FMLA)
- Bereavement leave
- Jury duty leave

Health and Safety: Guidelines related to workplace health and safety, including:

- Emergency procedures
- Injury reporting
- Ergonomics
- Workplace hazards

Employee Benefits: Detailed information about the benefits offered by the company, such as:

- Health insurance
- Dental and vision plans
- Retirement plans (401(k), pension)
- Disability insurance
- Flexible spending accounts (FSAs)
- Employee assistance programs (EAPs)

Employee Acknowledgment: A section where employees acknowledge receipt of the manual and agree to abide by its policies and procedures.

Appendices: Additional resources, forms, or legal disclosures related to employment with the company.

It's essential for organizations to keep their HR manuals updated regularly to reflect changes in laws, regulations, and company policies. Additionally, HR manuals should be easily accessible to all employees and provided to new hires during the onboarding process.

CHAPTER THIRTY-NINE

Sample HR Manual or Employee Handbook Template

<Company>

Human Resources Manual

Table of Contents

<Company Overview>. 3
Policy & Procedures Manual 3
1. PERSONAL CONDUCT 4
1.1 Dress Code. 4
1.2 Personal Communications 5
1.3 Gifts & Gratuities 7
2. EQUAL EMPLOYMENT OPPORTUNITY. 8
3. SEXUAL HARASSMENT 9
4. BUSINESS EXPENSES. 12
5. INDUCTION.. 13
6. HEALTH, SAFETY & ENVIRONMENT 14
6.1 Smoking. 14
6.2 Alcohol, Drug (& Other Substance Abuse) 15
6.3 Manual Handling. 15

6.4 Workers' Compensation. 16
6.5 Total & Permanent Disability. 16
7. PERFORMANCE MANAGEMENT SYSTEM.. 17
7.1 Introduction. 17
7.2 Performance Management Philosophy. 17
7.3 Position Descriptions 17
7.4 Probationary Period Reviews 18
7.5 Performance Appraisals 19
7.6 Professional & Personal Development 20
7.7 Superannuation. 21
8. LEAVE POLICY: 22
8.1 Annual Leave. 22
8.2 Personal Leave. 23
8.3 Compassionate/Bereavement Leave. 23
8.4 Long Service Leave. 23
8.5 Maternity Leave. 24
8.6 Paternity Leave. 25
8.7 Adoption Leave. 25
8.8 Study Leave. 26
8.9 Time in Lieu. 26
8.10 Leave Without Pay. 26
8.11 Blood Donor Leave. 27
8.12 Jury Duty. 27
8.13 Emergency Services Leave. 27
9. TRAVEL & ACCOMMODATION.. 29
9.1 Air Travel 29
9.2 Accommodation. 30
9.3 Travel Other Than By Air 30
9.4 Motor Vehicle Rental 31
9.5 Taxi Fares 31
9.6 Parking Charges 31
9.7 Work Events 32
10. EMPLOYEE RELATIONS. 33
10.1 Discipline. 33
10.2 Disciplinary Appeal 36
10.3 Grievance. 37
11. POST TRAUMA COUNSELLING.. 38
12. INTELLECTUAL PROPERTY AND SECURITY. 40

13. CONFLICT OF INTEREST 41
14. PRIVACY. 42

<Company Overview>

Insert some information on your company including:

- **history:** when did your business start and how has it changed over time
- **market:** what is your competition like?
- **general employment philosophy:** what type of employment do you offer (contracting, full-time, part-time etc), what work environment do you encourage

Policy & Procedures Manual

The <Company> Human Resources Policy and Procedures Manual has been developed to facilitate the implementation and clearly define <Company>'s policies on human resource management.

The Manual provides guidelines to be followed in the administration of these policies, and assists all employees in defining who is responsible for each human resource management decision, and the correct procedure which is to be followed.

The policies specified within are consistent with those of best practice management principles. They have the full support and commitment of <Company> management.

HR policies must be kept current and relevant. Therefore, from time to time it will be necessary to modify and amend some sections of the policies and procedures, or for new procedures to be added.

Any suggestions, recommendations or feedback on the policies and procedures specified in this manual are welcome. This should be provided by email.

These policies and procedures apply to all areas of operations within <Company> and related entities.

1. PERSONAL CONDUCT

Policy Statement

<Company> expects its employees to achieve and maintain a high standard of ethics, professional conduct and work performance to ensure the Company maintains its reputation with all internal and external stakeholders.

Objective

To enhance <Company's> reputation as a quality service provider and an enjoyable, stimulating and challenging place to work.

Application

The policy will be seen to be successfully applied when all employees are seen to perform their duties professionally with skill, care and diligence.

This includes:

- observing <Company> policies and procedures
- treating colleagues with courtesy and with respect for their rights, duties and aspirations

- employees who do not conform to this standard of conduct will be subject to disciplinary action as detailed in this manual

1. **Dress Code**

Dress choice is a matter of personal discretion, taking into account requirements for any protective clothing, customer/supplier interaction and professional environment.

Be aware that work attire will have an impact upon <Company's> image as well as your work colleagues.

As a minimum standard, dress should be clean, neat and professionally appropriate.

The following are examples of items that are not acceptable:

- ripped or torn clothing
- thongs or sports sandals
- sportswear or beachwear

<Company> reserves the right to request a staff member to dress to an appropriate standard as a condition of employment.

If you are in a work environment with inappropriate clothing you may be sent home to change, before returning to work.

1. **Personal Communications**

    i. **Phone Calls** [choose one of the following]

The making and receiving of personal phone calls must be limited to a maximum of five minutes in duration, unless otherwise approved by your manager.

Or

It is acknowledged that personal communication is inevitable and sometimes necessary. It is expected this will be kept to appropriate or reasonable levels.

    ii. **Email**

Email has legal status as a document and is accepted as evidence in a court of law. Even when it is used for private purposes, <Company> can be held responsible for the contents of email messages, including any attachments. Access to emails can be demanded as part of legal action in some circumstances.

It is therefore important that email is used within the following guidelines:

- email should mainly be used for formal business correspondence and care should be taken to maintain the confidentiality of sensitive information. Formal memos, documents and letters for which signatures are important, should be issued on company letterhead regardless of whether a physical or electronic delivery method is used
- if electronic messages need to be preserved, they should be printed out and filed
- limited private use of email is permitted, provided that such does not interfere with or distract from an employee's work. However, management has the right to access incoming and outgoing email messages to determine whether staff usage or involvement is excessive or inappropriate

- non-essential email, including personal messages, should be deleted regularly from the 'Sent Items', 'Inbox' and 'Deleted Items' folders to avoid congestion
- all emails sent should include the approved company disclaimer

In order to protect <Company> from the potential effects of the misuse and abuse of email, the following instructions are to be observed by all users.

1. No material is to be sent as email that is defamatory, in breach of copyright or business confidentiality, or prejudicial to the good standing of <Company> in the community or to its relationship with staff, customers, suppliers and any other person or business with whom it has a relationship.
2. Email is not to contain material that amounts to gossip about colleagues or that could be offensive, demeaning, persistently irritating, threatening, discriminatory, involves the harassment of others or concerns personal relationships.
3. The email records of other persons are not to be accessed except by management (or persons authorised by management) engaged in ensuring compliance with this policy, or by authorised staff who have been requested to attend to a fault, upgrade or similar situation. Access in each case will be limited to the minimum required to complete the task.
4. When using email a person must not pretend to be another person or use another person's computer without permission.
5. Excessive private use, including mass mailing, "reply to all" etc. that are not part of the person's duties, is not permitted.

Failure to comply with these instructions is a disciplinary offence and will be subject to appropriate investigation. In serious cases, the penalty for an offence, or repetition of an offence, may include dismissal. Staff need to be continually aware some forms of email conduct may also be open to criminal prosecution.

iii. **Internet**

The internet is a facility provided by <Company> for business use. Access is authorised by managers on the basis of business needs. Limited private use is permitted provided the private use does not interfere with or distract from a person's work. Management has the right to access the system to determine whether private use is excessive or inappropriate.

The following activities, using <Company>'s internet access are not permitted:

- attending to personal activities of a business nature
- viewing, other than by accident, sites of incoming emails portraying obscene, violent, defamatory and unlawful material and material that could cause <Company> to be in breach of equal opportunity or anti-discrimination legislation, verbally, in writing or pictorially
- downloading or printing material as described above
- showing to others, or allowing to be seen by others, items as described above
- repeated or prolonged use that is not directly relevant to the user's work
- introducing computer viruses by failing to follow company IT procedures
- downloading software from the internet or from unauthorised disks and CD ROMs on to the internal network

Failure to comply with these instructions is a disciplinary offence and will be subject to appropriate investigation. In serious cases, the penalty for an offence, or repetition of an offence, may include dismissal. Staff need to be continually aware some forms of internet conduct may also be open to criminal prosecution.

3. Gifts & Gratuities

<Company> is committed to ensuring all business relationships with suppliers and clients are legal and based on professional integrity.

Managers should be notified when a gratuity has been received. If the gratuity has been received as a thank you for work performed then it should be noted on the employee's personal file to ensure it is included in the employee's next appraisal.

No employee may give a gratuity to a client without prior approval from management, such gratuities must always be part of an approved program of customer relationship management and specific gifts will be purchased centrally in appropriate quantities with management approval.

2. EQUAL EMPLOYMENT OPPORTUNITY

Policy Statement

<Company> provides equal employment opportunity to all qualified persons without discrimination on the basis of age, sex, race, disability, marital status or religion in accordance with applicable local, state and national laws and regulations. <Company> will make reasonable job accommodation for persons with disabilities who can perform the essential functions of the position for which they are qualified and selected.

All employment and promotion decisions will be based solely upon individuals' qualifications, experience, prior contribution and demonstrated capacity to perform at higher or improved levels of performance and will be in accordance with the principle of equal employment opportunity. <Company> will take whatever affirmative action is necessary to attract and retain qualified persons.

Objective

The objective of the Equal Opportunity Policy is to support the attraction and retention of employees that contribute most to the development of the <Company> business.

Application

The Equal Employment Opportunity policy will be successfully applied when all roles are filled by the best qualified and experienced candidates available regardless of personal circumstances.

Process

The Equal Opportunity Employment process is reflected throughout <Company's> staff recruitment and retention processes.

3. SEXUAL HARASSMENT

Policy Statement

<Company> is committed to ensuring employees are treated fairly and equitably in an environment free of intimidation and sexual harassment. Sexual harassment is an unacceptable form of behaviour which will not be tolerated under any circumstances. It is also unlawful. All complaints of sexual harassment will be treated seriously and promptly, with due regard to confidentiality. Disciplinary action will be taken against any employee who breaches the policy.

Sexual harassment is any unwanted, unwelcome or uninvited behaviour of a sexual nature which makes a person feel humiliated, intimidated or offended. Sexual harassment can take many different forms and may include physical contact, verbal comments, jokes, propositions, the displaying of offensive material or other behaviour which creates a sexually tense or hostile working environment. Sexual harassment can occur between an employee and a co-worker, supervisor, manager, agent, consultant or contractor.

Sexual harassment is not just unlawful during working hours or in the workplace itself. The behaviour is unlawful in any work-related context, including conferences, work functions, business or field trips, and interactions with clients.

<Company> encourages any employee who feels they have been harassed to contact a company manager. The company aims to provide a working environment which is free of workplace harassment or intimidation.

<Company> recognises comments and behaviour which do not offend one person can offend another. Management accepts individuals may react differently and expects this right to be generally respected.

Any complaints or reports of sexual harassment will be treated promptly, seriously and sympathetically. They will be investigated thoroughly, impartially and confidentially. Managers and supervisors must act immediately on any reports of sexual harassment. Employees will not be disadvantaged in their employment conditions or opportunities as a result of lodging a complaint.

Appropriate disciplinary action will be taken against anyone in this company's employment who is found to have sexually harassed a co-worker. Depending on the severity of the case, consequences can include an apology, counseling, transfer, dismissal, demotion or other forms of disciplinary action. Immediate disciplinary action will also be taken against anyone who victimises or retaliates against a person who has complained of sexual harassment.

<Company> has a legal responsibility to prevent sexual harassment.

Therefore, managers and supervisors have a responsibility to:

- monitor the working environment to ensure acceptable standards of conduct are observed at all times
- model appropriate behaviour themselves
- treat all complaints seriously and take immediate action to investigate and resolve the matter

- refer complaints to another manager if they do not feel they are the best person to deal with the case (e.g. if there is a conflict of interest or if the complaint is particularly complex or serious)

All employees have a responsibility to:

- comply with the organisation's sexual harassment policy
- offer support to anyone who is being harassed and let them know where they can get help and advice (they should not approach the harasser themselves)
- maintain complete confidentiality if they provide information during the investigation of a complaint (employees who spread gossip or rumours may expose themselves to defamation action)

Objective

To foster a professional, open and trusting workplace.

Application

The sexual harassment policy will be successfully applied when all staff are treated on merit by their managers, by peers, by direct reports and by all other team members.

Process

Making a Complaint:

If you believe you are being, or have been, harassed, follow the procedure below:

- inform the offender the behaviour is offensive, unwelcome, and against company policy and should stop (only if you feel comfortable enough to approach them directly)
- keep a record of the incident(s)
- if the unwelcome behaviour continues, contact your supervisor or manager for support
- if this is inappropriate, you feel uncomfortable, or the behaviour still persists, contact your manager.

Receiving a Complaint:

When a manager receives a complaint, he/she should follow the procedure below:

- listen to the complaint seriously
- treat the complaint confidentially
- allow the complainant to bring another person to the interview if he/she chooses to
- ask the complainant for the full story, including what happened step by step
- take notes, using the complainant's own words
- ask the complainant to check your notes to ensure your record of the conversation is accurate
- explain and agree next action with the complainant
- if investigation is not requested:

    - act promptly
    - maintain confidentiality
    - pass your notes on to your manager

- if investigation is requested, or is appropriate, follow the procedure outlined

Investigating a Complaint:

When a manager investigates a complaint, he/she should follow the procedure below:

- interview all directly concerned, separately
- interview witnesses, separately
- keep records of interviews and investigation
- do not assume guilt
- interview the alleged harasser, separately and confidentially
- let the alleged harasser know exactly what he/she is being accused of
- give him/her a chance to respond to the accusation
- listen carefully and record details
- make it clear he/she does not have to answer any questions
- ensure confidentiality, minimise disclosure
- determine appropriate action based on investigation and evidence collected
- check to ensure the action meets the needs of the complainant and company

If resolution is not immediately possible, the complainant should be referred to more senior management.

If the resolution requires the authority of a more senior manager, the complainant should be referred to the appropriate level.

Outcomes as they affect the complainant should be discussed with the complainant to ensure that needs are met, where appropriate.

Potential Outcomes:

If the complaint is found to be justified, the complainant may be entitled to any or all of the following:

The complainant may receive:

- commitment the behaviour will cease
- private apology (verbal or written)
- re-credit of any leave taken due to the harassment
- payment of medical and counselling expenses
- transfer, with no job disadvantage
- other compensation

4. BUSINESS EXPENSES

Policy Statement

<Company> will reimburse employees for out of pocket business expenses incurred in the performance of their role, where prior approval has been received from a manager.

Tax receipts (showing an ABN if in Australia) must be provided for all expenses to be reimbursed.

Cash advances in advance of anticipated expenses can only be approved by senior managers.

Objective

The objectives of the business expenses policy are to ensure staff are not out of pocket in the course of fulfilling their responsibilities, and expenses can be correctly allocated to optimise the company's tax position.

Application

The business expenses policy will be successfully applied when all staff expenses are reported, allocated and reimbursed within 30 days.

Process

Minor one off expenses ($50 or less) may be reimbursed through petty cash. Where possible this should be in advance for a known requirement and receipts, along with change, should be returned to petty cash.

Expenses for more than $50 or for employees with ongoing individual expenses requirements should be submitted to Accounts on an Expenses Claim Form which has been signed off as approved by the employee's immediate supervisor.

All claims must be submitted by the seventh of the month for the previous month in arrears. Only one claim should be made per month. Exceptionally large expense claims may be submitted at the time of incurring them and not wait until the end of the month.

Payment of reimbursed expenses will be made directly into your nominated bank account (recorded with Accounts) generally by the 15th of the month but may take up until the end of the month they are submitted.

5. INDUCTION

Policy Statement

All new employees should complete an induction program upon their commencement. The induction period also refers to the three month probationary period during which it is recognised all staff may need ongoing familiarisation with their role, the business, systems and processes.

Objective

The objective of the induction policy is to familiarise the employee with the company, their job, the industry, colleagues, company systems, processes and policies with a view to ensuring they can make a contribution to business outcomes as quickly as possible.

The induction should be a combination of standard components as well as learning specifically tailored to the role.

Application

The induction policy will be successfully applied when all new employees meet their probationary period performance targets.

Process

Complete the induction planning format prior to the employee's commencement date.

Introduce the employee to the induction schedule and dates.

Review the progress against the schedule with the employee at the end of each week.

6. HEALTH, SAFETY & ENVIRONMENT

Policy Statement

<Company> is committed to providing and maintaining a safe work environment for the health, safety and welfare of our staff, contractors, visitors and members of the public who may be affected by our work.

We undertake to provide resources in terms of personnel, time and financial outlay commensurate with the commitment we place on OHS to achieve these objectives.

To do this, <Company> will:

- develop and maintain safe systems of work, and a safe working environment
- provide information and training at all levels in the organisation to enable all employees to support this policy
- require all risks to be assessed prior to engaging in new areas of operation, purchasing new equipment, and implementing new work methods, and that these risks continue to be reviewed

All persons who are responsible for the work activities of other employees will be held accountable for:

- identifying practices and conditions which could injure employees, clients, members of the public or our environment
- implementing steps to control such situations
- if unable to control such practices and conditions, reporting these to their superiors

<Company> demands a positive attitude and performance with respect to health, safety and the environment by all employees, irrespective of their position.

1. **Smoking**

<Company> employs a non smoking policy. Smoking is not permitted on <Company> property or offices at any time. Smoking is accepted to be harmful to the health of those who smoke and those around them (passive smokers). Consequently, smoking while on company premises will be considered as gross misconduct and will render an employee liable to instant dismissal.

Smokers who need to take breaks should do so during their allotted breaks (no more than two per day in addition to their lunch break). These breaks must be limited to 15 minutes from leaving the workplace to recommencing work.

These breaks must not be taken at the entrance to <Company> offices. This is a poor representation of the Company and people who may be visiting <Company>, visitors do not want to be walking through a cloud of smoke.

No special privileges will be afforded to smokers. Any additional breaks (outside of allotted breaks) must be approved by your manager - these must be limited to 10 minutes from leaving the workplace to recommencing work - and the time must be made up at the conclusion of the working day. Excessive smoking breaks will be regarded as absenteeism and disciplinary action may be taken.

2. **Alcohol, Drugs (& Other Substance Abuse)**

This policy applies to all levels throughout <Company>. The policy is not concerned with social drinking or the taking of prescribed drugs for medical purposes, the concern is directed to instances where alcohol or other drug dependence or abuse affects the job performance and or/safety of any employee(s).

<Company> is concerned by factors affecting an employee's ability to safely and effectively perform work to a satisfactory standard. The Company recognises alcohol or other drug abuse will cause short-term or long-term impairment to such work performance.

<Company> is committed to creating and maintaining a safe, healthy and productive workplace for all employees. <Company> has a zero tolerance policy in regards to the use of illicit drugs on their premises or the attending of other business related premises (e.g. clients) while under the influence of illicit drugs. Contravening either of these points may lead to instant dismissal.

Attending work under the influence of alcohol will not be tolerated and may result in disciplinary action or ultimately dismissal.

<Company>, at times, makes alcohol available to staff over the age of 18. Limiting the consumption of any alcohol made available is the responsibility of the employee. Driving under the influence of alcohol or any other illicit drug is illegal, it is your own responsibility to ensure you comply with this.

3. **Manual Handling**

It is the policy of <Company> to provide all employees with a safe and healthy working environment by identifying, assessing and controlling manual handling risks within the workplace.

While managerial staff are ultimately responsible for ensuring the health, safety and welfare of all staff, all employees are expected to participate by reporting potential and actual manual handling hazards within the workplace.

In all circumstances, do not lift or manually handle items larger or heavier than you can easily support. If you are in any doubt, ask for assistance.

4. Workers' Compensation

All employees, including part-time, temporary, and probationary employees, are eligible for workers' compensation benefits in the event of an injury arising from, or in the course and scope of, their employment.

The process to be followed if an injury occurs is as follows:

- the first priority in the event of an injury at work is medical attention
- the injured worker or nearest colleague should initially contact one of <COMPANY>'s registered first aid attendants
- in the event of any apparently serious injury an ambulance should be called
- any employee who sustains an on-the-job injury, experiences a safety incident or near miss must report the incident to their manager
- the manager must then complete a report in the Register of Injuries, Incidents and Near Misses
- this standard report must include:
    - employee details
    - time and location the injury/incident occurred
    - details of the injury including:
        - part of body injured
        - time lost
        - name of the first aid attendant
    - details of first aid treatment

- details of any investigation of the accident

5. **Total & Permanent Disability**

If an employee is injured while away from work, <Company> will allow them to exhaust their paid sick leave, accumulated annual leave or long service leave.

If the injured employee has used all leave owing, been off work for a lengthy period and is not fit enough to return to work then management will discuss with the employee their expectations of returning to work.

If the employee has an incapacity to perform their duties because of the disability, their employment will be terminated in compliance with the termination provisions in their employment contract.

<Company> will hold an injured worker's position open for a period of time as stated in the relevant legislation unless it is not reasonably practicable to do so.

Employees whose employment is terminated due to an incapacity to perform their duties because of a disability, will be paid all amounts owing to them, including accrued wages, leave entitlements, severance pay and superannuation.

7. PERFORMANCE MANAGEMENT SYSTEM

1. **Introduction**

At <Company> we aim to be an employer of choice– one where people want to work. As a business we are committed to giving all members of our team every opportunity to develop their careers, to contribute to our business and to share in its success.

The Performance Management System is designed to support the completion of the work of the organisation. It will also define, measure and recognise the contribution of individuals and help the organisation establish achievable goals for all of its people – it is a team based approach.

At any stage, if you have any questions or concerns you can raise them with your Manager.

2. **Performance Management Philosophy**

We believe everyone who comes to work really does want to realise their potential and develop their relationships with others (managers, colleagues and clients).

Work is characterised by feelings of satisfaction, frustration, opportunity, exasperation, stimulation, excitement and even feelings of fairness and dishonesty. To succeed and excel, we recognise people need to know what is expected of them, what authority they have and how they are performing. In addition the approach to managing them needs to be consistent.

If our organisation can help its people feel more of the positive emotions and eliminate most of the negative then we will have come a long way to being an employer of choice.

The Performance Management System is designed to be the foundation for fulfilling careers at <Company>.

3. Position Descriptions

All <Company> employees will have position descriptions, these will only be produced in an agreed format and amendments need to be approved by Management.

Objectives

The objective of all position descriptions is to provide an accurate picture of the responsibilities required within specific job roles, the authority levels attached to that role and a clear explanation as to how the output of the role is to be measured.

Application

The policy on position descriptions will be successfully applied when all position descriptions are used as the basis for performance appraisals and when amendments are completed within 14 days of a performance appraisal discussion. Any changes to position descriptions deemed necessary by managers will be communicated as soon as practicable to the employee and this will be implemented by both parties signing a copy.

Process

Introduction and Amendment of Position Descriptions

All employees will receive individual briefings on their position descriptions from their Manager.

Position descriptions will always be discussed in detail at job interviews and all new employees are to be given a copy of their position description with their letter of offer.

4. **Probationary Period Reviews**

Policy Statement

All new employees are appointed with the intention of the placement being permanent unless otherwise stated in the letter of offer.

All new employees will serve a three month probationary period to ensure both <Company> and the employee are happy with a permanent commitment to the role. Managers should engage new employees in informal performance based feedback regularly and have specific meetings to discuss progress after one and two months respectively.

Prior to the completion of the three month probationary period new employees will undergo a performance appraisal to provide feedback on performance, guidance on future direction and to set selected specific objectives for the next performance appraisal period.

Objectives

The objective of the probationary performance appraisal is to ensure both <Company> and the employee are satisfied the role is as agreed and a re-commitment to the permanent nature of the position can be made.

Application

The policy on probationary performance appraisals will be successfully applied when all probationary appraisals are completed within three months of employment commencing.

Process

1. The manager and the employee will agree on the date for a performance appraisal meeting. In the case of all probationary period appraisals, this must be before the completion of three months of service.
2. The manager will prepare a written performance appraisal in the approved format and provide this to the employee at least 48 hours before the meeting.
3. The manager and the employee will meet and agree any objectives for the next appraisal period.

Performance Appraisals

Policy Statement

All employees will undergo performance appraisals with their immediate managers on timing that is based on the level of their role. All performance appraisals will be timed from the date employment commenced. This is to ensure performance management is a regular, rather than occasional management responsibility. Performance appraisals are completely separate from remuneration reviews.

Objectives

The objective of the performance appraisal system is to constantly monitor progress of the capabilities and achievements of employees, to facilitate the ongoing development of team members and to identify when an employee has demonstrated readiness for greater responsibility.

The objective of individual performance appraisals is to review work performance on the basis of both capabilities and achievement of specific performance objectives. Performance appraisals also provide feedback to <Company> on the achievability of objectives and the capability of managers to manage their employees.

Application

The policy on performance appraisals will be successfully applied when all employees' appraisals are completed within the required time frames.

Process

1. The manager and the employee will agree on the date for a performance appraisal meeting. This must be within the allowable time frame for each role. The frequency of performance appraisals is noted on position descriptions.
2. The manager will prepare a written performance appraisal in the approved format and provide this to the employee at least 48 hours before the meeting.
3. The manager and the employee will meet and agree any objectives for the next appraisal period.

6. **Professional & Personal Development**

Policy Statement

<Company>, in partnership with the employee, will maintain a professional and personal development plan for each employee. <Company's> role in this is as a supportive facilitator. It will be up to the employee to take a leading role in managing their own development within

an approved structure.

Funding for professional and personal development will be considered for support by <Company> on its merits.

<Company> may, from time to time, require employees to attend specific training or instruction delivered by internal or external facilitators. This may be on or off-site.

Development may take the form of training, education, mentoring, coaching or counselling.

Objectives

The objective of the professional and personal development policy is to provide a structured environment for learning and development for the individual within and external to the company

Application

The policy on professional and personal development will be successfully applied when employees are managing their own development plans.

Process

1. During the appraisal process the manager will identify and document which areas the employee's performance may be enhanced by further training. The manager will identify specific courses where possible.
2. The employee and manager will then work together to complete a professional development plan for the employee.
3. In response to this the employee can source their own solutions instead of, or in addition to, the manager's suggestions. Requests to attend these should be submitted in writing to the employee's immediate manager and must include:

    - suggested dates
    - costs
    - anticipated outcomes

Superannuation

Policy

<Company's> policy is to provide superannuation benefits to all employees to assist them to prepare for retirement and provide options for coverage in the event of death or permanent incapacity. <Company> will as a minimum, comply with legislation in this area.

Process

Employees can nominate a super fund of their choice when they commence with the Company. All employees must belong to a superannuation fund whilst employed by <Company>. Contributions made by the company and employee will cease when the employee is of an age in accordance with occupational superannuation standards.

Employees may make their own contributions in addition to those made by <Company>.

Procedure

On commencement an employee should complete a super choice form.

Superannuation contributions will be deducted directly from an employee's salary. These deductions will terminate when the employee is 65 years of age.

8. LEAVE POLICY:

Policy Statement

<Company>'s policy is all employees are entitled to leave in accordance with the relevant awards/agreements and statutory provisions. Where the attached practices conflict with employment law for an employee, or group of employees, the law will take precedence. Leave for full time employees will generally be 20 days per annum plus gazetted public holidays in the workplace jurisdiction.

Annual Leave

All employees are entitled to a minimum of 20 days annual leave a year on completion of 12 months of service. Leave entitlements are calculated from date of commencement.

It is preferred annual leave is not accrued from year to year. Employees are expected to co-operate in taking annual leave as requested when the business closes for the Christmas break.

In the first 12 months of employment, employees can only take annual leave once it has accrued (or at management's discretion), unless required by management to take annual leave over the Christmas period.

In some circumstances, leave in advance of accrual may be approved and each request will be assessed individually by the relevant manager. This may be conditional on the individual agreeing to the Company deducting any advance in the event of termination, or to the employee accepting leave without pay.

Applications for annual leave should be lodged four weeks in advance. Leave application forms should be filled out and forwarded to payroll for action. Annual leave will count towards continuous service.

Any annual leave requests in excess of two weeks continuous leave must be signed off by management.

Employees may request to cash out up to two weeks of their credited annual leave entitlement every 12 months (or the pro-rata equivalent for part-time employees). A request to cash out annual leave must be made in writing and given to your manager for approval.

2. **Personal Leave**

As per the *Workplace Relations Amendment (Work Choices) Act 2005*, personal leave, carer's leave and sick leave have all been aggregated under the title personal leave.

An employee should notify his/her manager as soon as possible if he/she is unable to attend work due to illness or injury. Absences of two or more days in a row require a medical certificate.

Employees are entitled to 10 days of personal leave every 12 months.

Paid personal leave accrues on a pro-rata basis and is cumulative.

Personal leave for illness immediately prior to or following a gazetted public holiday requires a medical certificate.

If all personal leave accumulated has been taken, then an employee is entitled to a period of up to two days unpaid personal leave per occasion (e.g. when a member of the employee's immediate family or household requires care or support).

3. **Compassionate/Bereavement Leave**

Compassionate leaveis paid leave taken by an employee for the purposes of spending time with a family member/member of employee's household, who has a personal illness, or injury, that poses a serious threat to his/her life, or after the death of a family member/member of the employee's household.

Each employee is entitled to a period of two days paid compassionate leave for each occasion where a family member has died or the employee needs to spend time with a seriously ill family member

Each application for compassionate leave will be assessed individually by management.

Compassionate leave will count towards continuous service.

4. **Long Service Leave**

You will be entitled to long service leave in line with the provisions of the appropriate legislation in your state.

Employees should give reasonable notice of intention to take long service leave and payment will be made at the normal hourly rate of pay.

Long Service Leave will count towards continuous service.

5. **Maternity Leave**

Female employees with at least 12 months of continuous service are entitled to maternity leave.

Maternity leave is unpaid leave which is available for a minimum period of six weeks and for a maximum period of 52 weeks if the employee is the primary carer. Other types of leave can be taken in conjunction with maternity leave providing the total period of absence does not exceed 52 weeks.

Any employee taking maternity leave is required to take at least six weeks continuous leave after the date of the birth of her child. The employer may, with 14 days notice, require the employee to commence maternity leave within six weeks of the presumed confinement date.

Applications for maternity leave should include personal details, a medical certificate detailing the expected date of confinement or birth, proposed commencement date and duration of leave. Advice as to whether superannuation payments will continue should be given by the employee.

Where the pregnancy is terminated other than by birth of a living child and the employee has not commenced maternity leave, her entitlement to such leave ceases to exist. However, an employee may be entitled to special maternity leave, as specified by her doctor, if the pregnancy has extended beyond 28 weeks, and is terminated other than by birth of a living child.

Details of return to work date must be given four weeks in advance. The employee is entitled to return to the position held prior to taking maternity leave or to an alternative position of comparable status and pay.

Maternity leave will not count towards continuous service.

i. **Transfer to a Safe Job**

If a pregnant employee provides a doctors certificate stating she is fit to work but is unable to continue in her present position she is entitled to be transferred to a safe job. If transferring the employee to a safe job is not reasonably practicable then the employee is entitled to paid leave for the period during which she is unable to continue in her present position (as stated in the medical certificate).

A pregnant employee is only eligible to be transferred to a safe job if she is entitled to, and has formally applied for, maternity leave.

This entitlement is in addition to any other leave entitlement and does not reduce the period of maternity leave to which an employee is entitled.

6. **Paternity Leave**

Permanent male employees with at least 12 months continuous service are entitled to paternity leave.

Paternity leave is unpaid leave available for a minimum period of one week at the time of confinement and a maximum period of 52 weeks if the employee is the primary carer.

Other types of leave can be taken in conjunction with paternity leave providing the total period of absence does not exceed 52 weeks.

Applications for paternity leave should include personal details, a medical certificate detailing the date of confinement or birth, proposed commencement date and duration of leave. Additionally, the employee will need to provide a Statutory Declaration stating he will be the primary carer. Advice as to whether superannuation payments will continue should be given by the employee.

Where the pregnancy is terminated other than by the birth of a living child and the employee has not commenced paternity leave, his entitlement to such leave ceases to exist.

Details of the return to work date must be given four weeks in advance. The employee is entitled to return to the position he held prior to taking paternity leave or to an alternative position of comparable status and pay.

Paternity leave will not count towards continuous service.

Adoption Leave

An employee seeking to adopt a child may take up to two days of unpaid pre-adoption leave to attend any interviews or examinations required to obtain approval for the adoption.

Employees adopting a child under the age of five years are entitled to take up to 52 weeks of unpaid adoption leave (shared between both parents). This leave is only available when the adopted child has not previously lived continuously with either parent for at least six months and is not a child or step child of either parent. Parents may take up to three weeks unpaid leave simultaneously when an adopted child is placed with them.

Other types of leave can be taken in conjunction with adoption leave providing the total period of absence does not exceed 52 weeks.

Study Leave

Employees are entitled to study leave to undertake further education courses relevant to <Company's> business and approved by the Company.

The maximum amount of study leave that should be approved is four hours per week to attend lectures or 10 full days per year for those who are studying by correspondence and who are required to attend residential courses. Applications should be lodged four weeks in advance by filling out a training course application form and forwarding to payroll.

Employees are entitled to paid leave to sit an examination.

Days in excess of this entitlement are at the discretion of the manager.

Study leave will count towards continuous service.

9. Time in Lieu

Time-in-lieu will be granted to those employees who are required by their manager to work outside of their normal job function. All time-in-lieu granted will be added to the employee's annual leave.

The <Company> will maintain time-in-lieu accounts which will record time-in-lieu credits and debits. This allows management to provide time-in-lieu as a discretionary benefit. Generally, time-in-lieu should be taken within the same financial year within which it is accrued.

Time-in-lieu must be pre-approved by the appropriate manager.

10. Leave Without Pay

Approval of leave without pay is at the discretion of management.

An application giving personal details, employment details, the amount of time and the reason for the leave should be submitted by the employee.

Other types of appropriate paid leave should be used before approval for leave without pay can proceed.

Failure to return to work on the date stipulated may result in loss of continuity or termination. Extension of leave will be considered on an individual basis. An exchange of letters is required setting out all conditions.

Leave without pay will not count towards continuous service.

11. Blood Donor Leave

Employees may donate blood during working hours without loss of pay provided that:

- the payment will be for up to two hours, once in each quarter of the year
- the time fits in with work requirements
- it is with the approval of their immediate supervisor on presentation of an attendance card authorised by the Red Cross Transfusion Service

12. Jury Duty

Employees are entitled to paid leave to serve on a jury. An employee on jury service should provide official evidence of requirement to attend and attendance at the court.

Employees should declare the amount paid to them by the court and <Company> will reimburse them the difference between the amount received and their base salary.

Jury duty leave will count towards continuous service.

13. Emergency Services Leave

If an employee needs to take temporary absence from work because of voluntary emergency management activities (e.g. dealing with an emergency/natural disaster on a voluntary basis, as a member of SES, CFA, Army Reserve etc) then they must make a request to management for leave.

The total absence for such leave must be reasonable (take into account current work deadlines etc) and must be agreed between the employee and management.

<Company> may refuse a request by an employee to attend emergencies if they are urgently required at work. If an employee does not accept the

decision of the directors and leaves work without permission, they may be subject to disciplinary proceedings including dismissal.

Objective

The objectives of the leave policy are to ensure all staff have adequate time away from work for family holidays, special events, rest and recreation while avoiding the build up of large amounts of annual leave not taken on the Company balance sheet.

Application

The leave policy will be successfully applied when staff take appropriate breaks from work and when all annual leave is taken within the calendar year.

Process

All planned leave will be taken at a mutually agreed time and will take into account workload requirements and an employee's individual needs.

Leave must be approved in advance with the exception of sick leave or special leave where absences cannot be anticipated.

A leave form should be completed, signed by the employee's manager and forwarded to payroll for action.

9. TRAVEL & ACCOMMODATION

Policy Statement

All staff should adhere to the travel and accommodation policy when travelling on Company business. The Company recognises business travel is generally an inconvenience and seeks to make such inconvenience more comfortable at a cost that is appropriate for the Company's size and cash flows.

Objective

The objective of the travel and accommodation policy is that the employee can be in the required location to do business and be ready to do business. All travel arrangements are intended to be comfortable, practical and economical ensuring the employee endures no discomfort when they are required to travel or stay away from home.

Application

The travel and accommodation policy will be successfully applied when travel is completed within budget at no discomfort to the employee.

1. **Air Travel**

Policy

<Company's> policy is to use a preferred airline for approved business travel.

All our travel, both domestic and international is to be booked at economy class rates or the lower available discount fare, unless otherwise approved by management.

Process

Booking requests are to be made on the booking/authority form which should be forwarded to the nominated booker.

At least three days notice and wherever possible, the maximum period of notice of bookings required, should be given, to allow maximum use of available discounted fares.

2. **Accommodation**

Policy

<Company> has arrangements with various hotel/motel groups. Persons requiring accommodation should enquire from the nominated booker as to the availability of current deals in various locations.

Capital city and major provincial city accommodation should be booked wherever practicable through the previously nominated bookers.

Accommodation in country areas will be at the discretion of the traveller but should take maximum advantage of available corporate membership plans and lowest available rates.

All accommodation and meal charges are to be paid by the user, unless an alternative arrangement has been previously agreed by the relevant manager. Where there is more than one employee present, meal charges should be paid by the most senior employee.

The preferred method of payment is by an accepted credit card. Expenditure will be reimbursed on production of a personal expenses claim form.

No accounts will be opened in the Company name. No charges are to be invoiced directly to the Company, unless previously authorised by the relevant manager. Under no circumstances are accounts to be opened or operated at restaurants, hotels etc.

Process

See Expenses Reimbursement.

Travel Other Than By Air

Policy

If it is necessary to travel by rail or coach, arrangements and authorisation as for air travel will apply.

4. **Motor Vehicle Rental**

Policy

Approval must be obtained from the employee's manager before any vehicle is rented.

Car rental may not be the most cost effective form of local transportation, considering rental, insurance, fuel, mileage and parking charges. For short distances in a day, taxis may be the more economical form of transport.

<Company> does not have accounts with any car rental firms. All rentals are to be paid for by the employee and claimed as personal expenses.

Car rental is to be used only when other means are unavailable, more costly or impractical. The class of car should be a small sedan, unless a larger vehicle is absolutely necessary. Insurance for car rental must be incurred on the rental contract and signed for. If an accident occurs, the rental company should be advised promptly.

5. **Taxi Fares**

Policy

Employees who are travelling on work related business and who require the use of a taxi for travel should pay the fare and then forward an expenses form with receipt to accounts to be reimbursed

6. **Parking Charges**

Policy

Unless required for permanent parking of a particular vehicle, no reserved parking places are to be maintained for general use. It is more cost effective to pay casual rates or catch taxis.

Parking fees will be reimbursed for business purposes. However, parking infringement penalties or fines will not, in any circumstances, be paid for by the Company.

Work Events

Work social events are optional events for employees. All employees need to organise their own transportation to and from the venue unless previously organised by management.

10. EMPLOYEE RELATIONS

1. **Discipline**

Policy Statement

<Company> has a human resources' strategy that recognises the value of its people. Part of this strategy is the fair treatment of all employees. This requires a minimum standard of conduct and performance be agreed, set and communicated with all employees. If employees do not meet this standard, appropriate corrective action, such as training, should be undertaken. Discipline should only be engaged with an employee on a performance issue if all other corrective action has failed to achieve the desired result.

Where an employee has deliberately breached a Company policy or procedure, or engaged in misconduct, disciplinary procedures should be initiated.

Employees should be treated fairly and the proper procedures should be followed.

Employees must be made aware of their responsibilities, counselled and given the opportunity to reach the standards expected of them and the chance to defend themselves before action is taken.

It is a requirement to have a third party attend a disciplinary meeting, and notes taken be signed as a true record of discussions.

The expected standard must be clearly defined and the measurement criteria understood. A reasonable date for achievement of standards must be agreed. This should be shown as a minimum time, e.g. within one month.

For serious issues, employees must be advised in writing and such advice should be recorded on the employee's personnel file.

Process

a. **Poor Performance**

Wherever possible the Performance Management System should be used to manage employee performance. However, there may be times when performance, conduct or employee attitude need to be immediately addressed.

If employees fall below required performance standards and performance management processes have not been adequate to address the issue they must be personally counselled and then given written confirmation of their deficiencies in performance (a written warning).

Such written warnings must clearly define the deficiency, the expected standard, by when it should be achieved, how the company will help the employee achieve the improvement required and the consequences of failing to do so.

A record of all meetings, training and/or coaching given and a summary of discussions must be kept by the manager concerned and a copy placed on the employee's personnel file. This should include date, location and time of discussion.

If an employee consistently fails to meet agreed standards, he/she has been counselled and appropriate support/training has been offered and/or given, then further action is required. This may lead to the employee being dismissed.

If an employee has not been performing as required, and:

- all possible corrective action, including training and coaching, has been undertaken
- the manager concerned has documentation showing the conversations taken place, agreed action plans, and other communication with the employee
- the employee has been informed of the standards required and his/her performance deficiency(ies) with action plans in writing on at least two occasions and the consequences of failing to met the required standards
- the employee has been given the opportunity to appeal or respond to the issues highlighted on each occasion
- no other suitable option, or other appropriate positions, are available

If all these processes have been followed and the employee's performance still has not improved, then the employee may be dismissed*.

b. **Misconduct**

Managers are expected to investigate misconduct and proceed through the following steps:

- a verbal warning should be given to an employee for minor misconduct. A record of the warning must be kept by the manager and should be signed by the employee. The employee must be given the opportunity to respond
- if the unacceptable behaviour continues, a written warning will be issued, and signed by the employee as being received and understood. The employee must be given the opportunity to respond
- a second written warning should be given to an employee if he/she requires further discipline for the same or a related issue, and also signed by the employee as being received and understood. The employee must be given the opportunity to respond
- employees who have been disciplined three times are subject to dismissal*
- details of disciplinary actions should be recorded on the employee's personnel file and removed after six months if further disciplinary action is not required

If a manager considers the allegation to be serious, and it requires further investigation, an employee should be suspended on base pay for a maximum of two weeks while an investigation takes place. The individual must be informed, in writing, of the details of the allegation and advised he/she is under investigation. The employee must sign this notice as being received and understood.

This letter should invite the employee to present his/her version of events to the investigating officer and inform he/she may be accompanied by a representative. The only purpose of the representative's visit is to observe – they are not participants.

Should we consider an employee's conduct likely to lead to a situation in which we may wish to dismiss without notice, a diary must be kept at all times to record incidents and conversations and associated matters which may be needed in subsequent proceedings. The relevant manager is responsible for keeping this diary. This manager should also issue a written warning that a continuance of such behaviour will lead to instant dismissal.

c. **Gross or Serious Misconduct**

Summary (instant) dismissal for gross or very serious misconduct is possible (depending on the facts involved) for the following:

insubordination, drunkenness, dishonesty, assault, deliberately endangering the safety of others, commission of a criminal offence on our site, and objectionable language**. ***Managers must, however, consult with senior management prior to taking this action*.***

In such cases follow the procedure below:

- investigate the alleged offence thoroughly, including talking to witnesses, if any
- ask the employee for his/her response to the allegation (taking notes of this discussion)
- consult with the next most senior manager regarding possible action
- if still appropriate, following a thorough investigation, terminate/dismiss the employee
- keep a file on all evidence collected and action taken in these circumstances

All procedures must be followed in accordance with employment equal opportunity/anti-discrimination legislation.

***Note:** In all such cases ‘procedural fairness’ guidelines will apply. This means the warning and dismissal process must allow the employee to offer their view of the events concerned. The employee must have every chance to defend himself/herself and has the right to appeal a decision made. If this process is not followed the dismissal may be overturned by an Industrial Relations authority.

****Note:** For some offences <Company> retains the right to report the matter to the police where charges may be laid. The police will be notified with regard to any criminal act against the Company or another member of staff. Management has a duty of care to shareholders and staff and at all times will be subordinate to legal process.

2. **Disciplinary Appeal**

Policy Statement

During all stages of the disciplinary process employees have the right to appeal against any disciplinary action taken against them.

An employee who believes the disciplinary action taken against them is unfair, is able to appeal the process.

An appeal will be treated fairly, dealt with discreetly and actioned promptly.

This policy should be read in conjunction with the grievance policy.

Process

An employee is entitled to lodge a written appeal to their supervisor's manager detailing his/her objections to the disciplinary action within three working days of notification.

Managers should:

- acknowledge receipt of the employee's objection
- investigate the matter thoroughly
- report back to the employee within seven days

If the appeal is disallowed an employee is entitled to appeal to the next most senior manager.

The next most senior manager should investigate the matter and report back to the employee within 10 working days.

The employee has no further right of appeal under this process if the second appeal is disallowed.

All procedures must be followed in accordance with employment equal opportunity/anti-discrimination legislation.

Grievance

Policy Statement

<Company> supports the right of every employee to lodge a grievance with his/her manager if the individual believes a decision, behaviour or action that affects their employment is unfair. We aim to resolve problems and grievances promptly and as close to the source as possible with graduated steps for further discussions and resolution at higher levels of authority as necessary.

Grievances should be actioned discreetly and promptly dealt with in an objective manner.

Process

The employee should attempt to resolve the complaint as close to the source as possible. This can be at a quite informal and verbal level. If the matter is not resolved then further steps need to be taken.

All available attempts to settle a grievance before starting the formal grievance process should be taken.

For the formal grievance process to begin, complainants must fully describe their grievance in writing, including dates and locations wherever possible and the remedies sought.

The person(s) against whom the grievance/complaint is made should be given the full details of the allegation(s) against them and should have the opportunity and reasonable time to respond before resolution is attempted. The duration of this should not exceed one week.

If resolution is still not reached, the matter will be referred to the Managing Director for consideration and final decision. A grievance taken to this level must be in writing from the employee.

The employee's manager will forward to the Managing Director any additional information thought relevant. The Managing Director will provide a written response to the employee and also communicate with any other parties involved.

If the matter is still not resolved, the employee will be advised of his/her rights to pursue the matter with external authorities if they wish.

In some circumstances, it may not be appropriate for an employee to discuss his/her grievance with the immediate manager. Grievances relating to harassment would fall into this category and an employee should be able to make their approach to a more senior manager.

All procedures must be followed in accordance with employment equal opportunity/anti-discrimination legislation.

The above procedure takes place for individual employee grievances. Whatever the final outcome, it will affect the attitudes of each party and their long-term relationship. The issues which sparked the grievance should be reviewed by management at executive level so the dispute does not reoccur.

11. POST TRAUMA COUNSELLING

Policy Statement

<Company>'s policy is to ensure all staff who are faced with a traumatic event in a work environment are provided with immediate support and counselling, by a professional, external provider.

Traumatic events can include being the victim of a robbery or assault, witness to such an event, witness to a significant injury, or death of another employee or any other person, within the work environment.

Post-trauma counselling must be provided to employees involved in such situations. In normal circumstances, such employees should be sent home, and referred to appropriate counselling agencies.

The company will pay for such counselling for a reasonable period.

Objective

The objective of the post trauma counselling policy is to provide immediate care to any staff affected and to support their return to work.

Process

1. Check employee(s) are okay etc.
2. Be prepared to listen:
3. to the facts
4. to how he/she is feeling

do not give advice, direction or comment on how they should act or react.

3. Identify local providers of post-trauma counselling and advice. In more serious cases, arrange an immediate telephone interview from a qualified counsellor. In all traumatic circumstances, encourage the employee to attend counselling. Arrange a time for counselling for him/her. A number of counselling sessions may be required or appropriate.
4. It is recommended a supervisor speaks directly to a counsellor after a telephone interview. This is to ensure support for the employee's well-being.
5. The counsellor may make recommendations on how the employee should get home and which family and friends should be contacted for additional support.
6. In consultation with a counsellor, maintain contact with the employee as recommended.
7. Following the employee's return to work, maintain vigilance regarding their state of mind and discuss any concerns with the counsellor prior to speaking to the employee.
8. Remember to fill in appropriate workers compensation reports where appropriate. Contact the insurance company early in the process as they do not cope well with a claim if there is no medical certificate.

12. INTELLECTUAL PROPERTY AND SECURITY

During your employment with <Company> all intellectual property developed by you, discoveries or inventions made by you in the performance of your duties related in any way to the business of

<Company> or any related bodies corporate will be the property of <Company> or its related bodies corporate. You will be required to do everything necessary to ensure <Company> or its related bodies corporate has ownership of such intellectual property (including, if required assigning such intellectual property to <Company>, a related body corporate or any entity that <Company> nominates).

From time to time during the course of your employment, you may be given access to sensitive information, data, company property, keys to premises or any other company related property/information. It is expected employees will treat this as intellectual property and therefore it should be stored securely either physically and/or electronically. Failure to properly look after company information or property will result in disciplinary proceedings including dismissal.

13. CONFLICT OF INTEREST

Prior to your employment with <Company>, you may be conducting business activities which potentially give rise to real or perceived conflict of interest with <Company's> objectives and future activities.

In such circumstances, any business or other external interests that have a real or perceived conflict of interest should be declared to <Company>.

The Company will review the potential areas of conflict with the employee and mutually agree on practical, commercial arrangements, which may include, but is not limited to, the following:

- <Company> purchases the intellectual property right of the business in question
- you combine your business into <Company> business and you are compensated accordingly
- you cease your business or remove yourself from active involvement

You will at all times advise management of any other interests you or any related bodies corporate in which you participate, have or are potentially entering into that could cause conflict with your employment, interests or commitment in <Company>.

Where there are external involvements that do not represent a conflict of interest, these must not affect performance or attendance whilst working at <Company>. If such involvement does affect performance or attendance it will be considered as a conflict of interest giving rise to the remedies described above or disciplinary proceedings including dismissal.

Approval must be given from management before approaching any customers for commercial or non-commercial external interests. This includes fund raising, sponsorship and similar activities.

14. PRIVACY

You are required to observe and uphold all of the Company's privacy policies and procedures as implemented or varied from time to time.

Collection, storage, access to and dissemination of employee personal information will be in accordance with the principles of the *Privacy Amendment (Private Sector) Act 2000.*

If you would like any clarification of any of the policies or procedures contained within this HR Manual, please contact internal management who will be glad to provide guidance and support.

HUMAN RESOURCES MANUAL AGREEMENT

I, ________________________________, have been provided with access to the <Company> HR Manual and have read and understood all of the policies and procedures contained within.

I acknowledge that these policies and procedures form part of my employment with <Company> and that I am bound by its procedures.

Signed______________________________ Dated_______________

CHANGES TO <COMPANY> HR MANUAL

I, ________________________________, have been advised of the changes to the policies and procedures (listed below) in the <Company> Manual. I acknowledge that these policies and procedures form part of my employment with <Company> and that I am bound by its procedures.

Changes made to HR Manual:

1.

2.

3.

Signed______________________________ Dated___________________

HR Metrics and HR Analytics

CHAPTER FORTY

Introduction to HR Metrics

HR metrics, or human resource metrics, are essentially quantitative measurements used to track and assess the effectiveness of various aspects within an organization's Human Resources (HR) department. These are also called **Key Performance Indicators (KPI's)** that are tracked and circulated across the organization. These measurements act as indicators of various aspects, including:

Recruitment and selection: This involves metrics like time-to-hire, cost-per-hire, and quality of hire.

Employee retention: This includes tracking employee turnover rate, reasons for leaving, and employee satisfaction levels.

Training and development: This involves measuring the effectiveness of training programs, return on investment (ROI) for training, and employee skill development.

Performance management: This involves tracking individual and team performance, setting clear goals, and providing feedback.

Employee engagement: This involves measuring employee commitment, motivation, and overall satisfaction with their work and the company.

By analyzing these metrics, HR departments can gain valuable insights and make data-driven decisions that improve:

Efficiency: Streamlining processes to save time and resources.

Effectiveness: Ensuring initiatives are actually achieving desired outcomes.

Strategic planning: Aligning HR practices with the overall business goals.

Overall, HR metrics provide a clear picture of the health and well-being of an organization's workforce, allowing HR professionals to make informed decisions that benefit both employees and the company.

HR Metrics and HR Analytics: Differences

Both HR metrics and HR analytics play crucial roles in understanding and managing an organization's workforce, but they differ in their approach and purpose:

HR Metrics:

Focus: Quantitative measurements of specific HR functions.

Purpose: Track performance, identify trends, and compare data against benchmarks.

Examples: Turnover rate, time-to-hire, cost-per-hire, employee satisfaction scores.

Benefits: Offer a quick and easy way to monitor HR operations and identify potential problem areas.

HR Analytics:

Focus: Deeper analysis of HR data to uncover relationships and insights.

Purpose: Gain a comprehensive understanding of the workforce, make strategic decisions, and predict future outcomes.

Techniques: Statistical analysis, data visualization, machine learning.

Benefits: Provides deeper insights into the "why" behind metrics, allows for better problem-solving and strategic planning.

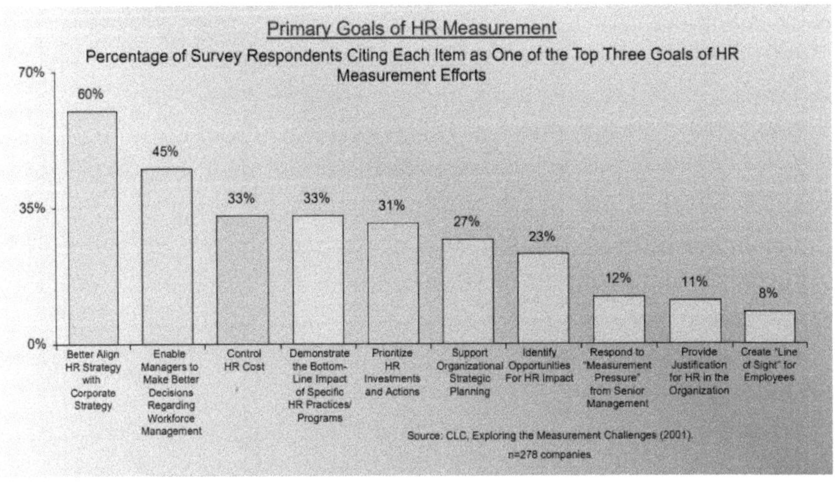

Goals of HR Measurement

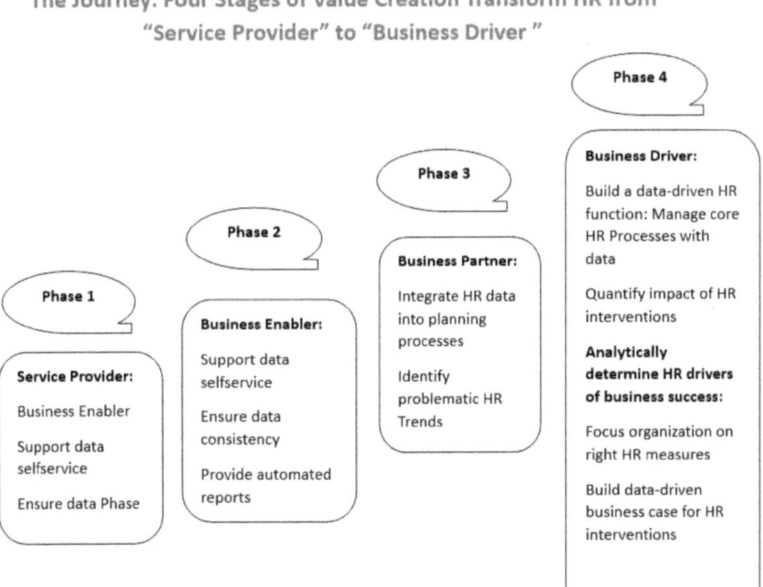

HR Transformation from Service Provider to Business Driver!

CHAPTER FORTY-ONE

Key HR Metrics or KPI's

HR Services & Software:

1. **Cost per Employee:** Total HR expenses divided by the number of employees, revealing overall HR spending efficiency.

Formula: Total HR expenses / Number of employees

HR Analytics Benefit: This metric helps assess the overall efficiency of HR spending. By comparing it to industry benchmarks or tracking it over time, you can identify potential cost-saving opportunities or areas requiring additional resources.

2. **HR Software Participation Rate:** Percentage of employees actively using HR software, indicating software adoption and potential benefits.

Formula: (Number of active users / Total number of employees) * 100%

HR Analytics Benefit: This metric indicates the adoption level of HR software among employees. A low rate could suggest usability issues, lack of training, or insufficient communication about its benefits. High participation suggests employees are finding value in the software, potentially leading to improved efficiency and engagement.

3. **HR Professional to Employee Ratio:** Number of employees per HR professional, providing insights into HR team workload and capacity.

Formula: Number of employees / Number of HR professionals

HR Analytics Benefit: This metric reflects the workload and capacity of the HR team. A high ratio (fewer HR professionals per employee) could indicate potential overwork and difficulty providing adequate support. Conversely, a low ratio (more HR professionals per employee) suggests the resources might be underutilized.

4. **Return on Investment (ROI) of HR Software:** Compares the software's cost against its financial benefits, like cost savings or revenue

generation.

Formula: (Benefits of software - Cost of software) / Cost of software * 100%

HR Analytics Benefit: This metric helps evaluate the financial effectiveness of investing in HR software. It's crucial to carefully define and quantify the benefits (e.g., cost savings from reduced administrative tasks, increased employee productivity) before calculating ROI.

Recruitment:

1. Acceptance Rate: Offer acceptance rate compared to the number of candidates, indicating the competitiveness of your offers.

Formula: (Number of accepted offers / Number of job offers made) * 100%

HR Analytics Benefit: This metric helps assess the competitiveness of your compensation and benefits package compared to the job market. A low rate could indicate the need to adjust your offer or improve communication about the position's value.

2. Cost per Hire: Average cost of hiring a new employee, encompassing internal and external hiring expenses.

Formula: Total hiring costs / Number of new hires

HR Analytics Benefit: This metric helps track the costs associated with recruiting and onboarding new employees. By monitoring it over time, you can identify potential cost-saving opportunities throughout the hiring process.

3. Workforce Demographics: Characteristics like age, gender, and education level, providing insights into diversity and workforce composition.

Formula: This metric doesn't require a specific formula as it involves analyzing and presenting data on various employee characteristics, such as:

- Age
- Gender
- Race/ethnicity
- Education level
- Tenure

HR Analytics Benefit: Analyzing workforce demographics provides insights into diversity, equity, and inclusion (DE&I) within your organization. It can help identify potential biases in recruitment practices and inform strategies to create a more diverse and inclusive workplace.

4. Headcount: Total number of employees within the organization or specific departments.

Formula: Total number of employees according to department, designation, location, units, etc.

HR Analytics Benefit: Headcount provides a simple yet crucial picture of your workforce size at various levels (e.g., entire company, department, location). This information helps in workforce planning, budgeting, and resource allocation.

5. New Hire Turnover: Percentage of new hires leaving within a set timeframe, highlighting potential onboarding challenges.

Formula: (Number of new hires leaving within a timeframe / Number of new hires) * 100%

HR Analytics Benefit: This metric highlights potential issues during the onboarding process or initial job experience. High turnover rates can indicate a need to improve onboarding programs, reassess job descriptions, or address underlying workplace dissatisfaction.

6. Time to Hire: Average time taken to fill an open position, indicating recruitment efficiency.

Formula: Total time from opening the position to filling it (average across multiple positions)

HR Analytics Benefit: This metric helps assess the efficiency of your recruitment process. A long time to hire can lead to increased costs, loss of top talent, and hinder business operations. By tracking this metric, you can identify bottlenecks and streamline the hiring process.

7. Time to Productivity: Time taken for new hires to reach full productivity, reflecting onboarding effectiveness.

Formula: This metric doesn't have a universally established formula due to the difficulties in defining and measuring "full productivity." However, various approaches can be used:

Manager surveys: Managers can estimate the time it takes for new hires to reach a specific performance level.

Performance data: Analyze how long it takes for new hires to consistently meet performance targets.

Self-reported data: New hires can self-report when they feel fully productive, though this may be subjective.

HR Analytics Benefit: Time to productivity helps assess the effectiveness of onboarding programs. A long time to productivity can indicate a need to improve training, mentorship programs, or support systems for new hires.

8. Applicant Demographics: Percentage of applicants from underrepresented groups within your overall talent pool.

Formula: (Number of applicants from underrepresented groups / Total number of applicants) * 100%

HR Analytics Benefit: This metric helps track the diversity of your applicant pool and identify potential gaps in attracting talent from underrepresented groups. Analyzing these demographics alongside hiring demographics (see below) allows you to assess progress towards diversity goals and identify potential biases in the hiring process.

9. Hiring Demographics: Percentage of new hires from underrepresented groups.

Formula: (Number of new hires from underrepresented groups / Total number of new hires) * 100%

HR Analytics Benefit: This metric reflects the actual representation of underrepresented groups within your new hires. Comparing it to applicant demographics can reveal potential biases in the selection process and inform strategies to promote diversity and inclusion in hiring decisions.

Engagement & Retention:

1. Employee Satisfaction: Measured through surveys or Net Promoter Scores (NPS), indicating overall employee sentiment and satisfaction.

Formula: This metric requires various methods to capture data, not a single formula:

Employee satisfaction surveys: Design surveys with specific questions and scoring mechanisms to measure employee sentiment on various aspects of work life.

Employee Net Promoter Score (eNPS): Ask employees "On a scale of 1-10, how likely are you to recommend this organization as a place to work?"

HR Analytics Benefit: These measures help understand employee sentiment and satisfaction with their work, company culture, and leadership. Monitoring changes over time can inform strategies to improve employee engagement, reduce voluntary turnover, and foster a positive work environment.

2. Retention Rate: Percentage of employees staying with the company over a period, reflecting workforce stability.

Formula: [(Number of employees at the end of the period) - (Number of new hires) / (Number of employees at the beginning of the period)] * 100%

HR Analytics Benefit: This metric reflects the stability of your workforce and the likelihood of employees staying with the company. A high retention rate indicates a positive work environment and engaged employees, while a low rate suggests potential issues that need to be addressed.

3. Retention Rate per Manager: Retention rate broken down by individual teams and managers, identifying areas needing improvement.

Formula: Use the same retention rate formula but calculate it for individual teams or specific managers instead of the entire company.

HR Analytics Benefit: This breakdown allows you to identify specific teams or managers with low retention rates. Analyzing reasons behind these low rates can help tailor improvement strategies and provide targeted support to managers struggling to retain their team members.

4. Talent Turnover Rate: Rate at which high-performing and high-potential employees leave, highlighting potential talent management issues.

Formula: This metric doesn't have a universal formula due to the difficulty in defining "high-performing" and "high-potential" employees. However, you can approach it by:

Identifying key talent: Define criteria for identifying high performers and high-potential employees based on performance data, skills, and future potential.

Track their turnover: Monitor the rate at which these individuals leave the company compared to the overall turnover rate.

HR Analytics Benefit: Tracking talent turnover helps identify potential problems with talent management and development. It highlights areas for improvement to retain your most valuable employees and ensure a strong talent pipeline for the future.

5. Total Turnover Rate: Percentage of employees leaving compared to the average employee count, showing overall turnover rate.

Formula: (Number of employees leaving the company during a period / Average number of employees during the period) * 100%

HR Analytics Benefit: This metric reflects the overall rate at which employees leave the company, regardless of their performance level. It helps benchmark your turnover against industry standards and identify potential issues causing employees to leave.

6. Voluntary Turnover Rate: Rate of employees leaving voluntarily, excluding involuntary terminations.

Formula: (Number of voluntary terminations / Average number of employees during the period) * 100%

HR Analytics Benefit: This metric focuses specifically on employees who choose to leave the company on their own accord, excluding terminations due to factors like layoffs, performance issues, or disciplinary actions. Analyzing voluntary turnover helps identify: **Employee satisfaction:** A high voluntary turnover rate could indicate issues with job satisfaction, compensation, work-life balance, or career development opportunities. **Engagement:** Low employee engagement can lead to higher voluntary turnover, as employees may not feel connected to the company or their work. **Management concerns:** Ineffective leadership, lack of communication, or a negative work environment can contribute to voluntary turnover.

Time Tracking:

1. Absence Rate: Average employee absence days (excluding approved PTO), indicating potential health or well-being concerns.

Formula: (Total number of absence days / Total number of working days) * 100

HR Analytics Benefit: By calculating the absence rate, HR can gain insights into the overall health and well-being of the workforce. High absence rates may indicate potential issues such as burnout, stress, or dissatisfaction among employees. Analyzing absence trends over time can help HR identify patterns and implement strategies to improve employee wellness and reduce absenteeism.

2. Absence Rate per Manager: Absence rate broken down by individual teams and managers, identifying potential team-specific issues.

Formula: (Total number of absence days for a specific manager's team / Total number of working days for that team) * 100

HR Analytics Benefit: This metric allows HR to assess absence patterns at the team level, providing valuable insights into potential managerial effectiveness and team dynamics. By identifying managers with consistently high absence rates among their team members, HR can offer targeted support, training, or interventions to address underlying issues and improve team performance and morale.

3. **Overtime Hours:** Total number of overtime hours worked by employees, providing insights into workload and potential burnout risks.

Formula: Total number of overtime hours worked by employees

HR Analytics Benefit: Tracking overtime hours helps HR understand workload patterns and identify potential risks of employee burnout or fatigue. High levels of overtime may indicate inadequate staffing levels, poor workload distribution, or inefficient processes. By analyzing overtime trends across departments or teams, HR can address workload issues, optimize resource allocation, and promote a healthier work-life balance for employees.

Performance Management:

1. **Company Performance:** Comparison between employee performance and employee engagement/satisfaction levels, highlighting potential correlation.

Formula: Comparison between employee performance and employee engagement/satisfaction levels

HR Analytics Benefit: By comparing employee performance with engagement and satisfaction levels, HR can identify potential correlations between these factors. High levels of employee engagement and satisfaction may indicate a positive impact on company performance, while low levels may suggest areas for improvement. Analyzing this metric allows HR to understand how employee experiences and perceptions influence overall organizational success, enabling targeted interventions to enhance employee engagement and drive performance improvements.

2. **Employee Performance:** Measured through self-assessments, peer reviews, or manager assessments, providing individual performance insights.

Formula: Measured through self-assessments, peer reviews, or manager assessments

HR Analytics Benefit: Tracking employee performance through various assessment methods provides valuable insights into individual strengths, areas for development, and overall contribution to organizational goals. By analyzing performance data, HR can identify high-performing employees, recognize achievements, and provide targeted support or development opportunities to enhance performance.

Additionally, comparing performance ratings over time allows HR to track progress, evaluate the effectiveness of performance management initiatives, and make data-driven decisions regarding talent management and succession planning.

3. Goal Tracking: Monitoring employee goals and their alignment with company goals, assessing goal-setting effectiveness and progress.

Formula: Monitoring employee goals and their alignment with company goals

HR Analytics Benefit: Tracking employee goals and their alignment with company objectives helps HR assess goal-setting effectiveness, employee productivity, and progress towards organizational priorities. By analyzing goal attainment rates and alignment metrics, HR can identify areas of alignment or misalignment between individual and organizational goals, enabling targeted interventions to realign priorities, enhance goal-setting processes, and improve overall organizational performance.

Additionally, goal tracking facilitates transparency, accountability, and communication within the organization, fostering a culture of goal-oriented performance and continuous improvement.

4. Performance & Potential: Nine-box model categorizing employees based on performance and potential, aiding succession and leadership planning.

Formula: Nine-box model categorizing employees based on performance and potential

HR Analytics Benefit: The nine-box model helps HR categorize employees into different segments based on their performance and potential, allowing for targeted talent management strategies. This model aids in succession planning, leadership development, and talent retention efforts. By identifying high-performing employees with high potential for growth, HR can invest in their development, groom them for leadership positions, and ensure a pipeline of talent to fill critical roles within the organization.

Similarly, employees in need of improvement can receive targeted support and development opportunities to enhance their performance and potential, ultimately contributing to the organization's long-term success.

5. Revenue per Employee: Total revenue divided by the total number of employees, indicating overall employee productivity and contribution.

Revenue per Employee:

Formula: Total revenue divided by the total number of employees

HR Analytics Benefit: Calculating revenue per employee provides insights into overall employee productivity and contribution to organizational performance. A higher revenue per employee ratio indicates that employees are generating more value for the organization, while a lower ratio may suggest inefficiencies or underutilization of resources.

By analyzing this metric, HR can assess workforce productivity, identify opportunities for improvement, and optimize resource allocation strategies. Additionally, tracking changes in revenue per employee over time allows HR to evaluate the impact of workforce-related initiatives, such as training programs, workforce optimization efforts, or changes in staffing levels, on organizational performance and profitability.

Diversity, Inclusion and Equity

1. Overall Workforce Diversity: Percentage of employees from underrepresented groups (based on gender, race/ethnicity, disability status, veteran status, sexual orientation, etc.) across the entire organization.

Formula: (Number of employees from underrepresented groups / Total number of employees) * 100

HR Analytics Benefit: This metric provides insights into the inclusivity of the organization's workforce across various dimensions of diversity. By measuring the percentage of employees from underrepresented groups, HR can assess progress towards diversity goals, identify areas for improvement, and track the impact of diversity initiatives over time.

Analyzing workforce diversity helps organizations foster a culture of inclusivity, enhance employee engagement, and leverage diverse perspectives to drive innovation and business success.

2. Diversity by Level: Distribution of diverse employees across job levels (entry-level, mid-level, management, leadership), highlighting potential barriers to advancement.

Formula: (Number of diverse employees in each job level / Total number of employees in each job level) * 100

HR Analytics Benefit: This metric examines the distribution of diverse employees across different job levels within the organization, highlighting potential barriers to advancement and opportunities for development. By analyzing diversity by level, HR can identify areas where representation of underrepresented groups may be lacking or where there are disparities in promotion rates. This information enables HR to implement targeted strategies to address barriers to advancement, promote diversity and inclusion, and cultivate a more equitable and diverse workforce.

3. Diversity in Leadership: Percentage of leadership positions held by individuals from underrepresented groups.

Formula: (Number of leaders from underrepresented groups / Total number of leadership positions) * 100

HR Analytics Benefit: Assessing diversity in leadership positions helps organizations gauge the inclusivity of their leadership team and identify opportunities to promote diversity at the highest levels of the organization. By measuring the percentage of leadership positions held by individuals from underrepresented groups, HR can evaluate progress towards diversity goals, identify gaps in representation, and implement strategies to foster diverse leadership pipelines. Diverse leadership teams bring a range of perspectives and experiences to decision-making processes, driving innovation, and driving organizational success.

4. Diversity in Key Roles/Teams: Representation of diverse talent in critical business functions or teams.

Formula: (Number of diverse employees in key roles or teams / Total number of employees in key roles or teams) * 100

HR Analytics Benefit: This metric assesses the representation of diverse talent in critical business functions or teams, ensuring that key roles are filled by individuals from diverse backgrounds. By measuring diversity in key roles or teams, HR can ensure that diverse perspectives are represented in decision-making processes, enhance creativity and problem-solving, and drive innovation.

Additionally, fostering diversity in key roles helps organizations better serve diverse customer bases, improve employee engagement, and strengthen the organization's reputation as an inclusive employer.

5. Pay Equity: Conduct regular pay gap analyses by gender, race/ethnicity, and other demographics to ensure fair compensation practices.

Formula: (Average salary of Group A - Average salary of Group B) / Average salary of Group A * 100

HR Analytics Benefit: Regular pay gap analyses by gender, race/ethnicity, and other demographics help ensure fair compensation practices within the organization. By calculating and monitoring pay gaps, HR can identify disparities in compensation between different demographic groups and take corrective actions to address inequities. This promotes fairness, equity, and inclusivity in the workplace, enhances employee morale and engagement, and reduces the risk of legal and reputational harm associated with pay discrimination.

6. Performance Evaluation Fairness: Examine performance ratings by demographic groups to detect potential bias in evaluations.

Formula: Compare average performance ratings across demographic groups

HR Analytics Benefit: Examining performance ratings by demographic groups helps HR detect potential bias in performance evaluations and ensure fairness in the performance management process. By analyzing performance ratings across different demographic categories (such as gender, race/ethnicity), HR can identify patterns of bias or disparities in ratings. This enables HR to implement measures to mitigate bias, enhance objectivity in performance evaluations, and promote a culture of fairness and inclusivity. Fair performance evaluations contribute to employee engagement, retention, and overall organizational success.

7. Access to Training and Development: Track participation rates in development opportunities across different employee groups to ensure equitable access.

Formula: (Number of employees from Group A participating in training and development / Total number of employees in Group A) * 100

HR Analytics Benefit: Tracking participation rates in training and development opportunities across different employee groups ensures equitable access to professional growth and development. By analyzing participation rates by demographic groups (such as gender, race/ethnicity), HR can identify disparities in access to training and development initiatives.

This enables HR to address barriers to participation, tailor development programs to meet the needs of diverse employee groups, and promote a culture of learning and development for all employees. Equitable access to training and development opportunities fosters employee engagement, career advancement, and organizational success.

Training & Development

1. Completion Rate: Percentage of employees who complete assigned training programs. A high completion rate suggests successful program enrollment and completion.

Formula: Completion Rate = (Number of employees who completed the program) / (Number of employees enrolled in the program) * 100

Example: If 120 employees were enrolled in a training program and 108 completed it, the completion rate would be:

Completion Rate = (108 / 120) * 100 = 90%

HR Analytics Benefit: Completion rate helps track program participation and identify potential issues with program accessibility, engagement, or motivation.

2. Learner Satisfaction: Measured through surveys or feedback forms, assesses employee satisfaction with the training content, delivery method, and overall learning experience.

Formula: Learner Satisfaction Score = (Average score on satisfaction survey) / (Highest possible score) * 100

Example: If a satisfaction survey uses a 5-point scale (1= least satisfied, 5= most satisfied) and the average score for a training program is 4.2, the learner satisfaction score would be:

Learner Satisfaction Score= (4.2 / 5) * 100 = 84%

HR Analytics Benefit: Learner satisfaction helps assess the quality and effectiveness of training programs from the participant's perspective, allowing for improvements to content, delivery, or overall experience.

3. Knowledge Retention: Assessed through pre- and post-training assessments, measures the effectiveness of knowledge transfer and skill development.

Formula: Knowledge Retention = ((Average score on post-training assessment) - (Average score on pre-training assessment)) / (Highest possible score - Average score on pre-training assessment) * 100

Example: If the average score on a pre-training assessment is 60 (out of 100) and the average score on the post-training assessment is 85, the knowledge retention would be:

Knowledge Retention = ((85 - 60) / (100 - 60)) * 100 = 50%

HR Analytics Benefit: Knowledge retention measures how well training programs transfer knowledge and develop skills, aiding in identifying knowledge gaps or areas needing further reinforcement.

4. Application of Learning: Observed through performance improvement, project outcomes, or task completion rates, this metric reflects how effectively employees apply their acquired knowledge and skills on the job.

Formula: While there's no single formula due to its qualitative nature, application of learning is typically measured through:

Performance improvement: Analyzing changes in relevant metrics like productivity, quality of work, or error rates after training.

Project outcomes: Assessing the success of projects leveraging the skills acquired through training.

Task completion rates: Evaluating how quickly and effectively employees complete tasks related to the training content.

HR Analytics Benefit: Application of learning measures the ultimate impact of training programs, indicating how effectively employees utilize their acquired knowledge and skills on the job. This helps assess the program's overall effectiveness in achieving business objectives.

5. **Return on Investment (ROI):** Compares the financial benefits of training programs (e.g., increased productivity, reduced errors) against the cost of development and delivery. A positive ROI indicates a valuable return on the investment in training.

Formula: ROI = ((Benefits of training - Cost of training) / Cost of training) * 100

Example: Benefits: Increased productivity leading to $10,000 additional revenue per employee annually.

Cost: Training development & delivery: $5,000 per employee.

ROI = ((10,000 - 5,000) / 5,000) * 100 = 100%

HR Analytics Benefit: ROI helps evaluate the financial performance of training programs, aiding in cost-benefit analysis and resource allocation decisions.

6. **Performance Improvement:** Measures employee performance changes after completing specific training programs. This could involve quantitative data like productivity metrics or qualitative observations from managers.

Formula: While there isn't a single formula due to varied metrics, it can be assessed through:

Quantitative data: Track changes in relevant metrics like sales figures, productivity rates, or error reduction percentages before and after training.

Qualitative data: Conduct surveys to gauge employee self-reported improvements, or gather feedback from managers on observed performance changes.

Example: If productivity (measured in units produced per hour) increases by 10% after training, the improvement would be: Performance Improvement = (10% increase)

HR Analytics Benefit: Performance improvement measures the effectiveness of training in enhancing employee capabilities and contributing to organizational goals.

7. Skill Development: Evaluates whether employees acquire the desired skills and knowledge they need to be successful in their roles and contribute to organizational goals. This can be assessed through skills assessments or feedback from managers and peers.

Formula: No specific formula exists, but it's typically assessed through:

Skills assessments: Pre- and post-training assessments to measure skill acquisition and proficiency.

Manager & peer feedback: Evaluations from supervisors and colleagues on observed improvements in relevant skills.

Example: Post-training skill assessments show a 70% increase in employees demonstrating mastery of key skills compared to pre-training assessments.

HR Analytics Benefit: Skill development helps ensure employees possess the necessary skills for their roles and contribute to achieving organizational objectives.

8. Time to Proficiency: Measures the time it takes for new hires to reach full productivity levels, which can be impacted by training effectiveness.

Formula: Time to Proficiency = (Time to reach full productivity level) - (Time spent in training)

Example: If it takes an average of 3 months for new hires to reach full productivity and they spend 2 weeks (0.5 months) in training, the time to proficiency would be:

Time to Proficiency = (3 months) - (0.5 months) = 2.5 months

HR Analytics Benefit: Time to proficiency helps assess training effectiveness in accelerating new hires' transition to productive roles, impacting overall operational efficiency.

9. Cost per Learner: Represents the average cost of training per employee, allowing for cost comparisons and resource allocation decisions.

Formula: Cost per Learner = (Total cost of training) / (Number of employees trained)

Example: If the total cost of training is $10,000 and 20 employees are trained, the cost per learner would be:

Cost per Learner = ($10,000) / (20 employees) = $500

HR Analytics Benefit: Cost per learner helps track training expenses and allows for cost comparisons between different programs or providers, facilitating informed resource allocation decisions.

Compensation, Rewards & Payroll

1. Total Compensation Cost: The overall cost of paying employees, including base salary, bonuses, commissions, and benefits, expressed as a percentage of total revenue. This metric indicates the cost of your workforce relative to your income.

Formula: Total Compensation Cost = (Total employee compensation costs) / (Total revenue) * 100

Example: Total employee compensation: $50 million

Total revenue: $100 million

Total Compensation Cost = ($50 million) / ($100 million) * 100 = 50%

HR Analytics Benefit: This metric helps analyze the relative cost of your workforce compared to your overall income. Identifying high compensation costs might prompt investigations into cost-saving measures or adjustments to revenue generation strategies.

2. Market Competitiveness: Analyzes how your compensation packages compare to competitors in your industry and location. This ensures you are attracting and retaining top talent.

Formula: While there's no single formula due to its comparative nature, it's typically assessed through:

Market salary surveys: Comparing your compensation packages to data on average salaries and benefits for similar positions in your geographic area and industry.

Benchmarking against competitors: Analyzing the compensation packages offered by your direct competitors to ensure you remain competitive in attracting and retaining talent.

Example: A salary survey reveals the average salary for a specific position in your industry and location is $80,000, while your company offers $75,000 for the same position. This indicates your package might be less competitive and require adjustments to attract top talent.

HR Analytics Benefit: Market competitiveness helps ensure you offer competitive compensation packages to attract and retain top talent, contributing to an engaged and high-performing workforce.

3. Retention Rate by Salary Band: Compares turnover rates across different salary bands to identify potential issues with compensation fairness and employee motivation.

Formula: Retention Rate = (Number of employees remaining at the end of the period / Number of employees at the beginning of the period) * 100

This formula can be applied to each salary band separately.

Example: Salary Band 1: 80 employees at the beginning, 75 remaining at the end, resulting in a retention rate of (75 / 80) * 100 = 93.75%

Salary Band 2: 50 employees at the beginning, 45 remaining at the end, resulting in a retention rate of (45 / 50) * 100 = 90%

HR Analytics Benefit: Retention rate by salary band helps identify potential compensation fairness or motivational issues. Consistently lower retention rates in specific bands might indicate the need to review compensation packages and address any concerns affecting employee satisfaction and loyalty.

4. Payroll Accuracy Rate: Measures the percentage of payroll checks or direct deposits issued without errors. Maintaining a high accuracy rate ensures employees receive their pay on time and correctly.

Formula: Payroll Accuracy Rate = (Number of accurate payroll checks/ direct deposits / Total number of payroll checks/direct deposits) * 100

Example: Total payroll checks/direct deposits: 1000

Number of accurate: 995

Payroll Accuracy Rate = (995 / 1000) * 100 = 99.5%

HR Analytics Benefit: This metric ensures timely and accurate payment to employees, fostering trust and avoiding financial discrepancies. A low accuracy rate necessitates investigating and rectifying any issues in payroll processing to prevent employee frustration and potential legal implications.

5. Benefit Costs as a Percentage of Revenue: Calculates the cost of employee benefits as a percentage of total revenue, providing insights into the financial impact of benefits.

Formula: Benefit Costs as a % of Revenue = (Total cost of employee benefits) / (Total revenue) * 100

Example: Total cost of benefits: $10 million

Total revenue: $100 million

Benefit Costs as a % of Revenue = ($10 million) / ($100 million) * 100 = 10%

HR Analytics Benefit: This metric helps understand the financial impact of employee benefits on your organization's overall revenue. It allows for comparisons against industry benchmarks and facilitates informed decision-making regarding benefit plans and their cost-effectiveness.

6. Employee Satisfaction with Benefits: Measured through surveys, assesses employee satisfaction with the range and quality of benefits offered by the company.

Formula: While there's no single formula due to its subjective nature, it's typically assessed through:

Employee surveys: Utilizing surveys with standardized or open-ended questions to gauge employee satisfaction with specific benefits or the overall benefits package.

Focus groups: Conducting focus groups with employees from diverse demographics to gather detailed feedback and gain deeper insights into their needs and preferences.

Example: A survey reveals an average satisfaction score of 4.2 out of 5 for the company's healthcare benefits, indicating generally positive employee sentiment.

HR Analytics Benefit: Measuring employee satisfaction with benefits helps understand their perception of the value and effectiveness of the offered benefits. This feedback can guide adjustments to benefit plans, improving employee morale and potential recruitment and retention efforts.

7. Cost of Turnover: Estimates the total financial cost associated with employee turnover, including recruiting, onboarding, and lost productivity. This highlights the financial implications of retaining talent.

Formula: While there's no single, universally accepted formula, a common approach estimates the cost of turnover through:

Identifying the total cost of replacing a departing employee: This includes recruitment, onboarding, and training expenses.

Estimating lost productivity during the transition period: This considers the time it takes for a new hire to reach full productivity.

Factoring in potential additional costs: These may include severance pay, lost knowledge and expertise, and impact on employee morale.

Example: Calculating the replacement cost might reveal an average cost of $20,000 per employee, with an additional $10,000 in lost productivity during the transition.

HR Analytics Benefit: Estimating the cost of turnover highlights the financial significance of retaining talent. It encourages efforts to minimize turnover by addressing potential causes like employee dissatisfaction, skill gaps, or inadequate compensation.

8. Participation Rate: Percentage of employees who participate in your reward and recognition programs, indicating program engagement.

Formula: Participation Rate = (Number of employees participating / Total number of employees) * 100

Example: Total employees: 1000

Employees participating: 750

Participation Rate = (750 / 1000) * 100 = 75%

HR Analytics Benefit: Participation rate helps assess the effectiveness of your reward and recognition programs. A low rate might indicate a lack of awareness, program misalignment with employee preferences, or accessibility issues. Monitoring participation aids in program optimization and ensures they effectively incentivize and appreciate employees, contributing to a more engaged and motivated workforce.

9. Frequency of Recognition: Tracks how often employees are recognized for their achievements and contributions, revealing the culture of appreciation within the organization.

Formula: While there isn't a single, universally accepted formula, it's typically measured through:

Tracking the number of recognition instances: This can involve monitoring formal recognition programs, manager recognition initiatives, or peer-to-peer recognition platforms.

Calculating the average recognition frequency per employee: Divide the total number of recognitions by the total number of employees over a specific period (e.g., month, quarter, year).

Example: Total recognitions: 500

Total employees: 100

Average Recognition Frequency per Employee = (500 recognitions) / (100 employees) = 5 recognitions per employee (over the considered period)

HR Analytics Benefit: Frequency of recognition helps assess the recognition culture within your organization. High recognition frequency can indicate a positive and appreciative environment, potentially boosting employee morale and motivation.

10. Impact on Performance & Engagement: Measures the correlation between recognition programs and desired outcomes like improved performance, increased engagement, and reduced turnover.

Formula: Due to the multifaceted nature of these concepts, a single formula isn't available. However, you can assess the impact through:

Analyzing trends in performance metrics: Compare relevant metrics like productivity, quality of work, or customer satisfaction before and after implementing recognition programs.

Conducting employee surveys: Gauge employee perceptions on recognition's impact on their engagement, motivation, and overall satisfaction.

Focus groups: Gather qualitative feedback from employees to understand their perspectives on how recognition programs influence their work and engagement.

Example: After implementing a recognition program, a company observes a 10% increase in employee productivity and a 5% decrease in turnover rate. This suggests a potential positive impact on performance and retention.

HR Analytics Benefit: Measuring the impact on performance and engagement helps evaluate the effectiveness of recognition programs in achieving desired organizational outcomes. Positive correlations can justify continued investment and program refinement.

11. Return on Investment (ROI): Compares the costs of implementing reward programs against the benefits they generate, such as increased employee motivation and retention.

Formula: ROI = ((Benefits of recognition programs - Cost of programs) / Cost of programs) * 100

Calculating the benefits can be challenging and requires careful consideration of various factors, including:

Improved employee retention: Estimate the cost savings associated with reduced turnover due to recognition.

Enhanced employee engagement: Quantify the potential benefits of increased engagement, such as improved productivity or customer satisfaction, and translate them into financial gains.

Reduced absenteeism: Estimate cost savings associated with lower absenteeism rates potentially linked to increased employee morale and satisfaction.

Example:

Program cost: $10,000

Estimated annual benefit: $20,000 (through reduced turnover and increased productivity)

ROI = ((20,000 - 10,000) / 10,000) * 100 = 100%

HR Analytics Benefit: ROI helps assess the financial value of recognition programs. A positive ROI indicates that the program generates more benefits than its implementation costs, justifying its continued use. However, accurately calculating benefits can be complex and requires careful consideration of various contributing factors.

Remember, the specific metrics most important to your organization will depend on its unique needs and priorities.

Activity for you:

List 5 hr metrics which are most important to be tracked and measured in your own organization (or any other organization if you are not working) and write its formula with an example calculation and its importance.

....

....

CHAPTER FORTY-TWO

Introduction to HR Analytics

Uncovering HR Analytics: A Beginner's Guide

The world of Human Resources (HR) is no longer just about paperwork and payroll. In today's data-driven world, HR professionals are increasingly leveraging HR analytics to gain valuable insights and make informed decisions about the workforce. But what exactly is HR analytics, and how does it benefit organizations?

What is HR Analytics?

Imagine HR as a treasure trove of information about your employees. HR analytics is the process of collecting, analyzing, and interpreting this data to gain a deeper understanding of your workforce. It involves measuring various aspects of employees' experience, from recruitment and onboarding to performance and retention.

Think of it like using a magnifying glass:

You gather data points, like the number of job applicants, average time to fill vacancies, or employee satisfaction scores.

You analyze these data points, identifying trends and patterns.

You interpret the findings, drawing insights and using them to improve HR processes, programs, and overall workforce management.

Why use HR Analytics?

HR metrics, the data points used in HR analytics, are like powerful tools that help you:

Make data-driven decisions: Instead of relying on intuition or gut feelings, HR professionals can use data to support their decisions, leading to more effective and strategic strategies.

Identify areas for improvement: By analyzing metrics, you can pinpoint strengths and weaknesses in your HR processes, like high turnover rates or low training effectiveness.

Measure the impact of HR initiatives: Implementing a new training program? HR analytics allows you to track its effectiveness and see if it's achieving its desired outcomes.

Predict future trends: By analyzing historical data and current trends, you can anticipate future workforce needs and challenges, allowing for proactive planning and resource allocation.

HR Analytics: Unveiling the Power of Data-Driven Workforce Management

In today's data-driven world, organizations are increasingly turning to HR analytics to gain valuable insights into their workforce, unlock hidden potential, and make informed decisions. But what exactly are the benefits and applications of HR analytics, and are there any ethical considerations or challenges associated with utilizing employee data?

Benefits of HR Analytics:

Improved decision-making: By analyzing data instead of relying solely on intuition, HR professionals can make more effective and strategic decisions regarding talent acquisition, training, performance management, and employee engagement.

Cost savings and resource optimization: HR analytics can identify areas where resources are under-utilized or misallocated, allowing for cost-effective strategies and improved resource allocation across various HR functions.

Enhanced employee engagement: By understanding employee sentiment, needs, and preferences through data, organizations can develop targeted initiatives to improve engagement, leading to a more motivated and productive workforce.

Reduced turnover: Identifying early signs of potential turnover through data analysis allows HR to implement retention strategies and address employee concerns before they leave, minimizing negative impacts on operations and costs.

Stronger ROI on HR initiatives: HR analytics allows you to measure the effectiveness of programs like training and development, enabling you to assess their return on investment and refine them for optimal impact.

Applications of HR Analytics:

Recruitment: Targeting job postings to the right audience, identifying effective recruitment channels, and evaluating the success of onboarding programs.

Training and development: Identifying skill gaps, measuring the effectiveness of training programs, and tailoring learning experiences for individual needs.

Performance management: Setting clear performance goals, tracking progress, providing data-driven feedback, and identifying areas for improvement.

Compensation and benefits: Ensuring fair and competitive pay practices, analyzing the effectiveness of benefit packages, and optimizing costs associated with compensation and benefits.

Succession planning: Identifying high-potential employees, analyzing skills and experience gaps, and developing talent pipelines for future leadership roles.

Ethical Considerations and Potential Challenges:

While HR analytics offers numerous benefits, it's crucial to address ethical considerations and potential challenges:

Data privacy: Organizations must adhere to relevant data privacy regulations and ensure employee data is collected, stored, and used ethically and transparently.

Algorithmic bias: The use of algorithms for data analysis can inadvertently perpetuate biases present in the data, leading to unfair or discriminatory outcomes.

Employee trust: Building trust and transparency regarding how data is used is crucial for employee buy-in and cooperation in data collection and analysis efforts.

Skill gap in data analysis: Equipping HR professionals with the necessary skills to analyze and interpret data effectively is essential for maximizing the benefits of HR analytics.

Conclusion:

HR analytics is a powerful tool that can unlock significant benefits for organizations. However, ethical considerations and potential challenges require careful attention to ensure responsible and effective use of employee data. By embracing data-driven decision-making while remaining mindful of ethical implications, HR professionals can leverage HR analytics to build a stronger, more engaged, and future-proof workforce.

CHAPTER FORTY-THREE

HR Analytics Communication

Building a Data-Driven HR Culture: Communicating HR Data Insights Effectively

In today's data-driven world, fostering a data-driven HR culture is no longer a choice, it's a necessity. This approach involves harnessing the power of data to inform strategic decisions, improve HR processes, and ultimately, enhance the employee experience. However, simply collecting data isn't enough. Effectively communicating the insights gleaned from HR data to stakeholders is crucial for ensuring buy-in, driving action, and maximizing the impact of your data-driven HR strategy.

Building the Foundation: Transparency and Trust

Before diving into communication strategies, it's essential to build a foundation of transparency and trust with your stakeholders. This involves:

Clearly outlining your data governance policies: Explain how data is collected, stored, and used, ensuring compliance with relevant regulations and demonstrating respect for employee privacy.

Promoting data literacy: Invest in training and workshops to equip HR professionals and other stakeholders with the basic skills to understand and interpret HR data.

Encouraging open dialogue: Foster a culture where stakeholders can ask questions, express concerns, and actively participate in discussions around HR data and its implications.

Communication Strategies for Effective Delivery:

Once you have a solid foundation, consider the following communication strategies to effectively present HR data insights to stakeholders:

Tailor your message to your audience: Understand the specific needs and interests of your audience (e.g., senior management, line managers, employees). Adjust the level of detail, technical jargon, and focus areas accordingly.

Focus on storytelling: Don't just present raw data; weave a compelling narrative that highlights the key insights, their significance, and potential impact on the organization and its people.

Utilize visuals effectively: Employ data visualization techniques like charts, graphs, and infographics to simplify complex data and make it easier to understand and retain key points.

Focus on actionable insights: Don't just present the problems; offer clear recommendations and practical solutions based on your data analysis. Be prepared to answer questions about implementation and potential challenges.

Utilize the right channels: Choose the communication channels most appropriate for your audience and message. This could include formal presentations, town halls, internal newsletters, or interactive dashboards.

Proactive communication: Don't wait for someone to ask. Regularly share relevant HR data insights and keep stakeholders informed about the evolving HR landscape and its implications.

Remember:

Focus on the "why" and "how": Explain not just what the data reveals, but also why it's important and how it can be used to improve individual and organizational performance.

Be open to feedback: Encourage stakeholders to provide feedback on your communication style and the content you present. This feedback can help you refine your approach and ensure your communication efforts are truly effective.

Building a data-driven HR culture requires a collaborative effort. By establishing a foundation of trust, tailoring communication to diverse audiences, and focusing on actionable insights, HR professionals can effectively share the power of data and drive positive change within their organizations.

CHAPTER FORTY-FOUR

Qualitative & Quantitative Data

Seeing Beyond Numbers: Unpacking Quantitative & Qualitative Data in HR Analytics

HR analytics delves into the depths of information to understand your workforce better. But this information isn't just a single entity. It encompasses two key types of data crucial for gaining a holistic view: quantitative and qualitative data. Let's explore what each type offers and how they work together, using real-life examples, to paint a comprehensive picture of your employees.

1. Quantitative Data: The Measurable World

Quantitative data refers to numerical information that can be easily counted, measured, and statistically analyzed. It's the realm of numbers and provides a concrete, objective perspective on various aspects of your workforce. Here are some examples:

Recruitment:

- Number of applications received per job posting (helps assess the effectiveness of sourcing strategies)
- Time to hire (indicates efficiency in filling vacancies)
- Training and Development:
- Average training completion rate (measures employee engagement in learning initiatives)
- Cost per training program participant (helps evaluate program cost-effectiveness)

Performance Management:

- Employee productivity metrics (e.g., sales figures, units produced) (tracks individual and team performance)
- Absenteeism rate (identifies potential issues with employee wellbeing or engagement)
- Compensation and Benefits:
- Average salary or hourly wage (ensures fair compensation practices)
- Cost of employee benefits as a percentage of total revenue (highlights the financial impact of benefits)

Real-life example:

A retail company analyzes its quantitative data and discovers that stores with higher employee engagement (measured by attendance rates and positive customer reviews) also have higher sales figures. This insight prompts them to invest in employee engagement initiatives across all stores.

2. Qualitative Data: The World Beyond Numbers

Qualitative data encompasses descriptive, non-numerical information that provides deeper insights into employee experiences, attitudes, and feelings. It captures the "why" behind the numbers and reveals valuable nuances often missed by quantitative data. Here are some examples:

Employee engagement surveys:

Open-ended questions: "What motivates you at work?" "What improvements would you suggest for the company culture?" (reveal employee sentiment and potential areas for improvement)

Exit interviews:

Reasons for leaving: "What led you to decide to leave the company?" (provide insights into employee retention challenges)

Focus groups:

Discussions on company culture, training programs, or specific initiatives: (uncover underlying employee perceptions and opinions)

Real-life example:

A technology company utilizes qualitative data from employee surveys and discovers a recurring theme of feeling undervalued. Based on this insight, they implement initiatives like skills development programs and recognition programs to address employee concerns and foster a culture of appreciation.

The Power of Combining Both:

By combining quantitative and qualitative data, HR professionals gain a comprehensive understanding of their workforce. Quantitative data provides the foundation (what), while qualitative data adds depth and context (why).

Imagine a scenario where you observe a low employee retention rate (quantitative data) through your HRIS system. But why are employees leaving? Conducting exit interviews (qualitative data) could reveal factors like lack of career development opportunities or a negative work environment, allowing you to address the root cause of the issue beyond just the numbers.

In conclusion, both quantitative and qualitative data are essential tools in HR analytics. By leveraging their unique strengths and using them together, you can gain a richer understanding of your workforce, make informed decisions, and ultimately, build a stronger, more engaged, and thriving organization.

CHAPTER FORTY-FIVE

Data collection methods and tools (surveys, HRIS, performance management systems)

Gathering the Clues: How HR Uses Tools to Understand Employees

Imagine you're trying to solve a mystery – but the clues are scattered everywhere! In HR, figuring out how to keep employees happy and productive is kind of like that. We need to gather information from different places to understand our "workforce mystery." Here are some of the tools HR uses to collect clues, like a detective:

1. Surveys:

Think of these like questionnaires. We ask employees questions about their work experience, like if they feel appreciated or have the training they need. This helps us understand their feelings and what we can do better.

Real-life example: A restaurant wants to know if its new employee wellness program is working. They ask employees in a survey if they like the program and if it helps them feel healthier.

2. HR Information System (HRIS):

Imagine a giant filing cabinet for employee information, like their address and job history. This system stores all this data in one place, making it easy to find what we need.

Real-life example: A factory sees a lot of employees leaving their jobs. They use their HRIS to see which departments have the most people quitting. This helps them figure out where to focus their efforts to keep employees happy.

3. Performance Management Systems (PMS):

These are like report cards for employees. They track things like goals, progress, and feedback from managers. This helps us see how employees are doing and how we can help them improve.

Real-life example: A store uses its PMS to find its top salespeople. They reward these employees for their hard work, which motivates others to do their best too.

Remember:

We only collect information that helps us understand how to make things better for employees.

We always ask permission before collecting any information.

We use information from different tools together to get the whole picture.

By using these detective tools, HR can gather the clues they need to create a happy and productive work environment for everyone!

CHAPTER FORTY-SIX

Data cleaning, analysis, and visualization techniques

Cleaning Up the Data Maze: How HR Makes Sense of Numbers

Imagine you have a box full of Legos, but they're all mixed up with other toys and pieces. It's hard to build anything cool until you sort them out, right? HR data is similar. We collect lots of information, but it needs to be cleaned and organized before we can use it to make smart decisions.

Step 1: Cleaning the Data Maze

Finding the Missing Pieces: Sometimes, information might be missing or incomplete. We have to find these missing pieces or decide if it's okay to use the data without them.

Fixing the Mixed-Up Pieces: Sometimes, there might be typos or mistakes in the data. We have to fix these errors so the information is accurate.

Taming the Wild Pieces: Sometimes, data might be formatted differently, like dates written in different ways. We need to make sure everything is consistent for easy analysis.

Step 2: Making Sense of the Pieces (Data Analysis)

Asking Questions: We use the cleaned data to answer specific questions about the workforce. For example, "Are employees happy with their jobs?" or "How long does it take to fill open positions?"

Looking for Patterns: We analyze the data to see if there are any trends or patterns. This helps us understand how things are related and what might be causing certain issues.

Step 3: Building with the Pieces (Data Visualization)

Turning Numbers into Pictures: Sometimes, numbers alone can be hard to understand. We use charts and graphs to turn the data into pictures, making it easier to see trends and patterns at a glance.

Sharing the Story: Once we have the insights, we share them with others in a clear and simple way. This helps everyone understand the information and make informed decisions.

Remember:

We only collect data that helps us improve things for employees and the organization.

We keep all data safe and secure.

We use data to help us make better decisions, not to judge individuals.

By cleaning, analyzing, and visualizing data, HR can turn a big pile of numbers into valuable information that helps everyone build a better workplace!

CHAPTER FORTY-SEVEN

Types of HR Analytics

Employee engagement is crucial for a thriving workforce. HR analytics can be used to understand and improve engagement in organizations through various approaches:

1. Descriptive Analytics:

Goal: Gain a baseline understanding of employee engagement at ABC Company.

Steps:

Data Collection: Gather data from employee surveys (engagement surveys, pulse surveys), exit interviews, and HRIS (e.g., absenteeism rates).

Analysis: Calculate metrics like employee satisfaction scores, turnover rates, and tenure. Identify areas with potentially low engagement (e.g., high absenteeism in a specific department).

Outcome: Provides a starting point for further analysis and highlights potential areas for improvement.

2. Diagnostic Analytics:

Goal: Identify the root causes behind low engagement in specific areas.

Steps:

Data Exploration: Analyze employee survey responses, focusing on open-ended questions and comments related to departments or teams with low engagement scores.

Focus Group Discussions: Conduct discussions with employees from identified departments to delve deeper into their concerns and suggestions.

Comparative Analysis: Compare engagement metrics across departments or teams to identify any significant variations.

Outcome: Provides in-depth insights into the reasons behind low engagement, allowing for targeted interventions.

3. Predictive Analytics:

Goal: Anticipate potential employee engagement issues and take preventive measures.

Steps:

Statistical Modeling: Develop models using historical data to identify patterns and predict employee flight risk (potential for leaving).

Targeted Interventions: Based on identified risk factors, implement personalized engagement strategies for high-risk employees (e.g., mentorship programs, career development opportunities).

Outcome: Proactive approach to address potential engagement issues before they escalate into turnover.

4. Prescriptive Analytics:

Goal: Recommend specific actions to improve employee engagement across the board.

Steps:

Cost-Benefit Analysis: Evaluate the potential impact and financial feasibility of different engagement initiatives based on historical data and industry best practices.

Action Plan Development: Develop and implement a comprehensive plan for improving employee engagement, including specific initiatives, timelines, and responsible parties.

Track & Monitor: Monitor the impact of implemented initiatives through employee surveys, focus groups, and updated engagement metrics.

Outcome: Provides a data-driven approach to improving employee engagement across the entire organization.

Remember:

Choose the appropriate HR analytics type based on the specific goal (e.g., understand current state vs. predict future trends).

Ensure data quality and combine data from multiple sources for richer insights.

Communicate findings clearly and involve employees in the process of improving engagement.

By implementing these types of HR analytics, organizations can develop a data-driven strategy to nurture a more engaged and productive workforce.

CHAPTER FORTY-EIGHT

Case Studies in HR Analytics

Background

Retaining key talent and providing a fulfilling work environment are critical to Experian's innovation and growth agenda. However, like with many businesses, staff turnover was an obstacle to meeting these ambitions. We addressed the problem by successfully applying what we do best – data and analytics.

Challenge

In 2016, Experian's global HR function found itself facing resignation rates globally that were 4% over the industry benchmark. The knock-on effect was significant. Financially every 1% increase was costing the business around $3million and ultimately putting a strain on growth and innovation. Financial impact aside, a major concern was the challenge it posed to Experian's most precious asset – its people. Experian prides itself on providing a fulfilling working environment that inspires a culture of high performance and innovation.

With more resource being diverted to recruitment and managing increasing resignation rates, HR was found it harder to maintain a focus on initiatives to benefit existing employees. The challenge boiled down to data. With a onedimensional view of its employee base, HR hands were tied. It had basic insights into why people were leaving, but with data in multiple systems and formats it was impossible to get a single source of truth.

A clear business case

Leading the project was Olly Britnell, Global Head of Workforce Analytics and HR strategy, alongside Wendy Cunningham from Experian's Global HR team. They set about building a data-driven analytics solution that would equip global HR teams with advanced insight into employee needs and motivations. This detail would enable a more tailored approach to providing the types of benefits that people value and enable more informed retention strategies.

According to Olly:

"We have a well-established methodology to building analytical insight models in other industries which could equally apply to the HR sector. We were confident that with our expertise and data assets we could create a solution to move the needle on employee retention, create a more fulfilling working culture and save a great deal of money." Olly Britnell, Global Head of Workforce Analytics and HR strategy.

A data-driven transformation

Since launch, the workforce analytics platform has been transformative, driving positive outcomes for employees and delivering significant cost savings. HR teams spend less time recruiting and on-boarding new employees. Instead they can focus on using the data available to ensure existing employees are fully engaged. Improved retention rates are testament to this shift in employee sentiment. Less disruption means the best talent remains within the business, relationships are improved, and teams are more motivated to deliver.

Having been recently included in Fortune's top 60 best workplaces in finance and insurance, the results speak for themselves:

- Global attrition has reduced by 4%, saving the business $14m over 2 years.
- The model has transformed the culture of HR from one which was reactive into a proactive and data-lead function. As a practical and transparent solution, nontechnical HR business users across our global network now use the tool.
- Via predictive modelling HR teams can proactively assess the possible impact of different scenarios and make better decisions about how to offer the best possible support to employees. Examples of this include training program implementation, support with pay reviews and building targeted strategies to individual regions where employee needs vary dramatically.
- Workforce Analytics has been the engine behind important strategic initiatives. One such example is a defence plan for diversity strategy where it's supported the retention of top female talent.

Source: experian website

CHAPTER FORTY-NINE

HR Analytics in Action: Example

Step-by-Step HR Analytics Process for Optimizing Recruitment at ABC Company:

1. Define the Problem & Goals:

Problem: ABC Company suspects its current recruitment strategies are inefficient and hindering their ability to attract high-quality talent.

Goals: Improve source of quality hires, reduce time to hire, and optimize cost-per-hire.

2. Identify Relevant HR Metrics:

Sourcing Channels: Number of applicants per channel, cost per applicant per channel, quality of applicants per channel (measured by interview conversion rate or offer acceptance rate).

Screening Methods: Time to screen per method, cost per candidate screened, effectiveness of screening methods in identifying qualified candidates (measured by interview conversion rate or offer acceptance rate).

Additional Metrics: Time to hire, cost per hire, offer acceptance rate.

3. Data Collection & Cleaning:

Gather data from Applicant Tracking System (ATS), historical hiring records, and financial records.

Clean the data by ensuring accuracy, consistency, and completeness.

4. Data Analysis & Interpretation:

Analyze data to identify trends and patterns.

Example: Analyze which sourcing channels attract the most applicants, and compare the quality of those applicants to the cost per applicant.

Example: Assess the effectiveness of different screening methods by comparing the time and cost per screened candidate with the resulting interview conversion rate.

Identify areas for improvement based on the data insights.

5. Develop & Implement Actions:

Based on the analysis, ABC Company might:

Optimize sourcing channels: Allocate resources towards high-performing channels and experiment with new channels.

Refine screening methods: Invest in more efficient methods or adjust existing methods to improve candidate selection.

Standardize hiring process: Streamline the recruitment process to reduce time to hire.

6. Communication & Monitoring:

Communicate the data-driven insights and planned actions to relevant stakeholders like hiring managers and recruiters.

Regularly monitor the impact of implemented actions by tracking the chosen HR metrics.

Refine the recruitment strategy further based on the ongoing analysis and monitoring.

Outcomes:

Improved quality of hires, leading to better employee performance and retention.

Reduced time to hire, resulting in cost savings and quicker filling of open positions.

Optimized cost-per-hire, maximizing the efficiency of recruitment efforts.

Remember:

This is a continuous process requiring ongoing data collection, analysis, and refinement based on evolving results.

Ethical considerations and data privacy regulations must be followed throughout the process.

By implementing this data-driven approach to recruitment, ABC Company can optimize its strategy, attract top talent, and build a stronger workforce.

CHAPTER FIFTY

HR Dashboards & Software Applications: Examples

HR departments utilize various types of HR dashboards to gain insights and monitor key metrics across different aspects of the workforce. Here are some common types of HR dashboards, their frequency of refresh, and how they are used:

1. Recruitment Dashboards:

Frequency: Daily or weekly refresh

Usage:

Track applicant flow through the recruitment process.

Monitor the effectiveness of different sourcing channels and screening methods.

Identify areas for improvement in the recruitment process (e.g., time to hire, cost per hire).

2. Employee Engagement Dashboards:

Frequency: Monthly or quarterly refresh

Usage:

Monitor employee sentiment and satisfaction levels.

Identify trends in employee engagement over time.

Measure the impact of employee engagement initiatives.

Track key engagement metrics, like turnover rate, absenteeism, and employee Net Promoter Score (eNPS).

3. Performance Management Dashboards:

Frequency: As needed, often tied to performance review cycles

Usage:

Track individual and team performance against goals.

Identify performance gaps and areas for development.

Monitor progress towards performance objectives.

Provide insights for conducting performance reviews and offering feedback.

4. Learning and Development Dashboards:

Frequency: Monthly or quarterly refresh

Usage:

Track employee participation in training programs.

Monitor the effectiveness of training programs (e.g., completion rates, skill development).

Identify skill gaps within the workforce.

Allocate resources for targeted training and development initiatives.

5. Compensation and Benefits Dashboards:

Frequency: Quarterly or annually, depending on changes

Usage:

Monitor payroll costs and benefits expenditure.

Analyze pay equity and identify potential pay gaps.

Compare compensation and benefits offerings to industry benchmarks.

Conduct cost-benefit analysis of proposed changes to compensation and benefits packages.

6. Workforce Analytics Dashboards:

Frequency: Customizable based on data needs, often real-time or daily

Usage:

Provide a comprehensive overview of key HR metrics across various areas.

Identify trends and patterns in the workforce data.

Support strategic decision-making related to workforce planning, talent management, and resource allocation.

Overall, the frequency of dashboard updates depends on the specific type of data and its volatility. Dashboards are used actively by HR professionals to monitor progress, identify areas for improvement, and inform strategic decisions across various aspects of HR management.

It's important to note that this is not an exhaustive list, and specific HR departments may utilize additional dashboards tailored to their unique needs and priorities.

Software Applications in HR Analytics & Dashboards:

HR dashboards can be created using a variety of software solutions, catering to different needs and budgets. Here are some popular options:

1. Business Intelligence (BI) Tools:

Features: Offer robust data visualization capabilities, data analysis tools, and integration with various data sources (e.g., HRIS, payroll systems).

Examples: Tableau, Power BI, Qlik Sense.

Pros: Powerful and flexible, suitable for complex data analysis and creating interactive dashboards.

Cons: Can be expensive, require some technical expertise for setup and maintenance.

2. HR-Specific Dashboarding Tools:

Features: Designed specifically for HR data, often pre-built with relevant templates and metrics for common HR functions (e.g., recruitment, training, performance).

Examples: Workday People Analytics, BambooHR, Zoho People Analytics.

Pros: User-friendly interface, readily available HR-specific metrics, often integrate seamlessly with existing HRIS.

Cons: May be less customizable and have fewer overall functionalities compared to general BI tools.

3. Spreadsheet Software:

Features: Familiar and readily available for most users, allows for basic data visualization and manipulation.

Examples: Microsoft Excel, Google Sheets.

Pros: Free or low-cost, relatively easy to learn and use.

Cons: Limited functionality for complex data analysis and visualization, can become cumbersome and prone to errors for large datasets.

4. Data Visualization Tools:

Features: Focus on creating visually appealing and interactive charts and graphs from various data sources.

Examples: Looker, Domo, Google Data Studio.

Pros: Easy to create visually engaging dashboards, often integrate with other BI tools or data sources.

Cons: May not offer in-depth data analysis capabilities and may require linking with separate data sources.

Choosing the right software depends on several factors, including:

Complexity of data needs: For simpler dashboards, spreadsheets might suffice, while complex data analysis might require robust BI tools.

Technical expertise: Consider the level of technical skillset available within the HR team.

Budget: Costs can vary significantly across different software options.

Integration needs: Ensure compatibility with existing HR software and data sources.

It's crucial to assess your specific needs and resources before selecting the most suitable software solution for creating effective HR dashboards.

Sample HR Dashboards - Data Visualization:

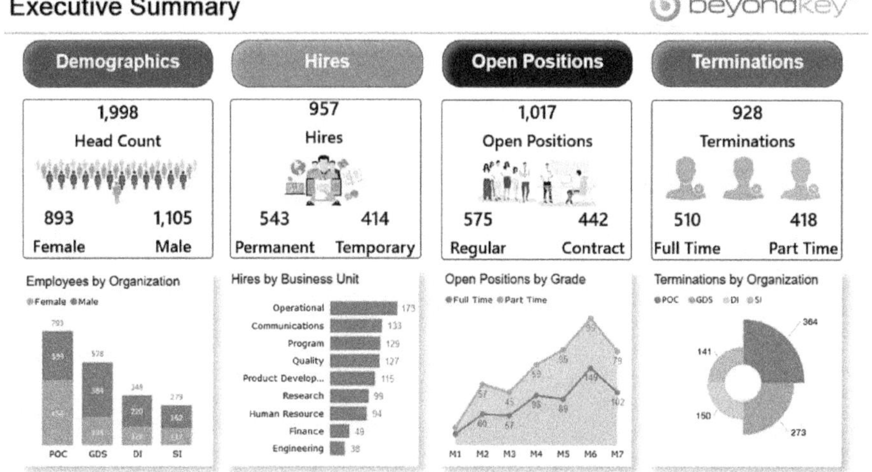

Executive Summary dashboard (beyondkey)

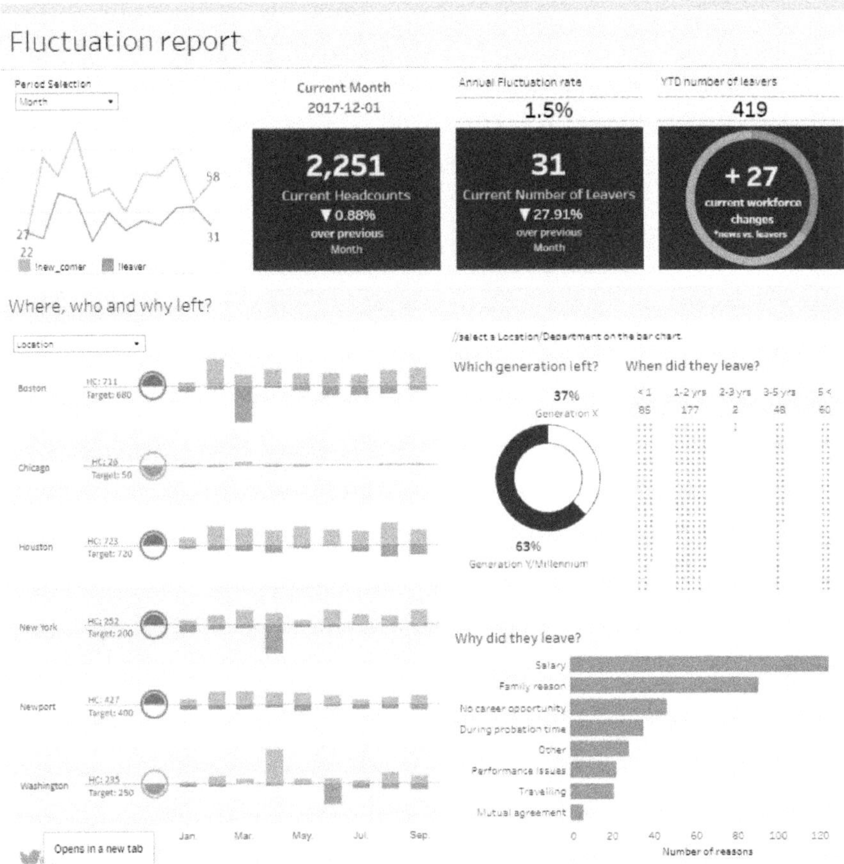

Fluctuation in Headcount (Tableau)

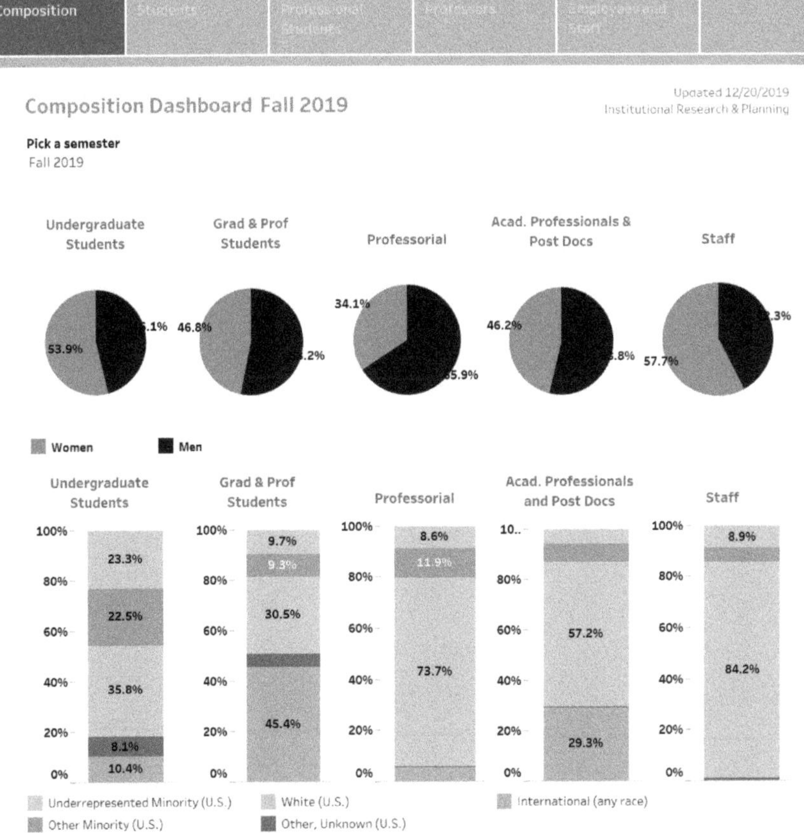

Cornell University Diversity Dashboard (Tableau)

Compensation, Benefits & Payroll Management

CHAPTER FIFTY-ONE

Compensation, Benefits & Reward System

Imagine your job is like a sundae. The base salary is the vanilla ice cream – a core element you receive for your work. But sundaes are more exciting with toppings, right? That's where compensation and benefits come in.

Compensation: This is the monetary value you receive for your work. It's like all the delicious toppings on your sundae! Here are some examples:

Base Salary: The fixed amount you get paid regularly, like weekly or monthly.

Bonuses: Extra payouts based on performance, exceeding targets, or company profits.

Commissions: Performance-based pay, often seen in sales roles, where you earn a percentage of what you sell.

Stock Options: The right to buy company stock at a certain price, potentially giving you a financial stake in the company's success.

Benefits: These are the non-cash rewards that add value to your total compensation package, like the cherry on top of your sundae! They can improve your work-life balance, well-being, and financial security. Here are some common benefits:

Health Insurance: Coverage for medical expenses, helping you stay healthy without breaking the bank.

Paid Time Off (PTO): Vacation days, sick leave, and personal days to rest and recharge.

Retirement Savings Plans: Employer contributions or matching programs to help you save for your golden years.

Tuition Reimbursement: Financial assistance for continuing education, allowing you to develop your skills.

Flexible Work Arrangements: Options like remote work or flex hours to create a better work-life balance.

Rewards: These are recognitions or incentives that go beyond regular compensation, like a special hot fudge drizzle on your sundae for exceeding expectations. Rewards can be monetary or non-monetary and often aim to motivate specific behaviors or achievements. Here are some examples:

Employee of the Month: Public recognition for outstanding performance.

Spot Bonuses: Small, immediate financial rewards for going the extra mile.

Gift Cards or Merchandise: Tangible appreciation for a job well done.

Team Outings or Events: Fun activities to boost morale and celebrate accomplishments.

A Company Example:

Let's say you work in marketing. Your base salary is the foundation. You might receive a bonus for exceeding quarterly marketing goals (compensation). The company also offers health insurance, paid vacation days, and a gym membership (benefits). If you consistently come up with great marketing ideas, you might be recognized as "Marketer of the Quarter" (reward) and get a gift card.

CHAPTER FIFTY-TWO

Introduction to International Payroll Management

Conquering Compensation Across the Globe: Your Guide to International Pay

The world's your business playground, but how do you pay your globetrotting team? Enter international compensation management, the secret weapon for attracting and keeping top talent worldwide. It's more than just throwing money across borders – it's about crafting a strategic pay plan that considers the unique challenges and complexities of a global workforce.

Why It Matters:

Global Talent, Global Rewards: Competitive pay isn't just a number anymore. It's about understanding the cost of living in Mumbai versus Munich and ensuring your compensation package reflects those differences. This helps you attract the best from anywhere in the world, not just your own backyard.

Fairness Across Borders: Your star engineer in India shouldn't feel undervalued compared to their counterpart in New York. International compensation management ensures internal equity, fostering a culture of respect and motivation across your global workforce.

Strategic Pay for a Global Workforce:

Balancing Act: It's a delicate dance – maintaining a consistent approach to core compensation principles while adapting to local needs. Think of it like a jazz band: everyone riffs on the same melody, but each instrument adds its own flavor.

Expat Perks: Going international comes with extra considerations. Expatriate compensation packages often include special allowances for housing, relocation assistance, and even equalizing tax burdens. It's all about making sure your international hires feel supported and valued throughout their assignment.

Understanding Local Pay:

Localization Explained: Imagine your employee in Tokyo – their salary needs to reflect the higher cost of living compared to someone in Seattle. Localization bridges that gap by adjusting expat pay to match the salary standards in their new country.

Grading Your Jobs Globally: How do you compare an engineering role in London to one in Lagos? Job evaluation methods help assess the relative worth of different positions within your global workforce. International job grading systems provide a consistent framework for aligning jobs with appropriate salary levels across countries.

Building a Global Pay Structure:

Market Matters: Setting pay ranges isn't a guessing game. You need to consider local market rates to stay competitive. A data scientist in Berlin deserves a salary that reflects the demand for their skills in that specific market.

Data Drives Decisions: Compensation surveys are your friends. They provide valuable data on prevailing salary levels and market trends across different regions and industries. This intel helps you benchmark positions, ensure external competitiveness, and make informed compensation decisions.

Staying Legal, Staying Ethical:

Navigating the Rules: Every country has its own labor laws and regulations. International compensation management means staying informed about minimum wage requirements, overtime regulations, and other legalities to avoid any nasty surprises.

Communicating Clearly:

Global Messages, Local Delivery: Don't assume a one-size-fits-all communication approach works. Tailor your message to different cultures and languages. A simple infographic might work wonders in France, while a detailed presentation might be better received in Germany.

The Future of Global Pay:

Tech & Talent: The world of work is changing. Remote work and digital nomads are on the rise. International compensation management needs to adapt, offering flexible compensation practices that cater to these evolving employee preferences.

Diversity Pays: It's not just about location anymore. Addressing gender pay equity and promoting diversity and inclusion in global compensation programs is gaining traction. A fair and inclusive compensation strategy fosters a positive work environment that attracts top talent from all walks of life.

Mastering international compensation management is your key to unlocking a world of talent. Embrace the complexities, and your global team will reward you with success!

CHAPTER FIFTY-THREE

Intro to Indian Payroll Components

Compensation is total of Cash and Non-cash payments that employees gets in exchange for the work

they do for a business.

Payroll is the system employer uses to process and manage salary payments to all employees.

Salary Components includes Earning & Deduction Heads

Earnings heads Ex: Basic, HRA, Conveyance, LTA, Medical Reimbursement, Other Allowance, Etc.

Deduction Heads: Statutory Deduction & Non Statutory Deductions

Payroll Head Categorisation

Earning Heads: 4 categories

1. **Master Heads** - Basic, HRA, Conveyance, Other Allowances

2. **One Time Payment** - Bonus, Gratuity, Leave Encashment, Night Shift Allowance, OT hours,Gratuity, etc

3. **Reimbursements** - Books & Periodicals Reimbursement, LTA, Telephone Reimbursement, etc.

Deduction Heads: 3 categories

1. **Statutory Deductions** are those which are mandatory as per Law.

Ex: PF, ESIC, Professional Tax, Income Tax, Labor Welfare Fund, etc.

2. **Non Statutory Deductions** : Master / One Time - Loan, Salary Advance, Notice Pay Recovery, Canteen

Deduction, Telephone Deduction, etc

3. **Third Party Deduction** - LIC, Loan etc which are paid from salary to third party.

FUNCTIONS OF PAYROLL DEPT

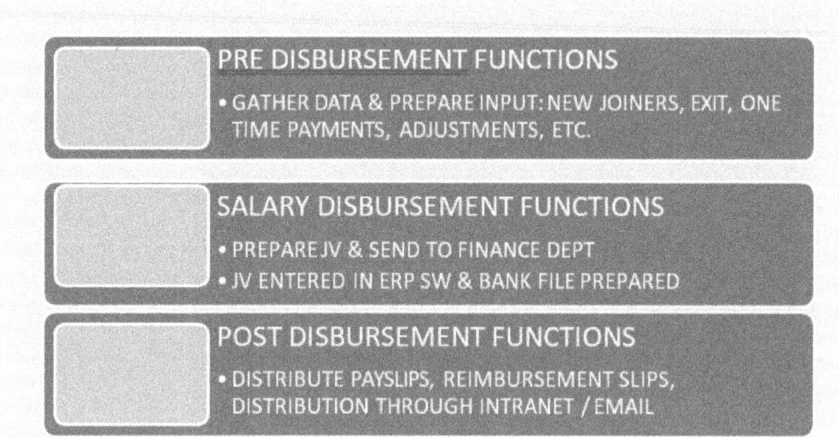

Functions of Payroll

POST SALARY DISBURSEMENT FUNCTIONS

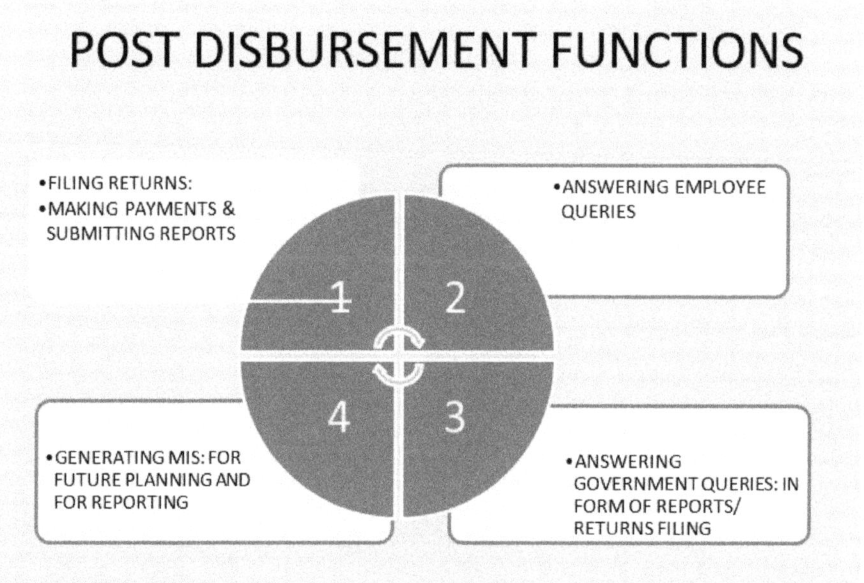

Post Payroll Disbursement Activities

TYPES OF COMPENSATION STRUCTURES

3 STRUCTURES :-

1. FIXED CTC STRUCTURES
2. FLEXIBLE CTC STRUCTURE
3. CONSOLIDATED PAY / GROSS PAY

Fixed CTC Structure and Flexible CTC Structure: *These structures are used commonly in most organizations. Management can decide on type of structure they would like to adopt and which salary components to be given. Consolidated Pay/ Gross Pay is not a well-defined method of payment.*

CTC :Total Cost of Company on Employee

CTC = **Direct Benefits + Indirect Benefits + Savings / Pension Contributions**

GrossSalary (Total before deductions):Grossisthe Basic + All Allowances/Reimbursements payable to an employee for a month, before deducting employee side contributions/deductions like Employee PF, Income Tax, Etc.

NetSalary (Take Home):GrossSalary–Total of all Employee side Deductions/Contributions

Activity for you:

List the different types of Payroll Activities:

....

....

CHAPTER FIFTY-FOUR

Compensation Structuring in India

Understanding Compensation & Benefits as per Indian payroll:

Types of CTC Structures

1. Fixed CTC Structure: In a fixed CTC (Cost to Company) structure, the total compensation offered to an employee is predetermined and fixed. This structure includes various components such as basic salary, allowances, and benefits, and these components remain constant throughout the employment period. The employee receives a fixed amount of money regardless of their performance or other factors.

Example: Let's say an employee is offered a fixed CTC of ?600,000 per annum, broken down as follows:

Basic Salary: ?400,000 per annum

House Rent Allowance (HRA): ?100,000 per annum

Conveyance Allowance: ?20,000 per annum

Medical Reimbursement: ?20,000 per annum

Provident Fund (PF): ?60,000 per annum

In this example, the employee's total compensation remains fixed at ?600,000 per annum regardless of any changes in performance or other factors.

2. Flexible CTC Structure: A flexible CTC structure allows employees to customize their compensation package based on their preferences and needs. Employees can choose from a range of benefits and allowances offered by the employer, adjusting their compensation according to their individual requirements. This structure provides employees with greater flexibility and control over their compensation package.

Example: An employer offers an employee a total CTC budget of ?800,000 per annum.

The employee can choose how to allocate this budget across various components such as basic salary, HRA, LTA, medical allowance, and others based on their prefences and Tax Saving needs. For instance, the employee may opt for a higher basic salary and lower allowances or vice versa, depending on their individual circumstances or tax saving purposes.

FBP (Flexible Benefit Plan) Components: These may include options like medical insurance, meal coupons, leave travel allowance (LTA), or top-up on HRA. Employees can choose benefits that best suit their circumstances.

3. Consolidated Pay / Non-CTC Based Pay Structure: This is less common and typically seen in contractual or project-based roles. The pay is a fixed amount for the entire project or contract period, and there's no breakdown of components like basic salary or allowances. Taxes are deducted from the gross pay.

Example (Consolidated Pay):

A freelancer receives a consolidated payment of Rs. 10 lakh for a 3-month project. The freelancer needs to calculate and pay taxes on this amount.

Choosing the Right Structure:

The choice of CTC structure depends on factors like industry, company policy, and employee preferences. Fixed structures offer predictability, while flexible structures provide customization. Consolidated pay is suitable for short-term engagements.

Compensation & Benefits:

CATEGORIES OF PAYMENT:

- **BASE (FIXED SALARY)**
- **VARIABLES**
- **BENEFITS**
- **EXTENDED BENEFITS**

1. Base or Fixed Salary:

Fixed Salary Components: This is the fixed amount paid monthly, independent of performance or additional hours worked. It's fully taxable income. This is the foundation of an employee's guaranteed compensation in India. It mainly consists of "basic salary" and forms a major portion (around 40-60%) of the total CTC (Cost To Company).

Key Points:

Fixed amount paid monthly, irrespective of performance or hours worked.

Generally includes Basic, HRA, DA (can be fixed DA or Variable DA also), Other Allowances which are fixed in nature, paid irrespective of performance such as certain Allowances / Reimbursements, etc.

2. Variables Salary Components:

These are components of your CTC that can vary based on performance, sales targets achieved, or other metrics. They are not guaranteed and are paid out on top of the base salary. Common variables in India include:

Performance Bonus: A reward for exceeding targets or achieving set goals.

Commission: Percentage-based incentive earned on sales or project completions (common in sales roles).

Stock Options: Employees are granted the right to buy company stock at a predetermined price in the future, potentially leading to gains.

3. Benefits:

These are non-cash perks offered by employers to supplement your base salary and attract talent. They can be categorized into two main groups:

Mandatory Benefits: These are required by law and employers must contribute towards them. Examples include:

Provident Fund (PF): A retirement savings scheme where both employer and employee contribute a portion of the base salary.

Employee State Insurance (ESI): Provides medical insurance coverage for employees and their dependents (applicable for companies with more than 10 employees).

Statutory Bonus: Employees earning monthly wages of up to Rs. 21,000 eligible for this. The higher of 8.33% of your annual salary/wages OR Rs. 100 will be paid. Maximum that can be paid is 20% of your annual salary/ wages. Generally paid at 8.33% of Annual Basic Salary.

Gratuity: Gratuity is a payment made by an employer to an employee upon their retirement, resignation, death, or termination after completing a minimum service period of 4.8 years. Gratuity = Basic x 15/26 x no. of years of service.

Voluntary Benefits: These are offered at the employer's discretion and can vary widely. Examples include:

Medical Insurance: Covers medical expenses for the employee and family.

Group Term Life Insurance: Provides financial security to the employee's family in case of death.

Meal Coupons: Allow tax-exempt purchase of meals at restaurants or groceries.

Leave Travel Allowance (LTA): Helps with travel expenses incurred during leave.

4. Extended Benefits:

These are additional perks beyond traditional benefits, often offered by larger companies or in specific industries. They can be:

Wellness Programs: Gym memberships, fitness classes, or on-site health services.

Work-Life Balance Benefits: Childcare assistance, parental leave policies, or flexible work arrangements.

Educational Assistance: Reimbursement for job-related courses or certifications.

Employee Discount Programs: Discounts on various products or services.

What is Basic Pay?

Basic is a fixed/base component in salary. If it's too high, it will increase pf & other statutory contributions for both employer and employees. It is completely taxable, hence it shouldn't be too high. If it's too low, you will not be meeting the statutory requirements to be in line with minimum wages act. Basic salary is taxable, and other allowances and benefits are often calculated as a percentage of the basic salary.

Basic is ideally largest component of salary, usually fixed at 33% to 50% on CTC. As per new wage code: Basic to be 50% of gross/CTC.

House Rent Allowance (HRA): HRA is provided to employees to meet the cost of renting a house. The amount of HRA can vary based on factors such as the employee's salary, the city of residence, and the organization's policies.

Dearness Allowance (DA): DA is an allowance paid to employees to compensate for the impact of inflation on their cost of living. It is usually linked to the Consumer Price Index and can vary based on changes in the index.

Conveyance Allowance: This allowance is provided to cover the cost of commuting between home and office. It is generally a fixed amount per month.

Medical Reimbursement: Medical allowance is provided to cover medical expenses incurred by the employee and their family. It may be provided as a fixed monthly amount or as reimbursement against actual medical expenses.

Leave Travel Allowance (LTA): LTA is provided to cover the cost of travel when an employee goes on leave with their family. It is usually tax-exempt up to a certain limit and is paid as a reimbursement of actual travel expenses.

Provident Fund (PF): PF is a retirement benefit scheme where both the employer and the employee contribute a certain percentage of the employee's basic salary towards a fund. The accumulated amount is paid out to the employee upon retirement or resignation.

Gratuity: Gratuity is a lump sum amount paid by the employer to the employee as a token of appreciation for the employee's long and meritorious service. It is usually payable when an employee completes five years of continuous service with the organization.

Bonus: Bonus is an additional payment made to employees as a reward for their performance. It can be paid annually, quarterly, or as per the organization's policies.

Other Allowances and Perquisites: Apart from the above components, CTC may also include other allowances such as special allowances, telephone/mobile allowances, food coupons, and perquisites such as company-provided accommodation, vehicles, or club memberships.

List of Fully and Partly Taxable Allowances in India:

Fully Taxable Allowances	
Basic	
D.A.	
V.D.A.	
Partly taxable Allowances	Exemption Limit
HRA	Actual HRA or Rent paid - 10% of B+DA or 40% of B+DA for Nmetro & 50% of B+DA for Metro
Meal Voucher	Rs. 100 per day.Rs.2200 per month or Rs. 2400 per month
Telephone & Internet Reimbursement	Actuals / As per Invoice
Child Education Allowance	Rs. 100 per child Max.2 children
Hostel Fees	Rs. 300 per child Max. 2 children
Petrol Reimbursment	2400 if vehicle above 1600 cc
Driver Allowance	Max 900 pm
Superannuation Fund	Max upto 15% of B+DA
NPS Employer Contribution	10% of B+DA
Purchase of Laptop/Mobile/ Computer	No Limit / As per Invoice
Performance Development Allowance	No Limit / As per Invoice
Books & Periodicals	No Limit / As per Invoice

List of Allowances in India

PARTLY TAXABLE ALLOWANCES CONTD..

Partly taxable Allowances	Exemption Limit
LTA – Leave Travel Allowance	Based on actual travel bills, maximum First Class Train fare (To & Fro) including all family members, excludes sight-seeing hotel, etc. Actual bills or LTA as per CTC whichever is lesser.
	Only twice in block of 4 years (2018-21) and only once in a single year
	Only travel within India
	If by Air, Maximum only economy class Indian Airways cost will be exempted
	All other mode of transport claims, like Bus, Road travel, etc. will be compared with Train and lowest fare will be considered

List of Allowances in India

Sample CTC Structure

CTC Components	CTC Structure
Basic Salary	50% of ctc
D.A	20% of Basic
HRA	40% of B+DA
Co. Contribution to PF	12% on PF Wages
Telephone Reimbursement	2000
LTA Reimbursement	10% OF BASIC
Special Allowance	Balance

Sample CTC Structure

Activity for you:

List the types of CTC structures and find CTC structures used by any 2 organizations on the Internet.

....

....

CHAPTER FIFTY-FIVE

Global Compensation Strategies

Conquering Compensation Across the Globe: Your Guide for Winning Talent

The world is your business oyster, but how do you pay your international team? Global compensation strategies are your secret weapon for attracting and retaining top talent worldwide. It's more than just one-size-fits-all salaries – it's about tailoring rewards to different countries and cultures.

Types of Global Compensation Strategies:

Global Standardization: Think "same pay, everywhere." This approach streamlines processes and ensures fairness, but might not account for higher living costs in some countries.

Localization: Tailor your compensation package to each location. This means adjusting salaries, allowances, and benefits to match the local market and attract top talent in each region.

Glocalization (Hybrid): The best of both worlds! This strategy combines a core global framework with flexibility to adapt to regional needs. It offers consistency while acknowledging local variations.

Why Are These Strategies Important?

Attract & Retain Talent: Competitive pay packages that consider local costs make you an employer of choice in any market.

Fairness for All: Ensure employees in different countries doing similar jobs are compensated equally, fostering a motivated and loyal workforce.

Simplify & Save: Standardized processes and clear policies streamline administration, saving time and money.

Stay Legal, Stay Ethical: Comply with local regulations to avoid fines and maintain trust with your employees.

Business Goals in Mind: Reward desired behaviors and performance to drive employee engagement and business success.

Mastering global compensation strategies is your key to unlocking a world of talent. Embrace the complexities, and your international team will reward you with success!

Activity for you:

Research on Google about the compensation strategies of 2 Indian and 2 International companies and list them here. Also go through their compensaiton policies and write key points from there:

....

....

CHAPTER FIFTY-SIX

Case Study in Compensation & Payroll Management

Case Study: Streamlining Payroll at Netflix

Source: https://jobs.netflix.com/search

The Challenge:

Netflix, the global streaming giant, experienced rapid growth in its subscriber base and employee headcount. This presented a challenge for their existing payroll system, which was manual and prone to errors. The manual processes were time-consuming, inefficient, and couldn't keep pace with the company's growth. Additionally, the lack of automation led to potential inaccuracies in tax calculations and deductions.

The Solution:

To address these challenges, Netflix implemented a new cloud-based payroll system. Key features of the new system included:

- **Automated workflows:** Streamlined processes for tasks like data entry, calculations, and tax withholdings.
- **Self-service portal:** Employees could access their paystubs, tax documents, and make changes to their personal information directly through the system.
- **Improved reporting:** The new system provided comprehensive reports on payroll data, allowing for better budgeting and forecasting.

The Results:

The implementation of the new payroll system led to several benefits for Netflix:

- **Increased Efficiency:** Automated workflows significantly reduced the time and resources needed for payroll processing.
- **Reduced Errors:** Automation minimized the risk of errors in calculations and deductions.
- **Improved Employee Experience:** The self-service portal provided employees with easier access to their payroll information.
- **Enhanced Reporting:** Comprehensive reports facilitated better financial planning and decision-making.

Why it's Valuable:

This case study by Netflix highlights the importance of a modern and efficient compensation and payroll management system. As a company grows, manual processes become unsustainable and can lead to errors and inefficiencies. By implementing a cloud-based solution, Netflix was able to streamline its payroll operations, improve accuracy, and enhance the employee experience.

This case study offers valuable insights for companies facing similar challenges:

- **Need for Automation:** Manual payroll processes become cumbersome with a growing workforce. Look for automation solutions to save time and resources.
- **Employee Self-Service:** Self-service portals empower employees and reduce the burden on HR teams.
- **Data-Driven Decisions:** Leverage reporting tools to gain insights from payroll data for better financial planning.

By adopting similar strategies, other companies can achieve a more efficient and accurate compensation and payroll management system.

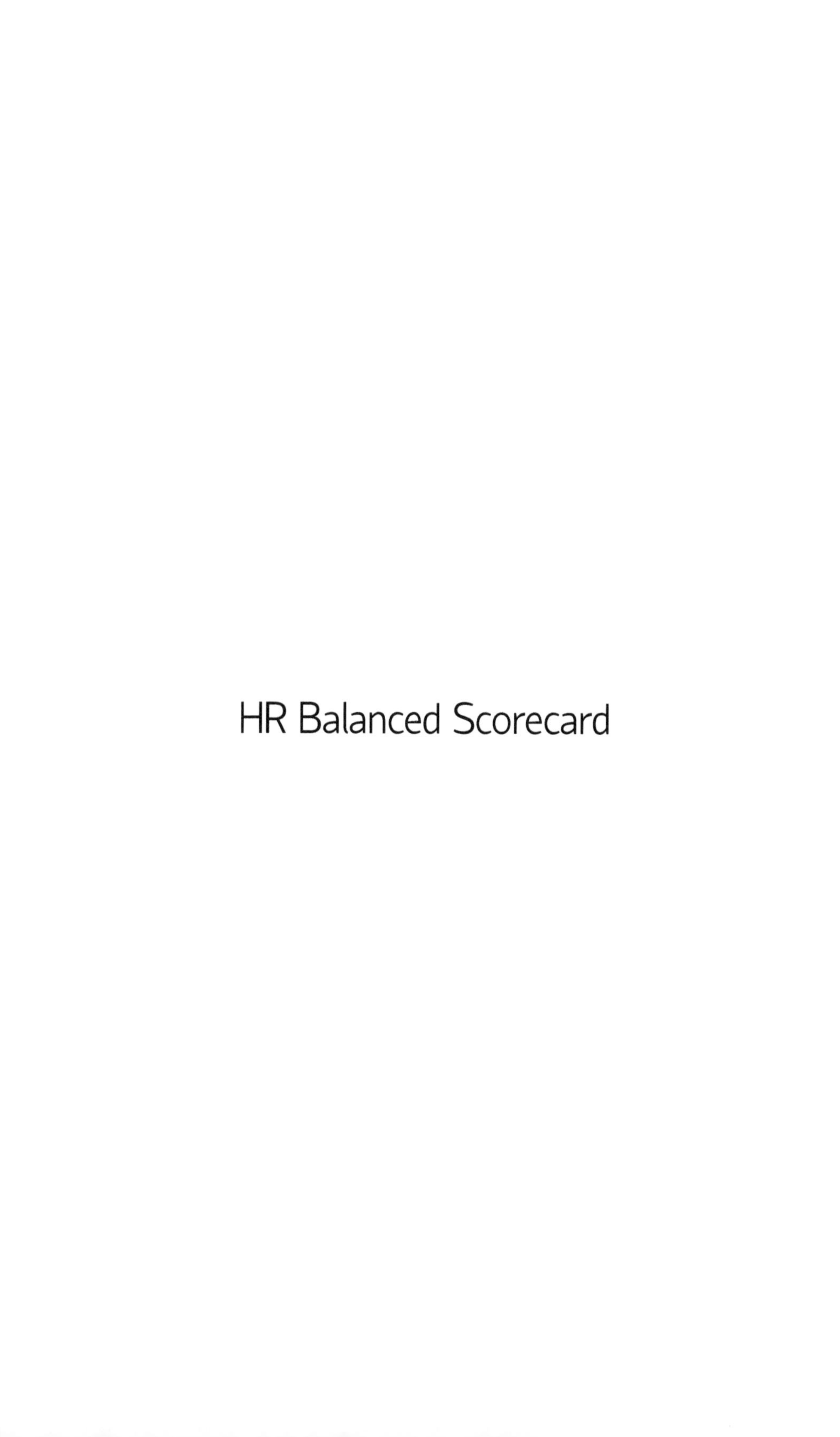

HR Balanced Scorecard

CHAPTER FIFTY-SEVEN

HR Balanced Scorecard

What is Balanced Scorecard?

A strategic management tool that provides a comprehensive view of an organization's performance by considering financial, customer, internal process, and learning and growth perspectives.

A Balanced ScoreCard looks like this:

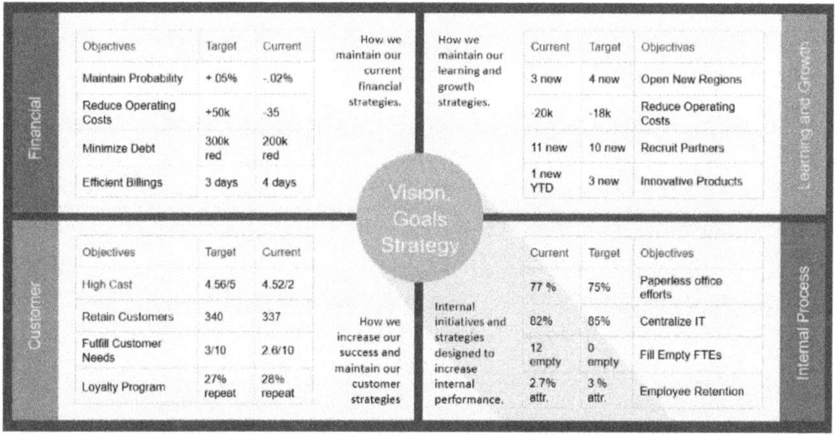

Balanced Scorecard

HR Balanced Scorecard: A specific application of the balanced scorecard concept to the human resources function, which helps HR departments to align their strategies and initiatives with the organization's overall goals and objectives. It evaluates HR performance through the same four perspectives as the balanced scorecard: financial, customer, internal process, and learning and growth.

To make a balanced scorecard, follow these steps:

Define your organization's vision and strategy: Start by identifying your organization's overall mission and goals, and the strategies that will help you achieve them.

Identify the key perspectives: Choose the four perspectives to be evaluated in the balanced scorecard: financial, customer, internal process, and learning and growth.

Identify key performance indicators (KPIs): For each perspective, determine the KPIs that will measure your organization's performance.

Set targets and priorities: Establish realistic targets for each KPI and prioritize them based on their significance to the organization's overall strategy.

Develop action plans: Based on the KPIs and targets, create action plans that outline the steps necessary to achieve your goals.

Implement and track progress: Implement the action plans and regularly track your organization's performance against the KPIs and targets.

Review and revise: Regularly review and revise your balanced scorecard to ensure that it continues to reflect your organization's evolving strategy and goals.

To make an HR balanced scorecard, follow these steps:

Align HR strategy with overall organizational strategy: Ensure that your HR strategy aligns with the overall goals and objectives of the organization.

Identify HR perspectives: Choose the four perspectives to be evaluated in the HR balanced scorecard: financial, customer, internal process, and learning and growth.

Identify HR KPIs: For each perspective, determine the KPIs that will measure HR performance. Examples could include employee satisfaction, turnover rate, training and development, and recruiting efficiency.

Set HR targets and priorities: Establish realistic targets for each HR KPI and prioritize them based on their significance to the organization's overall strategy.

Develop HR action plans: Based on the HR KPIs and targets, create action plans that outline the steps necessary to achieve your goals.

Implement and track HR progress: Implement the HR action plans and regularly track HR performance against the KPIs and targets.

Review and revise HR strategy: Regularly review and revise your HR balanced scorecard to ensure that it continues to reflect the organization's evolving strategy and goals.

The HR balanced scorecard has several uses, including:

1. **Aligning HR strategy with overall organizational strategy:** The HR balanced scorecard helps to ensure that HR initiatives and activities align with the overall goals and objectives of the organization.

2. **Measuring HR performance:** The HR balanced scorecard provides a comprehensive view of HR performance, allowing organizations to track progress and evaluate the impact of HR initiatives.

3. **Identifying areas for improvement:** By measuring HR performance across multiple perspectives, the HR balanced scorecard can help organizations identify areas where they can improve HR processes and practices.

4. **Communicating HR value:** The HR balanced scorecard can help HR departments to demonstrate their contribution to the organization's overall success by providing a clear and comprehensive picture of HR performance.

5. **Improving HR decision-making:** The HR balanced scorecard provides a structured and consistent approach to HR performance measurement, allowing HR departments to make informed decisions about their activities and initiatives.

6. **Prioritizing HR initiatives:** The HR balanced scorecard helps HR departments to prioritize initiatives and allocate resources effectively, based on the importance of each initiative to the organization's overall strategy.

HR Balanced Score Card example:

HR Scorecard	Objective	Measure	Target	Initiative
HR Deliverables	• Sales associates create exceptional buying experience	Mystery Shopper Ratings on: • product knowledge • helpfulness • courtesy	• average rating 90% • no rating below 70%	• Sales Training • Strategic Focus Initiative (Learning Map)
HR Efficiency	• Associate training by marketing deadline • Training costs at or below industry norm	• % associates trained by deadline • actual/ industry norm	• 100% trained • 90-100% of industry norm	• Sales Training • Strategic Focus Initiative (Learning Map)
HR Alignment	• Elements of HR system support strategic sales behaviors	• Alignment Index	• No negative ratings • average rating of +50	• Develop partnerships with line managers • Track progress of implementation
High Performance Work System	• HR practices are designed and implemented to support strategic objectives	• % receiving performance appraisal • % pay at risk for specified behaviors	• 100 % • 25%	• Develop partnerships with line managers • Track progress of implementation
HR Manager Competencies	• HR managers possess competencies that are linked to the needs of the business	• Rating on validated competency assessment tool (360)	• Average competency rating 85th percentile	• Targeted in-house and external development programs • Special developmental projects

HR Balanced Scorcard Example

What is balanced scorecard in hrm?

The balanced scorecard in HRM is a performance management tool that aligns an organization's human resource strategy with its overall business strategy. It measures the success of HR initiatives in four key areas: financial performance, customer satisfaction, internal processes, and employee learning and growth. This approach helps HR departments to demonstrate their value to the organization and ensures that HR practices are aligned with the company's goals.

A brief guide on HR Balanced Scorecard:

The HR balanced scorecard is a strategic management tool that provides a comprehensive view of an organization's human resources function. This tool helps HR departments to align their strategies and initiatives with the overall goals and objectives of the organization, and evaluate their performance through four key perspectives: financial, customer, internal process, and learning and growth. In this essay, we will examine the importance of the HR balanced scorecard, its components, and its benefits for organizations.

The HR balanced scorecard is an important tool for organizations because it allows HR departments to measure their performance in a way that is aligned with the overall goals and objectives of the organization. By focusing on the four key perspectives, the HR balanced scorecard provides a comprehensive view of HR performance, allowing organizations to track progress and evaluate the impact of HR initiatives. This helps to ensure that HR strategies and activities are aligned with the overall goals and objectives of the organization, and that HR is making a positive contribution to the organization's success.

The components of the HR balanced scorecard include key performance indicators (KPIs) for each of the four perspectives. For example, in the financial perspective, HR departments might measure their contribution to the organization's bottom line by tracking metrics such as the cost of turnover, the cost of benefits, and the cost of training and development. In the customer perspective, HR departments might measure employee satisfaction and engagement, and in the internal process perspective, HR departments might measure the efficiency of HR processes and practices. Finally, in the learning and growth perspective, HR departments might measure the impact of HR initiatives on employee development and the organization's overall learning and growth.

The benefits of the HR balanced scorecard are numerous. First, it allows organizations to measure HR performance in a way that is aligned with the overall goals and objectives of the organization, which helps to ensure that HR is making a positive contribution to the organization's success. Second, the HR balanced scorecard provides a comprehensive view of HR performance, allowing organizations to track progress and evaluate the impact of HR initiatives. This helps organizations to identify areas where they can improve HR processes and practices, and to prioritize HR initiatives based on their importance to the organization's overall strategy.

In conclusion, the HR balanced scorecard is a valuable tool for organizations that want to measure their HR performance in a way that is aligned with the overall goals and objectives of the organization. By focusing on four key perspectives and tracking KPIs, the HR balanced scorecard provides a comprehensive view of HR performance, allowing organizations to track progress, evaluate the impact of HR initiatives, and make informed decisions about HR activities and initiatives. Whether you are a small business or a large corporation, the HR balanced scorecard is an important tool for organizations that want to ensure that their HR strategies and activities are aligned with the overall goals and objectives of the organization.

Activity for you:

Briefly outline your learning of Balanced Scorecard:

....

....

CHAPTER FIFTY-EIGHT

Case Study: Balanced Scorecard

HR Balanced Scorecard: The Case of Dow Chemical

Source: https://www.youtube.com/watch?v=m9X6GGoLTDU

The Challenge:

Dow Chemical, a major player in the chemical industry, faced a critical need to align its HR practices with overall business strategy. Traditionally, HR metrics focused on internal activities like training hours, neglecting their impact on the company's bottom line. Dow needed a system to demonstrate the value HR brings to the organization.

The Solution:

Dow implemented a balanced scorecard approach specifically for HR. This balanced scorecard included four key perspectives:

- **Employee Perspective:** Measures aimed at employee satisfaction, engagement, and development. Metrics included employee retention rates, training completion rates, and employee satisfaction surveys.
- **Customer Perspective:** Focused on how HR practices impacted customer satisfaction. Metrics included customer satisfaction scores related to product quality and service.
- **Process Perspective:** Measured the efficiency and effectiveness of HR processes. Metrics included time-to-hire, cost-per-hire, and training program completion rates.
- **Financial Perspective:** Assessed the financial impact of HR activities. Metrics included return on investment (ROI) for training programs and cost savings from reduced employee turnover.

The Results:

The HR balanced scorecard at Dow Chemical yielded several positive results:

- **Strategic Alignment:** HR practices were directly linked to overall business objectives, demonstrating the value HR brings to the organization.
- **Data-Driven Decision Making:** The balanced scorecard provided data-driven insights to guide HR activities and resource allocation.
- **Improved Performance:** Metrics like employee retention and customer satisfaction showed improvement due to targeted HR initiatives.
- **Enhanced Communication:** The scorecard facilitated better communication between HR and other departments, fostering collaboration.

Why it's Valuable:

This case study by Dow Chemical showcases the benefits of implementing an HR balanced scorecard. By moving beyond traditional HR metrics, Dow was able to demonstrate the strategic value of HR and make data-driven decisions to improve employee engagement, customer satisfaction, and ultimately, the company's bottom line.

This case offers valuable insights for other organizations:

Strategic Alignment: Align HR activities with overall business goals to demonstrate HR's contribution.

Metrics that Matter: Use metrics that measure not just internal activities but also their impact on customer satisfaction and financial performance.

Communication and Collaboration: Utilize the balanced scorecard to foster better communication and collaboration between HR and other departments.

By adopting a similar approach, organizations can leverage the HR balanced scorecard to create a more strategic and impactful HR function.

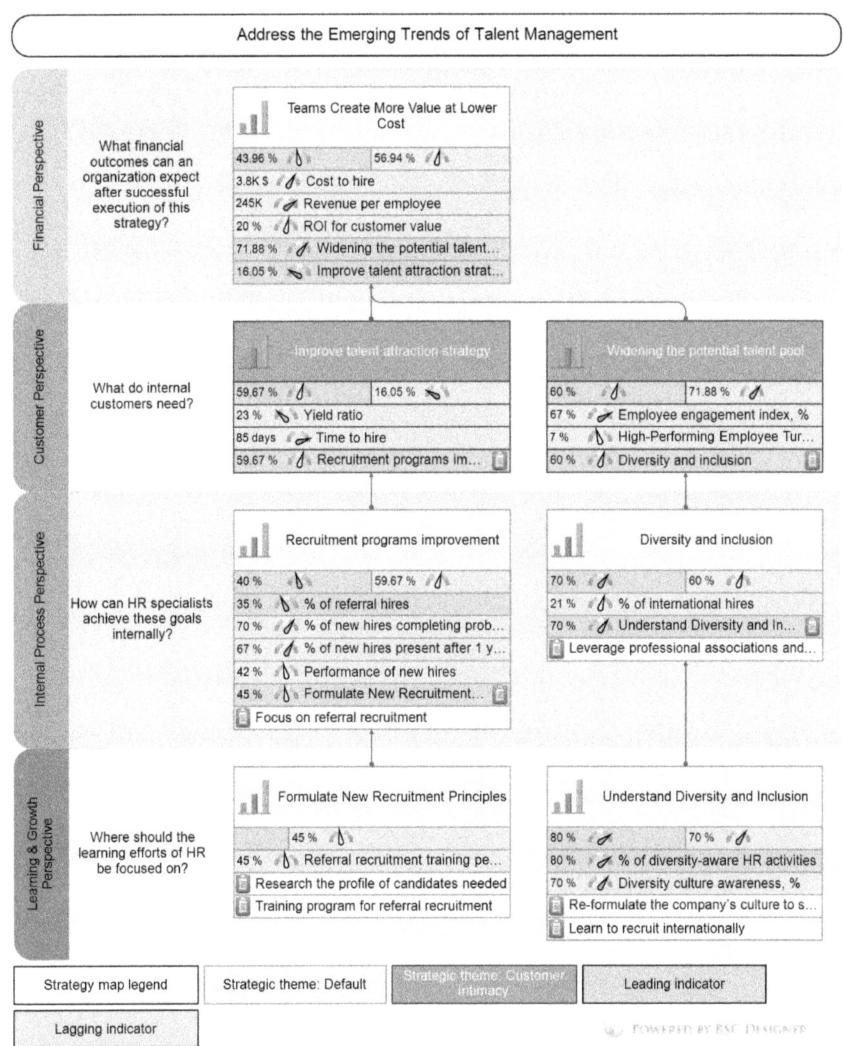

Sample Balanced Scorecard

Source: https://bscdesigner.com/hr-scorecard.htm

Performance Management System

CHAPTER FIFTY-NINE

Introduction to Performance Management Process

As employees, everyone wants to perform at their best. And of course, Organizations want their employees to do their best as well. Because High Performing Employees contribute to the bottom line of the organization. Most people feel **Performance Management & Appraisal** is synonymous Salary Hike or Compensation Revisions. Ofcourse Performance Management and Appraisal, helps measure employees' performance, which in turn helps management decide what kind of reward to be paid to the employee accordingly.

So let's delve into the topic and understand What is Performance Management?Performance management system is a process for evaluating an individual's job performance in an organization, including setting objectives, measuring progress, and providing feedback and coaching to help improve performance.

Performance Management helps managers and supervisors to monitor and evaluate employees' work.
Have you ever wondered if **Performance Management and Performance Management System (PMS) are one and the same?** Performance management and performance management system are related but not the same.

Key differences: Performance management refers to the overall process of evaluating employee performance, including setting goals and expectations, providing feedback and coaching, and determining compensation and promotions. Performance management aims to align employee performance with business goals.

Performance management system, on the other hand, refers to the specific tools and techniques used to support the performance management process, such as software applications, performance appraisal forms, and training programs.

Next, let us answer the question what is Performance Appraisal?
A specific event or process within the larger performance management system, typically done annually or semi-annually, in which an employee's performance is formally evaluated and documented. The goal of performance appraisal is to provide a comprehensive assessment of an employee's work and to inform decisions about pay, promotions, and other employment actions.

Difference between Performance Management and Performance Appraisal

Performance management is an ongoing process while performance appraisal is a specific step within that process.

Process of Performance Management: The process of performance management typically involves the following steps:-

1. **Setting goals and expectations:** Establish clear performance expectations and goals for each employee, aligned with the organization's mission and objectives.
2. **Monitoring and tracking performance:** Regularly collect data and metrics on the employee's performance and track progress towards their goals.
3. **Providing feedback and coaching:** Offer ongoing feedback and coaching to help the employee improve their performance and reach their goals.
4. **Evaluating performance:** Formally evaluate the employee's performance, using metrics and feedback, to assess their strengths and areas for improvement.
5. **Developing an action plan:** Work with the employee to develop an action plan to address any areas of underperformance, and provide support and resources to help them improve.
6. **Recognizing and rewarding performance:** Recognize and reward employees for their successes, such as through bonuses, promotions, or other forms of recognition.
7. **Continuously improving the process:** Regularly review and evaluate the performance management process to ensure it remains effective and

aligned with the needs of the organization.
The process of performance management should be ongoing, collaborative, and focused on continuous improvement, with the goal of enhancing employee performance and driving business results.

Objective of Performance Management:

This process helps companies ensure that their employees are meeting the company's expectations and contributing to its success. It aligns employee performance with the organization's goals and objectives. Providing a basis for compensation and promotion decisionsHelps Develop employee skills and abilities to meet performance goals Encouraging communication and collaboration between employees and management Identifying and addressing performance problemsPromoting continuous learning and development.

CHAPTER SIXTY

Methods in Performance Management: Traditional

The following are traditional methods of performance appraisal with examples:

1. Graphic rating scale - A rating system where supervisors rate an employee's performance by choosing from a list of pre-determined statements. The factors taken into consideration include both the personal characteristics and characteristics related to the on-the-job performance of the employees.

For example, a supervisor may rate an employee's performance in customer service using the following scale:

- Excellent
- Good
- Satisfactory
- Needs improvement
- Unsatisfactory

Pros:
Easy to understand and useProvides a clear benchmark for employee performanceEncourages employees to strive for higher ratings
Cons:
Can be subject to biases and inconsistencies in ratingsMay not provide enough detail or explanation of the ratingsMay not effectively capture an employee's full range of performance and skills

2. Forced distribution - A rating system where supervisors are required to rate a certain percentage of employees in specific performance categories (e.g. top 10%, bottom 10%).

For example, a supervisor may be required to rate the top 10% of employees as "outstanding," the next 20% as "above average," the next 50% as "average," and the bottom 20% as "below average."

Pros:

Encourages supervisors to distinguish high and low-performing employees. Provides a clear benchmark for employee performance. Helps to identify areas for improvement and training needs.

Cons:

Can create a competitive environment among employees. May not accurately reflect the true performance of employees. Can lead to inaccuracies if supervisors are forced to rate employees in specific categories who do not belong there.

3. Traditional rating scale - A rating system where supervisors rate an employee's performance on a numerical scale (e.g. 1-5, 1-10). **For example,** a supervisor may rate an employee's performance on a scale of 1 to 5, with 5 being the highest rating.

Pros:

Easy to understand and use. Provides a clear benchmark for employee performanceEncourages employees to strive for higher ratings.

Cons:

Can be subject to biases and inconsistencies in ratings. May not provide enough detail or explanation of the ratings. May not effectively capture an employee's full range of performance and skills

4. Narrative/essay evaluation - A written evaluation where supervisors provide a detailed description of an employee's performance, strengths, and areas for improvement. **For example,** a supervisor may write an essay outlining an employee's strengths in project management, such as their ability to effectively prioritize tasks and manage resources.

Pros:

Provides a more detailed and nuanced evaluation of an employee's performance. Encourages supervisors to think critically about an employee's performance. Helps employees to understand their strengths and areas for improvement.

Cons:

Can be time-consuming for supervisors to complete. May not provide a clear benchmark for employee performance. Can be subject to biases and inconsistencies in the written evaluations.

5. Critical incident method - A system where supervisors keep a record of specific incidents or behaviors that demonstrate an employee's strengths or areas for improvement. **For example,** a supervisor may keep a record of specific incidents where an employee demonstrated excellent communication skills or incidents where they struggled with time management.

Pros:

Provides a clear record of specific incidents that demonstrate an employee's performance. Encourages supervisors to observe and record employee performance regularly. Helps employees to understand their strengths and areas for improvement.

Cons:

May not provide a comprehensive evaluation of an employee's overall performance. Can be subject to biases and inconsistencies in the recorded incidentsMay not effectively capture an employee's full range of performance and skills.

6. Checklist - A system where supervisors use a pre-determined list of specific job tasks and rate an employee's performance on each task. For example, a supervisor may use a checklist to rate an employee's performance in tasks such as attending meetings, preparing reports, and meeting deadlines.

Pros:

1. Easy to understand and use. 2. Provides clear guidelines for evaluating performance. 3. Can be completed quickly.

Cons:

1. Does not allow for subjective or qualitative evaluation. 2. Can lead to rating errors, such as leniency or central tendency biases. 3. May result in an incomplete assessment of employee performance.

Note: The choice of method can depend on the specific goals of the appraisal, the type of work being evaluated, and the preferences of the supervisor and employee.

CHAPTER SIXTY-ONE

Methods in Performance Management: Modern

5 modern methods of performance appraisal:

- Management by objectives (MBO)
- 360 degree feedback
- Behaviorally anchored rating scale (BARS)
- Psychological appraisal.Assessment center.

1. Management by Objectives (MBO) The MBO method is all about boosting your organization's overall performance by setting clear objectives for the business. Both management and employees work together to set these goals.

Think of it like this: you and your manager team up to plan out specific, achievable goals for you to hit, usually within a set timeframe. And to make sure you're on track, you and your manager will have regular check-ins to discuss your progress and make any necessary adjustments.

Pros of Management by Objectives (MBO):

- **Clearly defined goals:** MBO helps employees understand what is expected of them and what they need to achieve.
- **Improved Communication:** Regular check-ins and feedback between employees and managers encourage open communication and collaboration.

- **Increased Motivation:** When employees understand their goals and how their performance will be evaluated, they tend to be more motivated and engaged.
- **Better Alignment with Business Goals:** MBO helps align an employee's performance with the organization's goals, which helps to improve overall performance.

Cons:

- **Time-consuming:** The goal-setting and evaluation process can be time-consuming and may divert resources away from other important tasks.
- **Lack of objectivity:** MBO relies heavily on subjective assessments and can be influenced by personal biases and opinions.
- **Unclear Performance Expectations:** Without clear guidelines, MBO can lead to misunderstandings and conflicting expectations between employees and managers.

2. 360 Degree Feedback The 360 Degree Feedback approach aims to gather feedback from everyone you interact with in your job — your managers, coworkers, subordinates, and even customers. You'll also give yourself a self-evaluation. This method is popular because multiple perspectives are taken into account when evaluating your performance.

Organizations usually gather feedback through an online form or questionnaire. And with tools like Jotform's free employee performance review form, collecting feedback and conducting evaluations has never been easier — whether you're using 360 Degree Feedback or another method.

Pros of 360 Degree Feedback:

- **Multi-perspective Feedback:** 360 degree feedback provides a comprehensive view of an employee's performance from multiple perspectives.
- **Improved Communication:** The feedback process encourages open and honest communication between employees, their managers, and their colleagues.
- **Increased Self-awareness:** By getting feedback from multiple sources, employees can gain a better understanding of their strengths and weaknesses.

Cons:

- **Time-consuming:** Collecting feedback from multiple sources can be time-consuming and may divert resources away from other important tasks.
- **Potential for Conflicts:** Feedback from multiple sources can sometimes lead to conflicting opinions and create conflict within the workplace.
- **Reliance on Surveys:** The effectiveness of 360 degree feedback depends on the accuracy and reliability of the survey data, which may be limited by response biases and other factors.

3. Behaviorally Anchored Rating Scale (BARS) BARS is a system that rates employees based on their performance and specific behaviors.
This is one of the most effective modern performance appraisal methods because it uses both quantitative and qualitative forms of measurement. The employer compares each employee's performance to specific behavioral examples, which are anchored to numerical ratings.

Pros of Behaviorally Anchored Rating Scale (BARS):

- **Combination of Quantitative and Qualitative Measurement:** BARS combines numerical ratings with specific behavioral examples, making the evaluation process more objective and reliable.
- **Improved Consistency:** By using specific behavioral examples, BARS helps ensure that evaluations are consistent across departments and managers.
- **Increased Objectivity:** The use of specific behavioral examples and numerical ratings helps to minimize subjectivity and biases in the evaluation process.

Cons:

- **Time-consuming:** Creating and implementing a BARS system can be time-consuming, particularly for large organizations with many departments and employees.
- **Limited Relevance:** BARS may not be relevant for all types of jobs and industries, making it difficult to use across the organization.

- **Potential for Resistance:** Some employees may resist the BARS system if they believe that their performance is being evaluated unfairly or inaccurately.

4. Psychological Appraisal The psychological appraisal method focuses on predicting an employee's future performance rather than just evaluating their past performance.

An experienced psychologist takes the lead in this approach, conducting in-depth interviews, psychological tests, and private conversations to assess an employee. The psychologist looks at various factors such as interpersonal skills, cognitive abilities, leadership skills, personality traits, emotional intelligence, and more.

Pros of Psychological Appraisal:

- **In-depth Analysis:** Psychological appraisal provides a thorough and in-depth analysis of an employee's strengths, weaknesses, and potential.
- **Improved Employee Development:** By identifying an employee's strengths and weaknesses, psychological appraisal can help organizations provide targeted training and development opportunities.
- **Improved Employee Retention:** By understanding an employee's strengths, weaknesses, and potential, organizations can provide them with opportunities for growth and development, which can improve employee satisfaction and reduce turnover.

Cons:

- **Time-consuming:** Psychological appraisal can be time-consuming and resource-intensive, particularly if the organization needs to hire a qualified psychologist.
- **Potential for Privacy Concerns:** Some employees may be concerned about the privacy of their personal and psychological information, which can impact the effectiveness of the appraisal process.
- **Limited Relevance:** Psychological appraisal may not be relevant for all types of jobs and industries.

5. Assessment Center The assessment center method tests both job capabilities and social interaction skills. Written tests evaluate ability, while situational exercises and role-playing scenarios help determine an employee's potential success in carrying out their day-to-day responsibilities.

Pros of Assessment Center:

- **Improved Predictive Validity:** Assessment centers combine various methods like simulations, presentations, and group exercises to assess a wider range of skills and behaviors compared to traditional interviews. This leads to a more accurate prediction of how an employee will perform in a specific role.
- **Fairness and Objectivity:** By using standardized exercises and multiple assessors, assessment centers help mitigate personal biases and create a more objective evaluation process. This fosters a sense of fairness among employees and ensures opportunities are based on merit.

Cons:

- **Cost and Time Investment:** Developing and conducting assessment centers can be expensive and time-consuming. The need for trained assessors, detailed exercises, and evaluation time can be a significant resource drain for organizations.
- **Stressful for Participants:** The pressure of being evaluated in an unfamiliar environment with various exercises can be stressful for participants. This can potentially impact their performance and lead to inaccurate assessments.

Activity for you:

Find out the Performance Management methods used by your organization (if you are working) and any 5 other organizations. Study the performance appraisal forms used by few organizations and highlight key points:

....

....

CHAPTER SIXTY-TWO

Performance Appraisal Forms: Templates

MANAGEMENT BY OBJECTIVES APPRAISAL FORM

Objective 1:

Standard for acceptable performance:

Results:

Special factors and other comments:

Objective 2:

Standard for acceptable performance:

Results:

Special factors and other comments:

Objective 3:

Standard for acceptable performance:

Results:

Special factors and other comments:

Objective 4:

Standard for acceptable performance:

Results:

Special factors and other comments:

Management by Objective (MBO) Form

360 degree feedback form template. This template allows a mixture of key skills comprising one, two, three, four, and up to six elements. The number of elements per key skill/capability varies of course, so if necessary adjust the size of the boxes in the first column accordingly to accommodate more or less elements. See the 360 degree appraisals notes for more explanation about the purpose of each column and heading, and the feedback scoring method.

Insert your own Feedback Form headings and instructions: appraisee name, date, feedback respondent name, position (if applicable) plus local instructions and guidelines for completion, etc.

key skill/capability area	skill/capability element	question number	feedback question	feedback score
		1		
		2		
		3		
		4		
		5		
		6		
		7		
		8		
		9		
		10		
		11		
		12		
		13		
		14		
		15		
		16		
		17		
		18		
		19		
		20		
		21		
		22		
		23		
		24		

360 Degree Feedback - Page 1

Employee Experience Design (EX-Design)

CHAPTER SIXTY-THREE

A Guide on Employee Experience Design in HR

What is Employee Experience Design (Ex Design) in HR and Why it is the most talked about topic in HR Fraternity?

Firstly Terminologies you need to know:

a. EX Design : Employee Experience Design

b. UX Design : User Experience Design

c. CX Design : Customer Experience Design

d. EX Design : Employee Experience Design

Objectives

Winning employees' hearts and minds Much as designing customer experience has dominated the thinking of companies competing in today's digital environment, organizations are now re-examining the employee experience. Recognizing the impact experience has on employee engagement and productivity, companies are taking a more comprehensive view of how to influence it.

The two most common goals when looking at EX are:

- Retaining talent by stimulating sustainable growth within the company.
- Boost productivity by having happy employees.

Areas where Employee Experience is created:

The employee experience is created through interactions in three areas:

- Employees' physical environment, Their social connections, and The work to be done.

Ex-Design Strategies:

Organizations can leverage five key strategies to enhance the overall experience for their employees:

Personalization: Tailoring the work environment and opportunities to individual needs and preferences.

Transparency: Fostering open communication and clear information sharing throughout the organization.

Simplification: Streamlining processes and procedures to reduce complexity and workload.

Authenticity: Building trust and credibility through genuine interactions and leadership.

Organizational Responsiveness: Demonstrating a willingness to adapt and address employee concerns in a timely manner.

Methods to Strengthen Employee Experience

In addition to the core strategies, four specific methods can further improve the employee experience:

Utilizing Analytics: Data-driven insights can help identify areas for improvement and measure the effectiveness of existing initiatives.

Identifying Differentiation Touchpoints: Pinpointing the unique interactions and experiences that set your company apart.

Building Cross-Functional Experience Teams: Bringing together diverse perspectives to design and implement a well-rounded employee experience strategy.

Applying Fast and Iterative Design Principles: Implementing changes quickly, gathering feedback, and continuously refining the employee experience based on that feedback.

What is Design Thinking?

Design thinking is a popular method for solving problems creatively. It results in innovative solutions that are more effective for people.

Design Thinking in HR

Design Thinking in HR

Human Resources (HR) professionals face challenges due to constant technological advancements, new applications, and information overload. Statistics show that people check their phones collectively over 8 billion times a day, yet productivity hasn't significantly increased.

To address employee overwhelm and develop helpful HR applications, HR can leverage design thinking. This approach prioritizes the employee experience by placing it at the center of the process.

Employee Engagement vs. Employee Experience Design: Key Differences

It's important to distinguish between employee engagement activities and employee experience (EX) design. Engagement initiatives often target short-term improvements in EX. While free lunches and flexible work schedules can be part of the picture, EX design goes much deeper.

It focuses on capturing the entire employee journey, encompassing critical interactions, decisions, emotions, and perceptions across all daily touchpoints. A well-designed EX fosters higher levels of engagement, involvement, and employer brand commitment in the long run. This positive impact will ultimately be reflected in engagement survey results.

Revamping HR with Design Thinking: 5 Key Principles

The modern workforce is changing rapidly, and HR needs to adapt. Design thinking offers a powerful framework to streamline HR processes and cater to this evolving landscape. Here are five key principles of design thinking that can revolutionize HR:

Human-Centric Design: Gone are the days of one-size-fits-all HR policies. Design thinking emphasizes understanding and prioritizing employee needs, wants, and well-being. It's a shift from "what's convenient for the company" to "what creates a great employee experience."

Collaborative Design: Building a strong employer brand goes beyond company-controlled messaging. Design thinking encourages collaboration with both current employees and future candidates. Happy employees become your best brand ambassadors. Imagine: A CEO praising the workplace culture might be nice, but a video of employees showcasing their positive Candidate Experience and work environment is far more impactful.

Creative Problem-Solving: In today's competitive talent market, fresh approaches are essential. Design thinking fosters creativity in attracting and retaining talent. New hiring strategies like inbound recruiting, social media recruitment, candidate relationship management (CRM), and data-driven recruiting are just a few examples.

Technology as a Tool: Technology offers incredible HR advantages, but it can also create roadblocks. Social media and online tools make candidates more informed about company culture. Design thinking helps HR leverage technology to create a seamless and positive Candidate Experience.

Prototyping and Iteration: HR policies and practices shouldn't be set in stone. Design thinking encourages testing and iterating on ideas. Experiment with different approaches, like showcasing employee testimonials, career stories, or team blogs on your careers page. Monitor results and refine your strategy for maximum impact.

By embracing these design thinking principles, HR can transform from a reactive department to a proactive force in attracting, engaging, and retaining top talent.

Applying Design Thinking in Human Resources

Design thinking can be a powerful tool for HR professionals across various areas:

Organizational Design: When restructuring roles or the organization itself, HR can integrate design thinking principles to ensure the new structure optimizes employee experience and efficiency.

Engagement & Involvement: Design thinking can guide efforts to make work easier, more efficient, fulfilling, and rewarding, leading to higher employee engagement and involvement.

Analytics: By combining data analysis with design thinking, HR can recommend solutions that directly address employee needs based on real data.

HR Skillset Expansion: To fully leverage design thinking, HR professionals should expand their skillset to include understanding of digital design, mobile app design, behavioral economics, machine learning, and user experience (UX) design.

Benefits of Design Thinking in HR

Design thinking offers several advantages for HR professionals:

Reduced Risk with New Ideas: By encouraging the exploration of multiple solutions quickly, design thinking prevents rigid attachment to the first idea. This allows for a more adaptable approach and reduces the risk of launching a flawed initiative.

Empathy-Driven Solutions: Design thinking prioritizes understanding the mindsets and needs of the target audience. In HR, this translates to solutions that truly address employee concerns and foster a positive work experience.

Opportunity Identification: By focusing on employee needs, design thinking helps identify opportunities to improve processes, increase engagement, and create a more fulfilling work environment. This translates to a more engaged and productive workforce.

How Organizations are using Design Thinking or Employee Experience Design?

Design Thinking in Action: How Cisco Created Winning Onboarding Solutions

This passage showcases how Cisco utilized design thinking to tackle a common challenge – improving the new hire onboarding process. Through their global "Breakathon" initiative, they fostered an environment for creative problem-solving, resulting in not just one, but two winning solutions.

The winning ideas – a mobile app named "YouBelong@Cisco" and a service called "Virtual Concierge" – exemplify the power of design thinking. YouBelong@Cisco provides a digital platform for new hires and managers to navigate the initial phases of employment. Virtual Concierge complements this by offering a human touch, creating a centralized point for face-to-face interaction alongside digital support. This innovative combination ensures a smooth onboarding experience that seamlessly blends digital and human elements.

This case study demonstrates the effectiveness of design thinking in generating successful solutions. By focusing on user needs and iterating on ideas, companies like Cisco can develop winning strategies to enhance employee experience.

Activity for you:

Explain Design Thinking in HRM. Write how it could be useful for HR activities in your organization or any other organization.

....

....

CHAPTER SIXTY-FOUR

How Employee Experience Design Works

Stages of Design Thinking

1. **Empathize:** Walk a mile in their shoes. Conduct interviews, observe workflows, and gather employee feedback to understand their needs and challenges.
2. **Define:** Frame the problem clearly. Analyze data, identify trends, and formulate a concise problem statement that captures the core issue faced by employees.
3. **Ideate:** Think outside the box. Brainstorm creative solutions with diverse stakeholders, encouraging unconventional approaches and wild ideas.
4. **Prototype:** Build a quick and dirty model. Develop a low-fidelity version of your proposed solution (e.g., wireframe, mock-up) to test with users and gather initial feedback.
5. **Test:** Learn and iterate. Implement the refined solution, continuously monitor employee feedback, and make adjustments based on user experience to ensure the solution effectively addresses the problem.

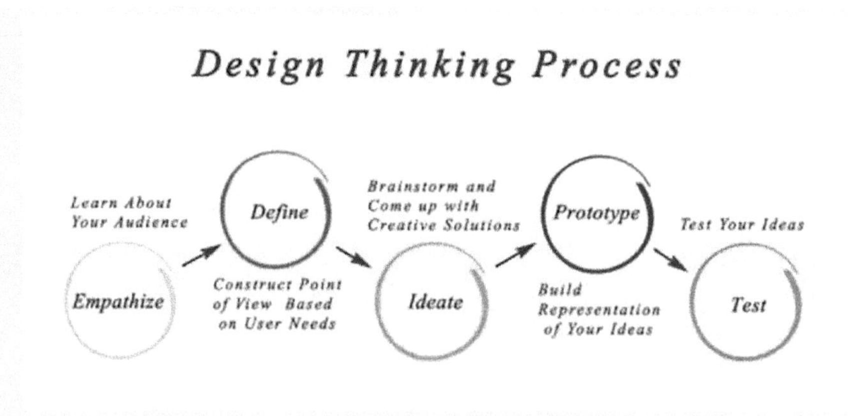

Design Thinking Process and Stages

How to Use Design Thinking in Employee Experience Design

The world of work is constantly evolving, and HR practices need to adapt accordingly. Enter design thinking: a human-centered approach to problem-solving that's revolutionizing HR departments. By focusing on employee needs and experiences, design thinking helps HR create innovative solutions to complex challenges.

We will explore five key stages of design thinking in HRM, along with real-world examples to illustrate their application:

1. Empathize: Understanding Your Workforce

This stage is all about putting yourself in your employees' shoes. Here's how:

Conduct Interviews: Talk to employees from different departments and seniority levels. Understand their daily struggles, frustrations, and desired work environment.

Observe Workflows: Shadow employees in their daily tasks. Witness firsthand the challenges they face with current processes or technology.

Employee Surveys: Gather broader data through surveys to identify common pain points and areas for improvement.

Example: An HR team notices a rise in burnout and low engagement among customer service representatives. Through empathy exercises, they discover the reps feel overwhelmed due to a clunky CRM system and unclear performance metrics.

2. Define: Framing the Problem

With all the gathered information, it's time to define the core problem you're trying to solve. Here's how:

Identify Trends: Analyze interview data and survey results to find recurring themes and frustrations.

Formulate a Problem Statement: Clearly articulate the central issue faced by your employees.

Prioritize: Focus on the most impactful problem with the highest potential for positive change.

Example: Based on their empathy research, the HR team defines the core problem as: "Customer service representatives lack efficient tools and clear performance goals, leading to frustration and disengagement."

3. Ideate: Brainstorming Solutions

Now that you understand the problem, it's time to unleash creativity! Here's how:

Brainstorming Sessions: Gather a diverse group of stakeholders (HR, IT, employees) to generate ideas for solutions. Encourage wild ideas and "out-of-the-box" thinking.

Think Outside the Box: Challenge assumptions and explore unconventional approaches. How can technology, gamification, or process redesign help?

Example: The HR team, along with IT and customer service representatives, brainstorm solutions. Ideas include implementing a user-friendly CRM system, introducing gamified performance dashboards, and providing mentorship programs for new hires.

4. Prototype: Building a Low-Fidelity Model

Before going all-in on a solution, design thinking emphasizes testing a stripped-down version. Here's how:

Develop a Prototype: Create a basic model of your proposed solution. This could be a wireframe for a new software interface, a mock-up of a training program, or a simplified version of a new workflow.

Test with Users: Get feedback from employees on the prototype. This helps identify flaws and refine the solution before a full-scale rollout.

Example: The HR team develops a prototype of the new CRM system with a simplified interface and automated performance tracking features. They test it with a small group of customer service representatives, gathering feedback on usability and efficiency.

5. Test: Refining and Iterating

The final stage involves testing the actual solution and iterating based on user feedback. Here's how:

Implement the Solution: Launch the refined solution across the organization.

Gather Feedback: Continuously monitor employee feedback on the implemented solution.

Iterate and Improve: Based on feedback, make adjustments and improvements to the solution.

Example: The CRM system is launched with the improved interface and performance tracking features. The HR team monitors employee reaction and usage data. Based on feedback, they introduce short training videos and further refine the automated metrics.

By incorporating design thinking into your HR practices, you can create solutions that truly address employee needs and foster a more engaged, productive, and fulfilling work environment. Remember, design thinking is an iterative process. Continuous improvement and adaptation are key to success!

Activity for you:

List Stages of Design Thinking in HRM. Explain how each stage is undertaken.

....

....

CHAPTER SIXTY-FIVE

Candidate Experience Design: Case Study

Case Study: Transforming Candidate Experience at Delta Company

Company: Delta Company (500+ Employees)

Challenge: Delta Company faced significant challenges in attracting and hiring qualified talent. They experienced:

High Hiring Costs: Extensive advertising and a lengthy interview process resulted in high recruitment expenses.

Low Quality Hires: The current process wasn't attracting the best fit, leading to frequent turnover and decreased productivity.

Candidate No-Shows: Many applicants wouldn't show up for interviews, wasting valuable time and resources.

Solution: Design Thinking for Candidate Experience

Delta Company embraced design thinking to revamp their candidate experience. Here's the process:

1. Empathize: The HR team conducted interviews with current employees, rejected candidates, and industry experts. They observed the application process and analyzed data on no-shows.

Key Findings:

- Job descriptions were lengthy and technical, deterring qualified candidates.
- The application process was cumbersome and outdated.

- Lack of communication with applicants throughout the process led to frustration and disengagement.

2. Define: The core problem was a poor candidate experience that discouraged top talent and resulted in wasted resources.

3. Ideate: A cross-functional team brainstormed solutions, including:

Revamping job descriptions: Using clear, concise language that highlighted company culture and growth opportunities.

Streamlining the application process: Implementing a user-friendly online platform for easy application submission.

Improved communication: Sending personalized updates to applicants at each stage and providing clear instructions for interviews.

Engaging content creation: Showcasing company culture and employee stories through social media and career pages.

4. Prototype: A pilot program incorporating the above solutions was launched for a specific open position.

5. Test: Data was collected through candidate feedback surveys and interview evaluations.

Results:

Reduced Hiring Costs: Streamlined process and targeted marketing lowered overall recruitment expenditure by 20%.

Improved Quality of Hires: The new approach attracted more qualified candidates, resulting in a 15% increase in successful hires.

Decreased No-Shows: Clear communication and a smooth process led to a 70% reduction in candidate no-shows.

Enhanced Employer Brand: Positive candidate experience resulted in increased applications and positive online reviews, strengthening Delta Company's employer brand.

Conclusion: Design thinking revolutionized Delta Company's candidate experience. By focusing on candidate needs, they attracted better talent, reduced hiring costs, and built a stronger employer brand. This case study demonstrates the power of design thinking in transforming HR practices and achieving positive outcomes.

Activity for you:

List some of the ways you have felt the interview candidate experience can be improvised in your own organization or some other

organization's. List your own experiences of attending an interview and how the experience could be improvised by the hiring company:

....

....

CHAPTER SIXTY-SIX

Case Studies in Employee Experience Design

Case Study: Rejuvenating Employee Experience at Delta Company

Case Study: Rejuvenating Employee Experience at Delta Company

Company: Delta Company (500+ Employees)

Challenge: Delta Company was experiencing a decline in employee morale.

Key issues included:

Lack of Motivation: Employees reported feeling unmotivated and disengaged, leading to decreased productivity.

Dissatisfaction with Appraisals and Salaries: Employees felt the appraisal system was unfair and salaries were not competitive, fostering resentment.

Gossiping Culture: A negative company culture with rampant gossip eroded trust and collaboration.

Solution: Design Thinking for Employee Experience

Delta Company recognized the need to improve employee experience. They adopted design thinking to address the issues:

1. Empathize: The HR team conducted focus groups, one-on-one interviews, and anonymous surveys to understand employee concerns.

Key Findings:

- Unclear career paths and limited growth opportunities demotivated employees.

- Opaque performance evaluation processes and lack of transparency regarding salary adjustments created frustration.
- A culture of fear and gossip discouraged open communication and collaboration.

2. Define: The core problem was a negative employee experience marked by a lack of motivation, frustration with compensation, and a toxic workplace culture.

3. Ideate: A cross-functional team brainstormed solutions, including:

Career Development Programs: Implementing mentorship programs, skills training, and clear career roadmaps to boost employee motivation.

Performance Review Revamp: Developing a transparent performance review system with clear criteria, regular feedback sessions, and opportunities for salary adjustments based on merit.

Culture Building Initiatives: Encouraging open communication, fostering team-building activities, and introducing internal recognition programs to promote a positive and collaborative work environment.

Anti-Gossip Training: Conducting workshops to raise awareness of the negative impacts of gossip and equipping employees with conflict resolution skills.

4. Prototype: Pilot programs were launched for specific departments, focusing on career development programs and team-building activities.

5. Test: Employee feedback was collected through surveys, focus groups, and one-on-one meetings.

Results:

Increased Motivation: Personalized career development plans and transparent performance reviews led to a 10% increase in employee self-reported motivation.

Improved Perception of Compensation: Fairer performance evaluations and adjusted salary structures improved employee satisfaction with compensation.

Reduced Gossip: Anti-gossip training and team-building activities fostered a more positive and collaborative environment, leading to a noticeable decrease in gossip.

Enhanced Employee Retention: Improved employee experience resulted in a lower turnover rate, saving Delta Company significant costs associated with recruitment and onboarding.

Conclusion: Design thinking empowered Delta Company to address the root causes of employee dissatisfaction. By focusing on employee needs and fostering a positive work environment, they boosted motivation, improved compensation perception, and built a more collaborative culture. This case study highlights the potential of design thinking to revitalize employee experience and create a thriving workplace.

Activity for you:

List some of the problems in your own company or any other well-known company, which can be solved using Design Thinking.

....

....

CHAPTER SIXTY-SEVEN

Real-Life Case Studies: Design Thinking

Here are 4 real-life examples of Design Thinking usage in different companies:

Airbnb: Revolutionizing Travel Lodging (Source: https://medium.com)

Challenge: How to connect travelers with unique and authentic accommodation options.

Solution: Design thinking helped Airbnb founders create a user-friendly platform where travelers could easily find and book stays, while homeowners could list and manage their rentals. By focusing on user needs (both travelers and hosts), Airbnb disrupted the traditional hospitality industry.

IDEO.org & Unilever: Tackling Sanitation in Ghana (Source: https://voltagecontrol.com)

Challenge: Provide affordable and accessible in-home sanitation solutions for low-income communities in Ghana.

Solution: Through design thinking, a team from IDEO.org and Unilever developed the "Clean Team" program. This involved creating a sanitation system with user-friendly toilets delivered and maintained in homes. The program not only addressed hygiene needs but also improved overall well-being and dignity for residents.

UberEats: Delivering Food, Designed for Efficiency (Source: https://www.hotjar.com/for-product-designer/)

Challenge: Design a seamless and efficient food delivery experience for both restaurants and customers.

Solution: UberEats uses design thinking to continuously improve its app and service. This includes activities like "Walkabouts" where designers shadow delivery partners to understand their challenges. User feedback is constantly incorporated to optimize the app for both restaurants (order processing, delivery management) and customers (ordering, tracking, feedback).

Intuit: Simplifying Taxes for Individuals and Businesses (Source: https://designthinking.ideo.com/)

Challenge: Make complex tax filing and financial management tools user-friendly for individuals and small businesses.

Solution: Intuit's design thinking approach focuses on user empathy. They conduct extensive research to understand user pain points and frustrations related to taxes and finances. This user-centric approach has led to the development of popular products like TurboTax and QuickBooks, which simplify complex financial tasks for millions of customers.

These examples showcase the diverse applications of design thinking across various industries. By focusing on user needs and iteratively creating solutions, companies can achieve innovative outcomes and gain a competitive edge.

Employee Engagement

CHAPTER SIXTY-EIGHT

Introduction to Employee Engagement

Employee Engagement is a critical factor in the success of any organization. Engaged employees are more productive, more committed to their work, and more likely to stay with the company for the long term. They are also more likely to provide high-quality customer service and help drive business growth. However, many organizations struggle to create a culture of engagement in the workplace.

Employee Engagement requires more than just offering competitive salaries and benefits. It requires a comprehensive approach that focuses on creating a positive work environment, providing meaningful work, recognizing and rewarding employee contributions, and fostering strong relationships between employees and managers. In this context, it is important for organizations to invest in employee engagement programs that help them build a thriving workplace culture and retain top talent.

What is Employee Engagement?

Employee engagement refers to the level of commitment, passion, and enthusiasm that employees have for their work and their organization. Engaged employees are emotionally invested in their jobs, feel a sense of purpose and fulfillment in their work, and are committed to achieving the organization's goals.

They are also more likely to be satisfied with their jobs, take pride in their work, and have a positive impact on their coworkers and the organization as a whole. Employee engagement is a critical factor in the success of any organization, as it is linked to higher productivity, better customer service, and greater employee retention. Engaged employees are more likely to stay with the organization for the long term and help drive business growth.

Employee Engagement

Employee Engagement Models:-

There are several models of employee engagement, each of which provides a framework for understanding the key drivers and outcomes of engagement. Here are three popular models:

1. Gallup's Q12 Model:

This model was developed by the Gallup organization and is based on a survey of employee engagement across a wide range of industries. It consists of 12 questions that measure factors such as employee recognition, opportunities for growth and development, and trust in senior leadership. This model emphasizes the importance of building a positive workplace culture and providing employees with meaningful work.

2. Aon Hewitt's Engagement Model:

Aon Hewitt's model is based on a survey of more than 7 million employees worldwide. It includes four key drivers of engagement: leadership, reputation, performance, and culture. This model emphasizes the importance of leadership in driving engagement and the role of organizational culture in shaping employee attitudes and behaviors.

3. Towers Watson's Engagement Model:

Towers Watson's model is based on a survey of more than 32,000 employees across a wide range of industries. It includes three drivers of engagement: employee enablement, employee engagement, and employee energy. This model emphasizes the importance of empowering employees to take ownership of their work and providing them with the resources and support they need to be successful.

Each of these models provides a useful framework for understanding the factors that contribute to employee engagement and can help organizations identify areas where they can improve. However, it is important to note that engagement is a complex and multifaceted concept, and no single model can capture all of its dimensions.

Employee Engagement Process Flow:-

Employee engagement is a continuous process that requires ongoing effort from both employees and employers. Here are the key steps involved in the employee engagement process:

1. **Define engagement**: The first step in the employee engagement process is to define what engagement means for the organization. This involves understanding the organization's mission, values, and culture and identifying the behaviors and attitudes that are associated with engagement.

2. **Measure engagement:** Once engagement is defined, the organization can measure it using tools such as surveys, interviews, or focus groups. These measurements help identify the areas where engagement is high or low and provide insights into what drives engagement in the organization.

3. **Analyze results:** The next step is to analyze the results of the engagement measurements and identify areas where action is needed. This may involve identifying specific departments or teams where engagement is low or looking for patterns across the organization.

4. **Develop action plans:** Based on the analysis of the engagement measurements, action plans are developed to improve engagement. These plans may involve implementing new programs or policies, providing training to managers and supervisors, or making changes to the work environment to make it more conducive to engagement.

5. **Communicate results and action plans:** It is important to communicate the results of the engagement measurements and the action plans to employees. This helps build trust and transparency and shows employees that their feedback is valued.

6. **Implement action plans:** The next step is to implement the action plans developed in step 4. This may involve working with various departments or teams to roll out new programs or policies or providing training to managers and supervisors.

7. **Monitor progress:** Finally, it is important to monitor progress and measure the impact of the action plans on engagement. This may involve

conducting follow-up surveys or focus groups to assess progress and identify areas where additional action is needed.

Overall, the employee engagement process is a continuous cycle of measurement, analysis, action, and monitoring. By following this process, organizations can create a culture of engagement that drives business success and employee satisfaction.

Employee Engagement Survey:-

Employee engagement surveys are a common tool used by organizations to measure the level of engagement among their employees. Here is a general overview of the process:

1. **Develop a survey questionnaire:** The first step in conducting an employee engagement survey is to develop a questionnaire that includes questions designed to measure various aspects of employee engagement, such as job satisfaction, sense of purpose, and connection to the organization. The questions should be clear, concise, and unbiased.
2. **Choose a survey administration method:** There are several ways to administer an employee engagement survey, including online surveys, paper surveys, and interviews. The chosen method should be convenient for employees and should provide anonymity to encourage honest responses.
3. **Distribute the survey:** Once the survey is developed and the administration method is chosen, the survey is distributed to employees. This may involve sending out an email with a link to an online survey or providing paper surveys to employees.
4. **Collect and analyze responses:** Once employees have completed the survey, the responses are collected and analyzed to identify patterns and trends. This may involve using statistical software to analyze the data and identify key insights.
5. **Communicate results and take action:** The results of the survey are communicated to employees, and action plans are developed to address areas where engagement is low. This may involve implementing new programs or policies to improve engagement, providing training to managers and supervisors on how to foster engagement, or making changes to the work environment to make it more conducive to engagement.
6. **Follow up and monitor progress:** Finally, it is important to follow up with employees to ensure that the action plans are having a positive

impact on engagement. This may involve conducting follow-up surveys or focus groups to assess progress and identify areas where additional action is needed.

Employee Engagement Survey Report / Results: How to Measure Engagement Level?

1. eNPS — Employee net promoter score

Employer Net Promoter Score, or eNPS, is a scoring system designed to help employers measure employee satisfaction and loyalty within their organizations. Employee Net Promoter Score (eNPS) is a method of measuring how willing your employees are to recommend their workplace to others.

One score/metric to measure your employee satisfaction and to identify the number of promoters, detractors, and passives through our reporting of employee engagement survey results.

2. Employee survey participation score

Employee engagement survey results reporting that throws a spotlight on your survey response rate, for you to pick it up and improve to gain a better perspective of your engagement levels.

3. Employee engagement score by drivers

Employee engagement heat map, a part of employee engagement survey results, which segments your employee engagement survey results into driver scores —work-life balance, rewards, recognition, wellness, communication— measurable across teams, locations, reporting managers, gender, and employee type.

CHAPTER SIXTY-NINE

HR Metrics in Engagement and Engagement Survey

HR Metrics that measure Employee Engagement:-

There are various employee engagement metrics that organizations can use to measure and track employee engagement levels. Here are some common employee engagement metrics along with their explanations:

Employee Engagement Index (EEI): The Employee Engagement Index is a comprehensive metric that measures employee engagement levels by asking employees about their level of satisfaction with their jobs, their commitment to the organization, and their willingness to go above and beyond their job duties. The EEI is usually calculated as a percentage of the total number of engaged employees.

Net Promoter Score (NPS): The Net Promoter Score is a metric that measures employee loyalty and likelihood to recommend the organization as a place to work. Employees are asked to rate how likely they are to recommend the company as a great place to work, on a scale from 0-10. The NPS is calculated by subtracting the percentage of detractors (employees who give a score of 0-6) from the percentage of promoters (employees who give a score of 9-10).

Employee Satisfaction Score (ESS): The Employee Satisfaction Score is a metric that measures how satisfied employees are with various aspects of their job and workplace, such as compensation, benefits, work-life balance, management, and career development. The ESS is usually calculated on a scale of 1-5 or 1-10, with higher scores indicating higher levels of satisfaction.

Employee Net Promoter Score (eNPS): The Employee Net Promoter Score is similar to the NPS, but it specifically measures employee loyalty and likelihood to recommend the organization as a place to work. Employees are asked to rate how likely they are to recommend the company as a great place to work to friends or family members, on a scale from 0-10. The eNPS is calculated by subtracting the percentage of detractors (employees who give a score of 0-6) from the percentage of promoters (employees who give a score of 9-10).

Employee Retention Rate: The Employee Retention Rate measures the percentage of employees who remain with the organization over a certain period of time. A high retention rate indicates that employees are satisfied with their jobs and the organization, and are less likely to leave for other opportunities.

Employee Turnover Rate: The Employee Turnover Rate measures the percentage of employees who leave the organization over a certain period of time. A high turnover rate indicates that employees are dissatisfied with their jobs and the organization, and are more likely to leave for other opportunities.

Absenteeism Rate: The Absenteeism Rate measures the percentage of employees who are absent from work on any given day. A high absenteeism rate can indicate that employees are disengaged or experiencing burnout.

Employee Referral Rate: The Employee Referral Rate measures the percentage of job openings that are filled by employee referrals. A high employee referral rate indicates that employees are satisfied with their jobs and the organization, and are willing to recommend it to others.

Overall, these employee engagement metrics can help organizations understand their employees' level of engagement and satisfaction, and identify areas for improvement. By tracking these metrics over time, organizations can also monitor the effectiveness of their employee engagement initiatives and adjust their strategies accordingly.

Example of an Employee Engagement survey report:

Executive Summary:

This report presents the results of the Employee Engagement Survey conducted at Culture Corporation in June 2022. The purpose of the survey was to measure employee engagement levels, identify areas of strength and improvement, and provide actionable insights for the company's management to enhance the employee experience.

The survey achieved a response rate of 80% and gathered data from employees across all departments and levels of the organization. The survey results indicate that overall employee engagement levels are moderate, with room for improvement in some areas.

Key Findings:

- **Employee Engagement Index:** The Employee Engagement Index score for Culture Corporation is 64%, which indicates moderate engagement levels. While this is a decent score, there is room for improvement to increase employee engagement.
- **Communication:** Communication emerged as a key area for improvement, with only 60% of employees feeling that communication from senior leadership is effective. Additionally, only 50% of employees feel that their immediate supervisor provides clear and frequent feedback.
- **Career Development:** There is an opportunity to enhance career development opportunities at Culture Corporation, with only 45% of employees feeling that there are adequate opportunities for career growth.
- **Recognition and Rewards:** Recognition and rewards also emerged as an area for improvement, with only 55% of employees feeling that their contributions are recognized and rewarded appropriately.
- **Work-life Balance:** While overall work-life balance at Culture Corporation is good, there is still room for improvement, with only 65% of employees feeling that they can manage their work and personal responsibilities effectively.

Action Plan:

Based on the survey results, Culture Corporation will take the following actions to improve employee engagement:

- **Improve communication**: Senior leaders will work on improving communication with employees, including increasing the frequency and transparency of communication. Supervisors will also receive training on providing effective feedback and recognition.
- **Enhance career development opportunities:** The company will develop a career development plan for employees, including mentoring, training, and job shadowing opportunities.
- **Improve recognition and rewards:** The company will implement an employee recognition program to acknowledge and reward employees for their contributions.

- **Improve work-life balance:** The company will offer flexible work arrangements, including remote work options, to help employees manage their work and personal responsibilities.

Conclusion:

The Employee Engagement Survey has provided valuable insights into the employee experience at Culture Corporation. The company is committed to addressing the areas of improvement identified in the survey and creating a more engaged and productive workforce. By taking action on the survey results, Culture Corporation aims to improve employee satisfaction, retention, and overall business performance.

CHAPTER SEVENTY

Engagement Trends for 2024

The landscape of employee engagement continues to evolve in 2024, with a strong focus on building a workforce that feels valued, supported, and empowered. Here are some key trends to watch:

People-First Culture: Companies are prioritizing a culture that puts employee well-being at the center. This includes fostering work-life harmony, offering flexible work arrangements, and creating a sense of belonging.

Work-Life Harmony: With the rise of remote and hybrid work models, ensuring a healthy balance between work and personal life is crucial. Companies are offering flexible hours, compressed workweeks, and generous leave policies.

Engagement Trends

Technology for Good: Cloud-based HR tools are streamlining processes and creating a more connected work experience. Artificial intelligence (AI) and machine learning (ML) are being used to personalize learning and development opportunities, as well as to identify and address potential burnout.

Diversity and Inclusion (DE&I): Creating a workplace that is inclusive and equitable for all employees is not just a moral imperative, it's a business strategy. Companies are actively fostering DE&I initiatives to attract and retain top talent.

Employee Recognition: Recognition programs that go beyond traditional performance reviews are gaining traction. Regular, personalized feedback and recognition for a job well done are key to keeping employees motivated.

Employee Wellness: Companies are recognizing the importance of employee mental and physical health. This includes offering comprehensive health insurance plans, access to wellness programs, and promoting healthy habits.

Meaningful Work: Employees are increasingly seeking work that aligns with their values and purpose. Companies are finding ways to connect individual roles to the organization's mission and social impact.

Upskilling and Reskilling: The pace of change in today's workplace demands a continuous learning mindset. Companies are investing in training and development programs to help employees keep their skills current and advance their careers.

Employee Voice and Feedback: Leaders are understanding the importance of creating open communication channels where employees feel comfortable sharing their ideas and concerns. Regularly collecting and acting on employee feedback demonstrates that their voices matter.

By focusing on these trends, companies can create a more engaged and productive workforce in 2024.

CHAPTER SEVENTY-ONE

How to Enhance Engagement

Some ways of Enhancing Employee Engagement at Workplace:-

1. Encourage work autonomy: Empower employees by giving them autonomy and flexibility to complete their work. This allows them to take ownership of their work and feel a sense of accomplishment when they complete tasks.

2. Provide regular feedback: Regular feedback on performance can help employees understand their strengths and areas for improvement. This can also help them feel more connected to the organization and motivated to improve.

3. Create opportunities for collaboration: Encourage collaboration between employees and teams to foster a sense of community and teamwork. This can also help employees feel more invested in the organization's goals and objectives.

4. Prioritize work-life balance: Help employees balance their personal and work lives by providing flexible work schedules, time off, and resources to support mental and physical health.

5. Foster transparent communication: Be transparent with employees about organizational goals, performance, and changes. This can help build trust and increase employee engagement.

6. Provide opportunities for volunteerism: Encourage employees to give back to the community by offering opportunities for volunteerism or participating in charitable events. This can help employees feel more connected to their community and the organization's values.

7. Offer opportunities for skill development: Provide opportunities for employees to develop new skills or improve existing ones. This can help employees feel more invested in their work and develop a sense of loyalty to the organization.

8. Create a positive work environment: A positive work environment can increase engagement and productivity. This can be achieved by offering comfortable workspaces, natural lighting, and access to amenities like coffee and snacks.

9. Foster innovation and creativity: Encourage innovation and creativity by giving employees the freedom to explore new ideas and experiment with new approaches to work.

10. Recognize and celebrate milestones: Recognize and celebrate employee milestones such as birthdays, work anniversaries, and achievements. This can help employees feel valued and appreciated.

Employee engagement programs adopted by top companies:-

Google: Google offers a range of employee engagement programs, including wellness programs, employee resource groups, and volunteer opportunities. They also provide a range of perks and benefits, such as on-site childcare, free meals, and fitness classes.

Corporates' Engagement programs

Salesforce: Salesforce offers a range of employee engagement programs, including employee resource groups, mentorship programs, and volunteer opportunities. They also prioritize work-life balance by offering flexible work schedules and unlimited paid time off.

Marriott: Marriott has a program called "TakeCare," which focuses on employee well-being and development. They offer wellness programs, career development opportunities, and recognition programs to foster a positive work environment.

Deloitte: Deloitte offers a range of employee engagement programs, including career development opportunities, mentorship programs, and employee resource groups. They also prioritize diversity and inclusion, offering training and support for underrepresented groups.

Southwest Airlines: Southwest Airlines has a program called “Culture Services” that focuses on creating a positive work environment. They offer perks and benefits such as free travel for employees and their families, flexible work schedules, and employee recognition programs.

HubSpot: HubSpot offers a range of employee engagement programs, including wellness programs, employee resource groups, and flexible work schedules. They also prioritize career development, offering mentorship programs and a “HubSpot Academy” to help employees develop their skills.

Microsoft: Microsoft has a program called “Employee Resource Groups” that fosters employee engagement and community building. They also offer career development opportunities, flexible work schedules, and a range of perks and benefits such as free meals and on-site fitness facilities.

Cisco: Cisco has a program called “Connected Recognition” that allows employees to recognize and reward each other for their hard work and contributions. They also prioritize career development, offering mentorship programs and on-site training and development opportunities.

These are just a few examples of employee engagement programs adopted by top companies. By prioritizing employee engagement and creating a positive work environment, these companies are able to attract and retain top talent, foster a sense of community and teamwork, and drive innovation and productivity.

Common Employee Engagement Programs:-

There are a variety of employee engagement programs that companies can adopt to increase employee satisfaction, productivity, and loyalty. Here are some common employee engagement programs:

- **Wellness Programs:** These programs focus on employee health and well-being, and may include gym memberships, healthy snacks, and mental health resources.
- **Employee Resource Groups:** These groups provide a platform for employees to connect and build community based on shared interests, identities, or experiences.

- **Mentorship Programs:** These programs connect employees with experienced mentors to help them develop their skills and advance their careers.
- **Professional Development Programs:** These programs provide employees with training, education, and development opportunities to help them grow and advance in their careers.
- **Recognition Programs:** These programs reward and recognize employees for their hard work and contributions to the organization.
- **Flexible Work Arrangements:** These programs offer employees more flexibility in their work schedules, including options for remote work, flexible hours, or part-time work.
- **Volunteer Programs:** These programs encourage employees to give back to their communities by offering opportunities to volunteer or participate in charitable events.
- **Diversity and Inclusion Programs:** These programs promote a culture of diversity and inclusivity, and may include training, support, and resources for underrepresented groups.
- **Employee Surveys:** These surveys provide employees with a voice and an opportunity to provide feedback on their workplace experience and suggest areas for improvement.
- **Social Events:** These events provide opportunities for employees to connect and build relationships outside of work, such as company outings, team-building activities, or holiday parties.

By implementing these employee engagement programs, companies can create a more positive work environment that fosters employee satisfaction, productivity, and loyalty.

Activity for You: Be the Engagement Expert!

Employee engagement is crucial for a happy and productive workplace. But how can companies actually achieve it?

Question: You are a consultant brought in to advise a company on how to improve employee engagement. Choose two (one non-monetary and one monetary/benefit) strategies you would recommend and explain why they would be effective.

Consider these factors when developing your recommendations:

Non-Monetary:

- Opportunities for growth and development

- Recognition and appreciation programs
- Fostering a sense of community and belonging
- Encouraging open communication and feedback

Monetary/Benefit:

- Competitive salary and benefits package
- Flexible work arrangements
- Wellness programs and perks
- Profit-sharing or bonus opportunities

Also include: Briefly discuss any potential challenges a company might face when implementing these strategies and how they could be overcome.

....

....

CHAPTER SEVENTY-TWO

Employee Engagement Ideas

Buddy Program: Employee Engagement for New Employees:-

Refer to Employee Onboarding Section for complete guide

Buddy Program is One of the programs that has gained popularity in recent years.

A buddy program is an employee engagement initiative in which new hires are paired with experienced employees or mentors who can guide them through their onboarding process and provide support and resources. This program helps new employees to acclimate to the company culture, understand the expectations of their role, and build relationships with their colleagues.

There are many benefits of implementing a buddy program in the workplace:

- **Faster Onboarding:** New hires often feel overwhelmed and unsure of themselves during their first few weeks on the job. By providing them with a buddy, they can quickly learn the ropes and get up to speed, which can result in faster productivity.
- **Increased Employee Retention:** Employees who feel supported and connected to their colleagues are more likely to stay with the company long-term. A buddy program can help to build those connections and make new employees feel like they are a part of the team.
- **Better Communication**: A buddy program can facilitate better communication between new hires and their colleagues, which can help to avoid misunderstandings and ensure that everyone is on the same page.

- **Improved Job Satisfaction:** When employees feel like they have the support and resources they need to succeed, they are more likely to feel satisfied with their job and perform at their best.

Employee Engagement Ideas:-
How to keep your employees engaged? Try some of these ideas:-

1. **Team building activities:** Team building activities help to foster better relationships and promote communication among employees.
2. **Health and wellness programs:** Health and wellness programs encourage employees to lead a healthy lifestyle, which helps to reduce stress, increase productivity, and improve overall wellbeing.
3. **Social events:** Social events such as holiday parties, happy hours, and company outings promote a sense of community and allow employees to relax and bond outside of work.
4. **Recognition and rewards programs:** Recognition and rewards programs acknowledge and celebrate employee achievements, which boosts morale and encourages continued excellence.
5. **Training and development programs:** Training and development programs provide employees with opportunities to learn new skills and advance their careers, which helps to improve job satisfaction and retention.
6. **Mentorship programs:** Mentorship programs pair experienced employees with newer employees to provide guidance and support, which can help to increase engagement and retention.
7. **Employee volunteer programs:** Employee volunteer programs give employees the opportunity to give back to the community, which promotes a sense of purpose and can increase engagement.
8. **Employee-led initiatives:** Employee-led initiatives give employees a sense of ownership and empowerment over their work, which can increase engagement and motivation.
9. **Performance feedback and coaching:** Regular performance feedback and coaching sessions help employees understand their strengths and areas for improvement, which can lead to increased engagement and motivation.
10. **Open communication:** Open communication between managers and employees fosters trust and respect, which can increase engagement and job satisfaction.

11. **Diversity and inclusion programs:** Diversity and inclusion programs create an inclusive workplace culture where employees feel valued and respected, which can increase engagement and retention.
12. **Employee recognition and appreciation days:** Employee recognition and appreciation days provide a day to celebrate and acknowledge employee contributions, which can boost morale and increase engagement.
13. **Employee surveys:** Employee surveys allow companies to gather feedback on what is working and what needs improvement, which can increase engagement and improve job satisfaction.
14. **Flexibility in work arrangements:** Flexibility in work arrangements, such as remote work and flexible schedules, can increase job satisfaction and engagement by allowing employees to better balance their work and personal lives.
15. **Continuous learning opportunities:** Continuous learning opportunities, such as access to online courses and workshops, can increase engagement by promoting professional growth and development.
16. **Employee benefits programs:** Employee benefits programs, such as health insurance and retirement plans, can increase engagement by showing that the company cares about employee wellbeing and financial stability.
17. **Empowerment initiatives:** Empowerment initiatives, such as leadership training and career development programs, can increase engagement by giving employees a sense of ownership and control over their careers.
18. **Employee resource groups:** Employee resource groups provide employees with opportunities to connect with colleagues who share similar interests, which can increase engagement and sense of belonging.
19. **Mentor-mentee relationships:** Mentor-mentee relationships help employees to develop their skills and achieve their career goals, which can increase engagement and motivation.
20. **Skill-sharing sessions:** Skill-sharing sessions allow employees to teach and learn from each other, which promotes collaboration and can increase engagement.
21. **Cross-functional projects:** Cross-functional projects provide employees with opportunities to work with colleagues from different departments, which can increase engagement and improve communication.
22. **Gamification:** Gamification can increase engagement by making work tasks more fun and engaging, such as through leaderboards, badges, and

rewards.

23. **Personal development plans:** Personal development plans help employees to set goals and track progress, which can increase motivation and engagement.
24. **Health challenges:** Health challenges, such as step challenges and healthy eating challenges, can increase engagement by promoting healthy habits and competition among employees.
25. **Employee recognition programs:** Employee recognition programs, such as employee of the month or spot bonuses, can increase engagement by acknowledging employee contributions and accomplishments.
26. **Goal setting and tracking:** Goal setting and tracking help

Employee Engagement Activities / Games:-

1. **Office Olympics:** This is a fun and competitive game that involves employees competing in various physical and mental challenges, such as paper clip javelin, desk chair relay, and computer mouse shooting.
2. **Two Truths and a Lie:** This game involves each employee sharing two true facts and one lie about themselves, and the other team members have to guess which one is the lie.
3. **Scavenger Hunt:** A scavenger hunt is a fun and engaging way to encourage team building and collaboration.
4. **Pictionary:** Pictionary is a classic drawing game that can be played in teams to promote teamwork and creativity.
5. **Trivia:** Trivia games can be customized to fit the company's industry or culture, and can be a fun way to learn more about each other and the company.
6. **Escape Rooms:** Escape rooms are a popular team-building activity that requires collaboration and problem-solving skills.
7. **The Name Game:** The Name Game is a simple yet fun game where each person has to come up with an adjective or word that starts with the first letter of their first name, and then everyone has to remember and say each person's name and adjective.
8. **Bingo:** Employee engagement bingo can include company-specific terms or fun facts about the company, and can be a fun way to learn more about the company and each other.
9. **The Marshmallow Challenge:** The Marshmallow Challenge involves teams competing to build the tallest freestanding structure using

spaghetti, tape, and a marshmallow.

10. **Who Am I?:** This game involves each employee writing down the name of a famous person, character, or animal on a piece of paper, and then taping it to another employee's forehead. The person then has to guess who or what they are by asking yes or no questions.
11. **Minute to Win It Games:** Minute to Win It games are quick and fun challenges that can be played individually or in teams, and can include tasks like stacking cups, balancing an egg on a spoon, or blowing a ping pong ball across a table.
12. **Charades:** Charades is a classic game that can be played in teams to promote teamwork and creativity.
13. **Truth or Dare:** This game involves each person taking turns choosing to answer a personal question truthfully or perform a silly dare.
14. **Fantasy Football:** Fantasy Football is a fun and engaging way to promote team building and friendly competition among employees.
15. **The Alphabet Game:** The Alphabet Game involves each person taking turns saying a word that starts with the next letter of the alphabet, and can be played with company-related words or topics.
16. **Table Tennis Tournament:** A table tennis tournament is a fun and engaging way to promote teamwork and friendly competition among employees.
17. **Scrabble:** Scrabble is a classic word game that can be played in teams to promote collaboration and problem-solving skills.
18. **Lego Building Challenge:** The Lego Building Challenge involves teams competing to build the most creative and complex structure using Lego bricks.
19. **Video Game Tournament:** A video game tournament is a fun and engaging way to promote teamwork and friendly competition among employees.
20. **Karaoke Night:** A karaoke night is a fun and engaging way to promote team.

Activity for You: Design Your Dream Engagement Game!

Think back to the different employee engagement activities and games discussed. Now you get to design your own!

Question: Imagine you work at a company and want to boost teamwork and communication among your colleagues. Create a fun and engaging game or activity that can be done in the workplace.

Your game design should consider:

1. What are the goals of the game? (e.g., improve communication, problem-solving, creativity)
2. What type of activity is it? (e.g., trivia, competition, icebreaker)
3. What materials will you need? (Keep it simple - paper, pens, online tools)
4. How many people can play? (Adaptable for small or large groups?)
5. How will the game be played? (Clear instructions and flow)

Bonus:

1. Sketch out the game or provide a visual representation.
2. Explain how this game would contribute to a positive and engaging work environment.

....

....

CHAPTER SEVENTY-THREE

Case Studies: Improving Engagement

1. Case Study: Improving Employee Engagement in XYZ Inc.

Introduction:

XYZ Inc. is a leading multinational corporation that specializes in the production of consumer electronics. Despite having a reputation for producing high-quality products, the company has been facing a high turnover rate and low employee engagement levels. The management team recognized the need for improvement in employee engagement as it directly affects productivity, performance, and business outcomes.

Objective:

The main objective of this case study is to explore how XYZ Inc. improved employee engagement and reduced employee turnover rates.

Challenges:

The following challenges were identified as hindering employee engagement at XYZ Inc.:

- Lack of recognition and appreciation for employees' contributions
- Inadequate communication channels between management and employees
- Limited career growth opportunities for employees
- Poor work-life balance for employees
- Limited employee involvement in decision-making processes

Solutions:

Recognition and Appreciation:

XYZ Inc. implemented an employee recognition program to acknowledge and appreciate employees' contributions to the company. The program included weekly shout-outs, monthly awards, and annual recognition events. The recognition program motivated employees to go above and beyond their roles, resulting in increased productivity and employee engagement.

Improved Communication:

The management team at XYZ Inc. implemented regular employee feedback sessions, where employees were encouraged to share their concerns, suggestions, and feedback. The management team acted on the feedback received, ensuring employees‘ voices were heard, and they felt valued.

Career Growth Opportunities:

XYZ Inc. created a career development program to provide employees with opportunities to advance their careers. The program included training, mentorship, and a clear career path. The program improved employee retention and engagement as employees felt valued and invested in.

Work-life Balance:

The management team at XYZ Inc. implemented flexible work schedules, including remote work options and work-from-home policies. The policies helped employees balance work and personal commitments, leading to increased job satisfaction and engagement.

Employee Involvement:

The management team at XYZ Inc. implemented an employee involvement program, where employees were encouraged to participate in decision-making processes. The program increased employee engagement levels as employees felt valued and invested in the company's success.

Results:

The initiatives implemented by XYZ Inc. resulted in significant improvements in employee engagement levels and reduced employee turnover rates. The results included:

- Improved employee engagement scores, as measured by employee surveys
- Reduced employee turnover rates, resulting in cost savings and increased productivity
- Increased employee productivity, resulting from improved work-life balance, employee recognition, and career growth opportunities.

Conclusion:

In conclusion, improving employee engagement levels is crucial for business success. By addressing the identified challenges and implementing the solutions, XYZ Inc. was able to improve employee engagement and reduce employee turnover rates, resulting in a positive impact on the company's productivity, performance, and bottom line.

2. Case Study: Enhancing Employee Engagement at GREAT Corporation

Introduction:

GREAT Corporation is a leading manufacturing company that specializes in the production of heavy machinery. Despite its success in the market, the company was facing low employee engagement levels, which were affecting productivity and employee turnover rates. The management team recognized the need to improve employee engagement levels and implemented several initiatives to address the problem.

Objective:

The objective of this case study is to examine how GREAT Corporation enhanced employee engagement and reduced employee turnover rates.

Challenges:

The following challenges were identified as hindering employee engagement at GREAT Corporation:

- Lack of communication between management and employees
- Inadequate recognition and appreciation for employees' efforts
- Limited career growth opportunities for employees
- Poor work-life balance
- Lack of training and development programs

Solutions:

Improved Communication:

GREAT Corporation implemented several initiatives to improve communication between management and employees. The management team held regular town hall meetings where employees could voice their concerns and suggestions. The company also introduced an anonymous suggestion box where employees could share their feedback without fear of reprisal. The management team acted on the feedback received, resulting in improved employee morale and engagement.

Recognition and Appreciation:

GREAT Corporation introduced an employee recognition program to acknowledge and appreciate employees' contributions to the company Recognition and Appreciation:

The program included awards for outstanding performance, employee of the month, and team awards. The program motivated employees to go above and beyond their roles, resulting in increased productivity and employee engagement.

Career Growth Opportunities:

GREAT Corporation implemented a career development program to provide employees with opportunities to advance their careers. The program included training, mentorship, and a clear career path. The program improved employee retention and engagement as employees felt valued and invested in the company's success.

Work-life Balance:

GREAT Corporation implemented flexible work schedules, including remote work options and work-from-home policies. The policies helped employees balance work and personal commitments, leading to increased job satisfaction and engagement.

Training and Development:

GREAT Corporation introduced several training and development programs to improve employees' skills and knowledge. The company provided regular training sessions, mentorship programs, and educational opportunities to its employees. The programs improved employee engagement levels, as employees felt invested in their professional growth and development.

Results:

The initiatives implemented by GREAT Corporation resulted in significant improvements in employee engagement levels and reduced employee turnover rates. The results included:

- Improved employee engagement scores, as measured by employee surveys
- Reduced employee turnover rates, resulting in cost savings and increased productivity
- Increased employee productivity, resulting from improved work-life balance, employee recognition, and career growth opportunities.

Conclusion:

In conclusion, enhancing employee engagement levels is crucial for business success. By addressing the identified challenges and implementing the solutions, GREAT Corporation was able to improve employee engagement and reduce employee turnover rates, resulting in a positive impact on the company's productivity, performance, and bottom line.

3. Case Study: Employee Engagement at Google

Introduction:

Google is a multinational technology company that specializes in internet-related services and products. The company is known for its innovative work culture and employee engagement practices. Google's success can be attributed to its highly engaged and motivated workforce, which has helped the company achieve significant growth and success.

Objective:

The objective of this case study is to examine how Google fosters employee engagement and motivation in its workforce.

Challenges:

Google's employee engagement practices have been studied and emulated by many companies. However, the company faces some challenges in maintaining its work culture, including:

- Sustaining a highly engaged and motivated workforce
- Managing the increasing workforce size while maintaining a cohesive work culture
- Adapting to the changing needs and expectations of its employees

Solutions:

Empowering Employees:

Google empowers its employees by providing them with a high degree of autonomy and decision-making power. The company encourages its employees to take ownership of their work, providing them with the resources and support they need to succeed.

Employee Recognition:

Google values and recognizes its employees' contributions through several initiatives, including employee awards and recognition programs. The company also recognizes its employees' work through public recognition in company-wide emails and meetings.

Continuous Learning:

Google promotes a culture of continuous learning by providing its employees with access to training programs, mentorship opportunities, and educational resources. The company also encourages its employees to pursue their professional goals by providing them with resources and support.

Work-life Balance:

Google understands the importance of work-life balance and provides its employees with flexible work options, including remote work, flexible schedules, and on-site services like laundry and massage therapy. The company also offers paid parental leave, allowing its employees to balance work and family commitments.

Community Building:

Google fosters a sense of community and belonging by providing its employees with several opportunities to connect and build relationships with their colleagues. The company provides on-site amenities, including cafes, fitness centers, and game rooms, creating a collaborative and supportive work environment.

Results:

Google's employee engagement practices have resulted in several positive outcomes, including:

- High employee retention rates, resulting in cost savings and increased productivity
- Improved employee morale, leading to increased motivation and productivity
- Enhanced innovation and creativity, resulting in new product development and growth
- Improved customer satisfaction, resulting from a highly engaged and motivated workforce

Conclusion:

In conclusion, Google's employee engagement practices are a significant factor in the company's success. By empowering its employees, providing recognition and learning opportunities, promoting work-life balance, and building a sense of community, Google has created a work culture that fosters employee engagement and motivation. The company's practices serve as an excellent example for other companies to follow and emulate.

4. Case Study: Employee Engagement at Salesforce

Introduction:

Salesforce is a cloud-based software company that specializes in customer relationship management (CRM) and enterprise resource planning (ERP) solutions. The company is known for its innovative work culture and employee engagement practices. Salesforce's success can be attributed to its highly engaged and motivated workforce, which has helped the company achieve significant growth and success.

Objective:

The objective of this case study is to examine how Salesforce fosters employee engagement and motivation in its workforce.

Challenges:

Salesforce faces some challenges in maintaining its work culture and employee engagement practices, including:

Ensuring employee engagement and motivation in a remote work environment

Adapting to the changing needs and expectations of its employees

Managing employee burnout due to high workloads and increased demand for services

Solutions:

Creating a Strong Company Culture:

Salesforce values creating a strong company culture, which fosters a sense of community, shared values, and a mission-driven mindset. The company focuses on creating an inclusive and collaborative work environment, promoting employee well-being, and recognizing employees' contributions to the company's success.

Encouraging Employee Learning and Development:

Salesforce promotes employee learning and development by providing its employees with access to training programs, mentorship opportunities, and educational resources. The company encourages its employees to pursue their professional goals, providing them with resources and support to enhance their skills and knowledge.

Offering Competitive Benefits and Perks:

Salesforce understands the importance of offering competitive benefits and perks to attract and retain top talent. The company offers its employees comprehensive health insurance, retirement plans, paid time off, parental leave, and flexible work options. Salesforce also provides its employees with on-site amenities, including fitness centers, cafes, and wellness programs.

Prioritizing Employee Well-being:

Salesforce prioritizes employee well-being by providing mental health support, including access to an employee assistance program (EAP), counseling services, and wellness programs. The company also promotes work-life balance, allowing its employees to take time off when needed, and offering flexibility in their work schedules.

Supporting Employee Volunteering and Philanthropy:

Salesforce encourages its employees to give back to their communities through volunteering and philanthropy programs. The company offers paid time off for volunteering and matches employees' charitable donations, promoting social responsibility and community involvement.

Results:

Salesforce's employee engagement practices have resulted in several positive outcomes, including:

- High employee retention rates, resulting in cost savings and increased productivity
- Improved employee morale, leading to increased motivation and productivity
- Enhanced innovation and creativity, resulting in new product development and growth
- Improved customer satisfaction, resulting from a highly engaged and motivated workforce

Conclusion:

In conclusion, Salesforce's employee engagement practices are a significant factor in the company's success. By creating a strong company culture, promoting employee learning and development, offering competitive benefits and perks, prioritizing employee well-being, and supporting employee volunteering and philanthropy, Salesforce has created a work culture that fosters employee engagement and motivation. The company's practices serve as an excellent example for other companies to follow and emulate.

5. Case Study: Employee Engagement at Microsoft

Introduction:

Microsoft is a multinational technology company that specializes in software development, cloud computing, and hardware products. The company has a reputation for being a great place to work, with a strong focus on employee engagement and development. Microsoft's success can be attributed to its highly engaged and motivated workforce, which has helped the company achieve significant growth and success.

Objective:

The objective of this case study is to examine how Microsoft fosters employee engagement and motivation in its workforce.

Challenges:

Microsoft faces some challenges in maintaining its work culture and employee engagement practices, including:

- Attracting and retaining top talent in a highly competitive industry
- Adapting to the changing needs and expectations of its employees
- Managing the impact of rapid technological advancements on its workforce

Solutions:

Creating a Strong Company Culture:

Microsoft places a strong emphasis on creating a positive company culture that fosters collaboration, innovation, and employee engagement. The company focuses on promoting diversity, equity, and inclusion, providing employees with opportunities to connect with each other, and fostering a sense of purpose and meaning in their work.

Encouraging Employee Learning and Development:

Microsoft encourages employee learning and development by providing its employees with access to a wide range of training programs, mentorship opportunities, and educational resources. The company encourages its employees to pursue their professional goals, providing them with resources and support to enhance their skills and knowledge.

Offering Competitive Benefits and Perks:

Microsoft understands the importance of offering competitive benefits and perks to attract and retain top talent. The company offers its employees comprehensive health insurance, retirement plans, paid time off, parental leave, and flexible work options. Microsoft also provides its employees with on-site amenities, including fitness centers, cafes, and wellness programs.

Promoting Work-Life Balance:

Microsoft places a strong emphasis on promoting work-life balance, recognizing the importance of employee well-being and mental health. The company offers its employees flexible work schedules, allowing them to work from home or choose their work hours. Microsoft also provides employees with resources and support to manage stress, including mental health support, counseling services, and wellness programs.

Fostering Employee Engagement and Recognition:

Microsoft fosters employee engagement and recognition by providing its employees with opportunities to connect with each other, share their ideas, and contribute to the company's success. The company recognizes employee contributions through awards and recognition programs, and encourages employees to participate in company-wide initiatives and events.

Results:

Microsoft's employee engagement practices have resulted in several positive outcomes, including:

- High employee retention rates, resulting in cost savings and increased productivity
- Improved employee morale, leading to increased motivation and productivity
- Enhanced innovation and creativity, resulting in new product development and growth
- Improved customer satisfaction, resulting from a highly engaged and motivated workforce

Conclusion:

In conclusion, Microsoft's employee engagement practices are a significant factor in the company's success. By creating a strong company culture, promoting employee learning and development, offering competitive benefits and perks, promoting work-life balance, and fostering employee engagement and recognition, Microsoft has created a work culture that fosters employee engagement and motivation. The company's practices serve as an excellent example for other companies to follow and emulate.

6. Case Study: Employee Engagement and Productivity Link: Superior Company

In this case study, we will examine the effect of employee engagement on productivity, using a real-life example.

Case Study:

Superior Company is a mid-sized company that specializes in the production of automotive parts. The company employs around 500 people across two plants in different parts of the country. Superior Company has been struggling with low productivity and high employee turnover for the past few years. The company's management suspects that low employee engagement is the root cause of these problems.

To test this hypothesis, Superior Company conducted an employee engagement survey across the two plants. The survey measured employees' engagement levels, their satisfaction with their jobs, and their perceptions of the company's culture and leadership. The results of the survey confirmed the management's suspicions. Employee engagement levels were low, and many employees were dissatisfied with their jobs and the company's leadership.

Based on the survey results, Superior Company decided to launch an employee engagement program. The program had several components, including:

Leadership Training: The company provided training to its leaders to improve their communication skills, empathy, and ability to provide feedback and recognition to their team members.

Performance Management: The company introduced a new performance management system that was based on regular feedback, coaching, and goal-setting.

Employee Recognition: The company launched an employee recognition program to acknowledge and reward employees for their achievements and contributions.

Employee Feedback: The company set up regular channels for employee feedback, including suggestion boxes, town hall meetings, and employee surveys.

The company implemented these initiatives across both plants, and the results were impressive. Within six months of launching the employee engagement program, the company's productivity increased by 15%. Employee turnover also decreased significantly, which resulted in cost savings for the company.

Conclusion:

This case study demonstrates the strong link between employee engagement and productivity. By investing in employee engagement, Superior Company was able to improve its bottom line and create a more positive workplace culture. Companies that invest in employee engagement are likely to see similar benefits in terms of improved productivity, reduced turnover, and better overall business outcomes.

HRM Interview Questions & Answers: A Comprehensive Guide to crack HRM Interviews

CHAPTER SEVENTY-FOUR

Preparing for HR Professional Interview

Human resources (HR) managers play a crucial role in an organization, as they are responsible for overseeing and managing a company's HR policies, procedures, and programs. As a result, the qualities and skills that interviewers look for in HR manager candidates can vary depending on the specific organization and the needs of the HR department.

However, here are some of the most common qualities and skills that HR managers are typically evaluated on during an interview:

1. **HR Knowledge and Experience:** Interviewers look for HR managers who have a solid understanding of HR policies, laws, and regulations, as well as practical experience in implementing HR programs and initiatives.

2. **Communication Skills:** Effective communication is crucial for HR managers, who need to communicate effectively with employees, managers, and senior executives. Interviewers look for candidates who have strong written and verbal communication skills, as well as the ability to listen and respond to the needs of others.

3. **Leadership and Management Skills:** HR managers are often responsible for leading teams of HR professionals and managing the HR function for an entire organization. As a result, interviewers look for candidates who have strong leadership and management skills, as well as the ability to motivate and inspire others.

4. **Strategic Thinking:** HR managers need to be able to think strategically about how to align HR initiatives with the goals and objectives

of the organization. Interviewers look for candidates who are able to see the big picture and develop creative solutions to HR challenges.

5. **Emotional Intelligence:** HR managers must be able to work effectively with people from a wide range of backgrounds and with varying levels

of authority. Interviewers look for candidates who are empathetic, understanding, and able to build strong relationships with others.

6. Adaptability and Flexibility: The role of HR manager can be demanding, and the ability to adapt and be flexible in response to changing circumstances is essential. Interviewers look for candidates who are able to be nimble, adjust their approach as needed, and maintain a positive attitude in the face of challenges.

7. Technical Proficiency: In today's technology-driven world, HR managers need to be proficient in the use of HR-related software and tools. Interviewers look for candidates who have a good understanding of HR technology and are comfortable using it in their work.

Here are some tips to help you crack your interview for an HR manager position:

- **Research the company:** Before your interview, research the company and its culture, mission, and values. This will give you a better understanding of what the company is looking for in an HR manager and how you can demonstrate your fit with the company's goals and values.
- **Know your HR knowledge:** Brush up on your knowledge of HR best practices, including recruitment, training and development, compensation and benefits, employee relations, and HR compliance. Be prepared to talk about how you have applied this knowledge in your previous roles.
- **Prepare for behavioral questions:** Many HR interviews will include behavioral questions, which ask you to provide specific examples of how you have handled certain situations in the past. Prepare for these questions by thinking about examples of your past experiences that demonstrate your HR skills and abilities.
- **Show your enthusiasm:** An HR manager is responsible for building relationships with employees and helping to create a positive work environment. Show your enthusiasm for the role and your commitment to fostering a positive and productive workplace culture.
- **Be ready to ask questions:** Asking thoughtful and relevant questions demonstrates your interest in the company and your willingness to engage with the interviewer. Ask about the company's HR initiatives, the role of the HR manager, and how you can contribute to the company's goals.
- **Practice active listening:** Pay attention to what the interviewer is saying and respond thoughtfully. Show that you are listening and engaged by making eye contact, nodding, and asking follow-up questions.

• **Be yourself:** Be honest and authentic in your interview. Show your personality and let the interviewer get to know you as a person, not just a collection of skills and experience.

By following these tips, you can demonstrate your qualifications, knowledge, and enthusiasm for the HR manager role and increase your chances of landing the job.

Activity for you:

Rate yourself on a scale of 1 to 10 on the 7 areas important for HR professional mentioned above, such as Communication Skills. Develop a strategy to improvise your score.

....

....

CHAPTER SEVENTY-FIVE

Recruitment: HR Manager / Generalist Interview Questions and Answers Guide:

Commonly Asked Recruitment Interview Questions with Answers:

1. Walk me through your recruitment process from start to finish.

Answer: "My recruitment process begins with understanding the hiring manager's needs and the specific role requirements. I then develop a sourcing strategy utilizing various channels like job boards, social media, professional networks, and employee referrals. Once I receive applications, I screen them based on pre-defined criteria and conduct initial interviews. Shortlisted candidates undergo further assessments and interviews with relevant stakeholders. Finally, I facilitate offer negotiations and onboarding for the chosen candidate."

2. Describe a time you had to fill a difficult-to-fill position.

Answer: "In my previous role, I was tasked with recruiting a highly specialized software engineer with a specific skill set. I employed a multi-pronged approach, attending industry events, networking with professionals in the niche field, and utilizing targeted online job boards. Through persistent outreach and highlighting our company's unique offerings, I was able to attract qualified candidates and successfully fill the position."

Recruitment questions

3. How do you stay up-to-date on the latest recruitment trends and technologies?

Answer: "I stay informed by attending industry conferences, webinars, and workshops. I also subscribe to relevant publications and follow thought leaders in the HR and recruitment space. Additionally, I actively participate in online communities and forums to learn from other professionals and share best practices."

4. How do you build and maintain strong relationships with hiring managers?

Answer: "I believe in building trust and open communication with hiring managers. I take the time to understand their needs, expectations, and challenges. I also provide regular updates on the recruitment process and actively seek their feedback for continuous improvement."

5. How do you ensure a positive candidate experience throughout the recruitment process?

Answer: "I strive to be responsive and communicate clearly with candidates at every stage. I provide timely updates on the application status, even if they are not selected. I also ensure clear communication of the company culture and expectations in the job description and throughout the interviews."

6. Tell me about a time you had to deal with a difficult candidate.

Answer: "I once encountered a candidate who was frustrated with a delay in the interview process. I acknowledged their concern and explained the rationale behind the delay. I offered to schedule a call to address their specific questions and concerns, demonstrating empathy and transparency."

7. How do you measure the success of your recruitment efforts?

Answer: "I use a combination of metrics to measure success, such as time to fill, quality of hire, cost per hire, and candidate satisfaction. I also monitor metrics like the number of applications, interview conversions, and offer acceptance rates to identify areas for improvement."

8. What are your salary expectations for this role?

Answer: "Before discussing salary, I'd like to learn more about the specific responsibilities and expectations for this role. Based on my experience and qualifications, I am open to discussing a competitive compensation package that aligns with the market value for this position and my skills."

9. What are your biggest strengths and weaknesses as a recruiter?

Answer: "My strengths include strong communication skills, analytical thinking, and a talent for building relationships. I am also passionate about finding the right talent and ensuring a positive candidate experience. As for weaknesses, I am always working to improve my time management skills and delegate tasks effectively when juggling multiple roles."

10. Why are you interested in this specific HR recruitment role at our company?

Answer: "I am particularly interested in this role at your company due to [mention specific reasons, such as company culture, industry reputation, specific projects or initiatives you are aware of]. My skills and experience align well with your company's needs, and I believe I can contribute significantly to your ongoing success."

Remember, these are just sample answers. Tailor them to your specific experiences and skills, highlighting your strengths and qualifications for the role.

Activity for you:

Answer the above 10 questions in your own words:

....

....

CHAPTER SEVENTY-SIX

Employee Engagement: HR Manager / Generalist Interview Questions & Answers

10 Commonly Asked Employee Engagement Interview Questions with Answers:

1. What are your views on employee engagement and its importance in today's workplace?

Answer: "Employee engagement is crucial for a company's success. It fosters a positive work environment, increases productivity, and reduces turnover. Engaged employees are more motivated, innovative, and willing to go the extra mile."

2. How do you identify the key drivers of employee engagement in a specific organization?

Answer: "To understand the key drivers, I would use a multi-pronged approach. This could include conducting surveys, focus groups, and one-on-one interviews with employees at different levels. Analyzing data from existing sources like performance reviews and employee satisfaction surveys would also be crucial."

3. Describe a time you implemented a successful employee engagement initiative.

Answer: "In my previous role, I noticed a decline in employee morale due to limited recognition. I implemented a peer-to-peer recognition program where employees could nominate colleagues for their contributions. This fostered a sense of camaraderie and appreciation, leading to a significant increase in employee engagement."

4. How do you measure the effectiveness of employee engagement programs?

Answer: "I would track various metrics before and after implementing the program, such as employee satisfaction scores, absenteeism rates, productivity levels, and retention rates. Analyzing changes in these metrics would help assess the program's effectiveness."

5. How do you handle situations where employees are disengaged or unhappy?

Answer: "I would first try to understand the root cause of their disengagement through open communication and active listening. This may involve one-on-one meetings or confidential surveys. Based on the identified cause, I would collaborate with the individual and their manager to develop a personalized solution, which could involve addressing workload concerns, offering additional training, or improving communication channels."

6. How do you stay up-to-date on the latest trends and best practices in employee engagement?

Answer: "I actively participate in industry conferences, workshops, and webinars. I also read relevant publications and research from reputable sources, and connect with other professionals in the field through online communities and forums."

7. How do you build trust and credibility with employees across different levels and departments?

Answer: "Transparency, honesty, and open communication are key. I would actively listen to their concerns, provide timely and accurate information, and be readily available to address their questions and needs."

8. How do you handle conflicts between employees in a way that fosters engagement?

Answer: "I would first attempt to mediate the conflict by facilitating open communication between the involved parties. My goal would be to help them understand each other's perspectives and find a mutually agreeable solution. If necessary, I would involve HR leadership for further guidance and support."

9. What are your salary expectations for this role?

Answer: (Similar to previous answer) "Before discussing salary, I'd appreciate learning more about the specific responsibilities and expectations for this role. Based on my experience and qualifications, I am open to discussing a competitive compensation package that aligns with the market value for this role and my skills."

10. Why are you interested in this specific employee engagement role at our company?

Answer: "I am particularly interested in this role at your company due to [mention specific reasons, such as company culture, focus on employee well-being, specific initiatives you are aware of]. My passion lies in creating positive work environments where employees feel valued and empowered. I believe my skills and experience align well with your company's commitment to employee engagement, and I am confident I can contribute significantly to your success."

Remember, these are just sample answers. Tailor them to your specific experiences and qualifications, highlighting your strengths and passion for employee engagement.

Answer the above 10 questions in your own words. What other questions could be asked in the interview? Write 3 questions of your own.

....

....

CHAPTER SEVENTY-SEVEN

HR Administration: HR Manager / Generalist Interview Questions & Answers

5 Commonly Asked HR Admin Interview Questions:

1. Describe the process you follow for onboarding a new employee.

Answer: "My onboarding process begins with collecting pre-employment documents and facilitating necessary clearances. Then, I prepare welcome materials, schedule new hire orientation, and ensure access to necessary equipment and systems. Additionally, I guide them through company policies, benefits enrollment, and connect them with their supervisor and colleagues."

2. How do you handle the exit formalities for a departing employee?

Answer: "Upon receiving a resignation, I ensure the proper legal and administrative procedures are followed. This includes collecting company property, processing final payroll and benefits, and conducting exit interviews. I also strive to maintain a positive and professional experience for the departing employee."

3. Explain how you manage employee ID cards and access control.

Answer: "I work closely with the IT department to ensure proper ID card issuance and access control protocols. This includes verifying employee information, processing ID card requests, and coordinating access permissions for various systems and facilities."

4. How do you ensure the accuracy and security of employee data and paperwork?

Answer: "Data security and accuracy are paramount. I adhere to strict organizational guidelines and maintain accurate and up-to-date employee records. I also utilize secure storage systems and access controls to safeguard sensitive information."

5. Describe your experience with HR software and systems.

Answer: "I am proficient in various HR software and systems, including [list specific software you have experience with]. I leverage these tools for tasks like payroll processing, benefits administration, and employee data management. I am also adaptable and eager to learn new systems quickly."

Remember, these are just sample answers. Tailor them to your specific experiences and skills, demonstrating your knowledge of HR administration procedures and your ability to efficiently manage essential paperwork.

Answer the above 10 questions in your own words. What other questions could be asked in the interview? Write 3 questions of your own.

....

....

CHAPTER SEVENTY-EIGHT

Compensation, Benefits & Payroll (Indian): HR Manager / Generalist Interview Questions & Answers

10 commonly asked rewards, compensation, benefits, and payroll interview questions (Indian payroll) with sample answers:

1. Explain the core components of an Indian salary structure.

Answer: "A typical salary structure in India includes:

Basic Salary: The fixed portion, typically forming 40-50% of the gross salary.

House Rent Allowance (HRA): Provided by employers to cover housing costs.

Conveyance Allowance: To cover travel expenses between home and work.

Dearness Allowance (DA): An adjustment to offset inflation.

Other Allowances: May include special allowances, leave travel allowance (LTA), medical allowance, etc.

Statutory Deductions: Including Provident Fund (PF), Employee State Insurance (ESI), Professional Tax, etc."

2. How do you ensure compliance with India's complex payroll regulations?

Answer: "Staying updated is critical. I regularly monitor changes in tax laws, PF and ESI contribution rates, and other statutory regulations. I subscribe to relevant newsletters and publications and consult with legal experts when needed. Meticulous record-keeping ensures adherence to compliance requirements."

3. Describe your experience with managing employee Provident Fund (PF) and Employee State Insurance (ESI) contributions in India.

Answer: "I have substantial experience with calculating and deducting PF and ESI contributions, managing monthly challan generation, and ensuring timely submission. Additionally, I handle related administrative tasks and coordinate with various government agencies for PF and ESI purposes."

4. How do you handle payroll discrepancies and disputes in an Indian payroll context?

Answer: "I adopt a methodical approach, first verifying the discrepancy's nature – calculation error, incorrect data entry, or a misunderstanding of policies. I communicate transparently with the employee and relevant stakeholders and rectify the issue promptly while complying with regulatory guidelines."

5. How do you design competitive compensation packages to attract and retain top talent in India?

Answer: "I analyze market trends and industry benchmarks, understanding salary ranges and benefits packages offered by similar companies. I collaborate with HR leaders to design packages that align with the company's budget and values, offering a balance of core components, statutory benefits, and additional perks relevant to the Indian market."

6. Can you explain the concept of gratuity and how it is calculated in India?

Answer: "Gratuity is a long-term benefit for employees with at least five years of continuous service. It's calculated based on the employee's last drawn salary, tenure, and a factor of 15/26. I am familiar with applicable eligibility criteria and calculations under the Payment of Gratuity Act, 1972."

7. Describe your experience with any Indian payroll software. What features do you find most useful?

Answer: "I have worked with Ramco or SAP [name the payroll software]. Its most valuable features include automated tax calculations, PF/ESI compliance management, report generation, and integration with HR systems. Staying adaptable to different software environments is also a strength."

8. How do you maintain confidentiality and security of sensitive payroll information in India?

Answer: "I understand the importance of payroll data security. I adhere to the company's data protection protocols, ensuring limited access to sensitive information. I utilize secure file storage solutions, password protection, and follow established security procedures."

9. How do you communicate complex compensation and benefits information to Indian employees effectively?

Answer: "I believe in clear and transparent communication. I use simple language, break down complex terms, and provide examples relevant to employees' lives. I also offer multiple communication channels, such as presentations, written materials, and one-on-one consultations, to cater to different learning styles."

10. What motivates you to pursue a career in rewards, compensation, benefits, and payroll in India?

Answer: "I find the intersection of HR and finance within this field fascinating. Ensuring employees are compensated fairly and receive valuable benefits, while driving organizational success, is highly rewarding. Additionally, the dynamic nature of Indian payroll, with its regulations and complexities, presents a stimulating challenge."

Remember to tailor these answers further with specific examples from your own experience.

Answer the above 10 questions in your own words. What other questions could be asked in the interview? Write 3 questions of your own.

....

....

CHAPTER SEVENTY-NINE

Compensation, Benefits & Payroll (International): HR Manager / Generalist Interview Questions & Answers

10 Commonly Asked Rewards, Compensation, Benefits, and Payroll Interview Questions (International):

1. Explain the difference between salary, wages, and bonuses.

Answer: Salary is a fixed, regular payment typically received monthly or bi-weekly, regardless of hours worked. Wages are typically paid hourly and can fluctuate based on the number of hours worked. Bonuses are performance-based rewards that supplement regular compensation, often given annually or upon achieving specific goals.

2. How do you stay up-to-date on current compensation and benefits trends?

Answer: "I utilize various resources to stay informed, such as salary surveys, industry publications, and online databases. Additionally, I attend industry conferences and workshops to network with other professionals and learn about emerging trends in compensation and benefits."

3. Describe your experience with different benefit plans, such as health insurance, rctirement plans, and paid time off.

Answer: "I have experience administering various benefit plans, including health insurance with different coverage options, retirement plans like 401(k) with employer matching contributions, and paid time off policies, including vacation, sick leave, and personal days."

4. How do you ensure payroll is processed accurately and on time?

Answer: "Accuracy and timeliness are crucial in payroll processing. I adhere to strict procedures and utilize reliable software to ensure all deductions, taxes, and net pay are calculated correctly. I also double-check for errors and maintain open communication with employees to address any discrepancies promptly."

5. How do you handle employee inquiries about their paychecks or benefits?

Answer: "I welcome employee inquiries and strive to provide clear and accurate information. I am familiar with benefits plan details and can assist in navigating the enrollment process or addressing any concerns regarding paychecks, including deductions or tax withholding."

6. How do you develop and implement performance-based compensation plans?

Answer: "Developing such plans requires a collaborative approach. I work closely with managers to define clear performance metrics, set achievable goals, and determine appropriate rewards for exceeding expectations. I also ensure these plans are aligned with company objectives and legal compliance."

7. Describe your experience with payroll software and systems.

Answer: "I am proficient in various payroll software and systems, such as [list specific software you have experience with]. These tools facilitate efficient payroll processing, automate calculations, and manage tax compliance. I am also adaptable and can learn new systems quickly."

8. How do you ensure compliance with state and federal regulations regarding compensation and benefits?

Answer: "Staying informed about relevant regulations is crucial. I regularly review updates on federal and state laws impacting compensation and benefits. I also utilize compliance resources and seek guidance from HR leadership or legal counsel when necessary."

9. How do you explain complex compensation and benefits information to employees in a clear and concise manner?

Answer: "Effective communication is key. I utilize straightforward language, avoid jargon, and use practical examples to explain complex topics. I also encourage questions and welcome individual consultations to ensure every employee understands their benefits and compensation package."

10. Why are you interested in a career in rewards, compensation, benefits, and payroll?

Answer: "This field allows me to contribute to employee well-being and support organizational goals. I am passionate about ensuring fair and competitive compensation and providing employees with valuable benefits packages. Additionally, I enjoy the analytical and problem-solving aspects of payroll processing and compliance."

Remember, these are just sample answers. Tailor them to your specific experiences and skills, highlighting your understanding of compensation and benefits principles, your experience with payroll systems, and your commitment to compliance.

Answer the above 10 questions in your own words. What other questions could be asked in the interview? Write 3 questions of your own.

....

....

CHAPTER EIGHTY

Training & Development: HR Manager / Generalist Interview Questions & Answers

Here are 10 commonly asked training and development interview questions with sample answers tailored for an HR Generalist:

1. While your primary role is not L&D, how would you identify training needs within an organization?

Answer: "As an HR Generalist, I would identify training needs through various methods. This includes:

Performance reviews: Analyzing trends and identifying skill gaps hindering employee performance.

Employee surveys: Gathering feedback on desired training topics and areas for improvement.

Exit interview analyses: Understanding why employees leave and identifying potential training gaps that could have contributed to their departure.

Staying informed about industry trends: Identifying new skills and knowledge employees need to remain competitive in the market."

2. How would you collaborate with the L&D team or external vendors to develop training programs suitable for HR-related topics?

Answer: "I would actively collaborate with the L&D team or vendors to ensure training programs align with organizational goals and HR objectives. This collaboration would involve:

Sharing my knowledge and expertise on HR policies, regulations, and best practices.

Providing feedback on program content and delivery methods to ensure clarity and effectiveness for the target audience.

Assisting with program promotion and ensuring smooth communication with participants."

3. How would you promote a company's new training program to employees and encourage participation?

Answer: "I would utilize various communication channels to promote the training program. This may include:

Company intranet and internal email blasts: Providing clear information about the program's benefits, objectives, and eligibility criteria.

Department meetings and team huddles: Presenting the program and addressing any questions or concerns.

Internal communication tools like social media platforms: Sharing engaging content and testimonials from past participants.

Offering incentives: This could involve offering flexible schedules or recognizing participation through certificates or appreciation programs

4. How would you handle situations where employees are hesitant or resistant to participating in training programs?

Answer: "I understand that some employees might feel resistant to training. I would adopt a collaborative approach by:

Understanding their concerns: Openly communicating and addressing their specific anxieties about the program or the training process.

Highlighting the benefits: Explaining how the program will empower them with new skills, improve their job performance, or contribute to their career development.

Offering diverse learning options: Providing flexible scheduling options or exploring alternative learning methods like online modules or self-paced learning to accommodate individual preferences."

5. How would you measure the success of HR-related training programs implemented within the organization?

Answer: "I would utilize a mix of quantitative and qualitative measures to assess the program's effectiveness. This may include:

Pre- and post-training knowledge assessments: Evaluating learning gains and knowledge retention.

Employee satisfaction surveys: Gathering feedback on the program's delivery, content, and perceived usefulness.

Monitoring changes in key performance indicators (KPIs): Observing if the training resulted in improved performance metrics relevant to the program's objectives, such as efficiency, productivity, or employee engagement levels."

6. What role do you see HR playing in creating a culture of learning and development within an organization?

Answer: "HR plays a crucial role in fostering a culture of learning and development. This includes:

Championing the importance of learning: Highlighting the value of continuous learning for individual and organizational growth.

Collaborating with L&D and other departments: Identifying training needs, developing relevant programs, and integrating learning into everyday work practices.

Promoting learning opportunities: Encouraging employees to take advantage of available training resources, including internal programs, conferences, and professional development opportunities.

Recognizing and rewarding learning achievements: Appreciating employees' commitment to learning through awards, career advancement opportunities, or other forms of recognition."

7. How would you handle a situation where a manager is hesitant to invest in training for their team due to budget constraints?

Answer: "I would understand the manager's perspective while advocating for the value of training. My approach would involve:

Demonstrating ROI (Return on Investment): Presenting data or case studies that demonstrate the potential cost savings or increased productivity associated with specific training programs.

Highlighting cost-effective options: Exploring alternative learning methods like online modules, group learning, or leveraging internal resources, like subject matter experts within the team.

Tailoring training needs: Collaborating with the manager to identify essential skills and focus the training program on maximizing impact within budget limitations."

8. How would you ensure accessibility and inclusivity in training programs offered by the organization?

Answer: "Accessibility and inclusivity are crucial for effective learning. I would strive to:

Offer diverse learning formats: Providing accommodations like closed captioning for videos, translated materials for non-native speakers, and alternative formats for printed materials.

Ensure accessibility for individuals with disabilities: Make reasonable adjustments to facilitate participation, such as offering physical access modifications or alternative testing methods.

Consider diverse learning styles: Utilize various teaching methods and encourage interactive learning to cater to different learning preferences, ensuring everyone has equal opportunity to participate and benefit from the training."

9. How would you leverage technology to enhance the training experience for HR-related topics?

Answer: "Technology can significantly enhance the training experience. I would explore using:

E-learning platforms: Providing access to self-paced learning modules, allowing for flexibility and convenience.

Learning Management Systems (LMS): Facilitating program administration, tracking employee progress, and delivering online assessments.

Collaboration tools: Utilizing video conferencing or online platforms for interactive workshops and discussions, even with a geographically dispersed workforce."

10. How would you stay up-to-date on emerging trends in training and development, specifically relevant to the HR field?

Answer: "Staying informed is essential. I would utilize various resources to stay updated, such as:

Attending HR conferences and webinars: Participating in learning opportunities focused on emerging trends in training and development within the HR domain.

Subscribing to industry publications and online resources: Reading articles and research papers on best practices and innovative approaches in HR training.

Networking with other HR professionals: Participating in online communities or professional groups to exchange knowledge and learn about new trends from colleagues facing similar challenges."

Remember to tailor these answers to your own experiences and highlight how your understanding of training and development principles can complement your HR Generalist role, emphasizing collaboration, communication, and a focus on employee development as part of your broader HR responsibilities.

Answer the above 10 questions in your own words. What other questions could be asked in the interview? Write 3 questions of your own.

....

....

CHAPTER EIGHTY-ONE

Performance Management System: HR Manager / Generalist Interview Questions & Answers

13 Commonly Asked Performance Management Interview Questions with Sample Answers (HR Generalist Role):

1. Describe your experience with performance management processes.

Answer: "In my previous role, I assisted with [mention specific tasks, e.g., performance goal setting, performance reviews, feedback delivery, or managing performance improvement plans]." I understand the importance of a clear and structured performance management process and am familiar with best practices in this area.

2. How do you ensure a fair and consistent performance management process for all employees?

Answer: "Fairness and consistency are crucial. I would advocate for:

Standardized performance appraisal forms and evaluation criteria.

Training for managers on effective goal setting, feedback delivery, and conducting fair performance reviews.

Providing opportunities for self-assessment and employee involvement in the process.

Utilizing a system that promotes transparency and facilitates communication throughout the process.

3. How do you effectively handle situations where employees disagree with their performance evaluations?

Answer: "I would approach such situations with empathy and professionalism. I would:

Encourage open communication: Schedule a meeting with the employee to understand their concerns, allowing them to express their perspectives.

Review the evaluation details: Facilitate a review of the evaluation process and ensure all procedures were followed fairly.

Offer mediation: Act as a neutral facilitator to discuss the concerns with the manager and collaborate towards a solution acceptable to both parties.

4. How do you promote a culture of continuous feedback within an organization?

Answer: "A culture of continuous feedback is essential for growth and development. I would:

Encourage managers to provide ongoing feedback throughout the year, not just during formal review periods.

Promote tools and resources to facilitate regular feedback exchange, such as online feedback platforms, anonymous surveys, or one-on-one conversations.

Train managers on effective feedback delivery techniques, focusing on constructive criticism, positive reinforcement, and clear communication.

5. Explain the importance of setting clear and measurable performance goals.

Answer: "Clear and measurable goals are essential for effective performance management. They help:

Motivate employees and provide clear direction.

Ensure alignment with organizational objectives.

Facilitate fair and objective performance evaluations.

Track progress and measure success.

6. How do you ensure performance management supports employee development?

Answer: "Effective performance management should be linked to employee development. I would advocate for:

Utilizing performance reviews to identify skill gaps and development needs.

Recommending training and development opportunities based on individual performance evaluations.

Encouraging managers to connect performance feedback with career development conversations and goal setting for the next review period.

7. How would you handle a situation where an employee's performance consistently falls below expectations?

Answer: "Addressing underperformance requires a structured approach. I would:

Support the manager in following established performance improvement plans (PIPs), ensuring clear communication of expectations and timeframes for improvement.

Help facilitate constructive conversations between the employee and manager to identify underlying reasons for underperformance and explore solutions.

Offer relevant resources and support, such as training or coaching, to assist the employee in meeting performance expectations.

8. Describe your experience with different performance management software or systems.

Answer: (Adjust based on your experience) "While I haven't directly used specific performance management software, I am familiar with the functionalities of Greytip software [mention software names or types]. Understanding these systems allows me to quickly adapt and learn new tools that can optimize the performance management process."

9. What role do you see HR playing in ensuring the effectiveness of the performance management process?

Answer: "HR plays a crucial role. This includes:

Developing and communicating clear performance management policies and procedures.

Training managers on effective feedback delivery, goal setting, and performance reviews.

Providing guidance and support to managers and employees throughout the process.

Monitoring and evaluating the effectiveness of the performance management system and making necessary adjustments.

10. Why are you interested in a role where performance management is an aspect of the job?

Answer: "Effective performance management is crucial for employee engagement, organizational success, and individual growth. I am passionate about creating a framework that fosters a culture of feedback, development, and continuous improvement. I believe HR plays a critical role in supporting this process, and I'm eager to contribute to its effectiveness."

11. List the types of performance management methods available or used in organizations today.

Answer: Organizations utilize various performance management methods, each with its own strengths and weaknesses. Here are some common approaches:

Management by Objectives (MBO): Collaborative goal setting between employees and managers, focusing on measurable objectives aligned with organizational goals.

360-Degree Feedback: Gathering feedback from various sources, including colleagues, supervisors, and self-assessment, to provide a multifaceted perspective on employee performance.

Behaviorally Anchored Rating Scales (BARS): Anchoring performance ratings to specific behavioral examples, ensuring consistency and objectivity in evaluations.

Peer Reviews: Employees within the same team or department provide feedback on each other's performance, fostering collaboration and team accountability.

Self-Appraisal: Encourages employees to reflect on their performance, identify strengths and weaknesses, and set personal development goals.

The most suitable method often depends on the organization's size, culture, and specific needs.

12. How do you ensure effective communication throughout the performance management process?

Answer: Clear and transparent communication is key. I would emphasize:

Clear communication of performance expectations at the beginning of the review period.

Regular check-ins and feedback discussions throughout the year.

Open communication channels for employees to express concerns or ask questions.

Providing feedback in a timely, constructive, and specific manner.

Utilizing multiple communication channels to cater to different preferences, such as one-on-one meetings, written reports, or online platforms.

13. How would you measure the effectiveness of a performance management system?

Answer: Evaluating the effectiveness of the system requires a multi-pronged approach:

Employee satisfaction surveys: Gauging employee perceptions of the fairness, clarity, and usefulness of the process.

Manager feedback: Gathering feedback from managers on the system's effectiveness in supporting them in evaluating and developing their team members.

Performance data analysis: Examining trends in performance metrics, such as engagement, retention, and productivity, to assess potential correlations with the performance management system.

Review completion rates and timeliness: Monitoring whether reviews are completed on time and by all participants.

Exit interview analysis: Identifying if any recurring themes point to potential shortcomings in the performance management process.

Remember to tailor these answers to your specific experiences and highlight your understanding of the importance of a fair, consistent, and development-oriented performance management process.

Answer the above 10 questions in your own words. What other questions could be asked in the interview? Write 3 questions of your own.

....

....

Diversity, Equity and Inclusion

CHAPTER EIGHTY-TWO

Defining Diversity, Equity and Inclusion

Everyone on the Team: Defining Diversity, Equity, and Inclusion

Have you ever felt like "**diversity, equity, and inclusion**" **(DE&I)** are just jargon used in meetings but don't really translate to everyday work life? You're not alone. These terms are important, but understanding what they mean in action is key to a thriving company culture.

DE&I

DE&I isn't a checklist, it's a **powerful philosophy** that celebrates the unique strengths everyone brings to the table and empowers them to excel.

Let's break it down:

Diversity: In HR, diversity refers to the variety of human qualities, experiences, and backgrounds that employees bring to the workplace. This encompasses visible aspects like race, gender, and age, as well as invisible characteristics like personality, skills, and socioeconomic background. A diverse workforce fosters a richer pool of ideas, strengthens decision-making, and allows companies to better connect with a wider range of clients and customers.

- Imagine a team brainstorming a new marketing campaign. A young designer with a social media background might have fresh ideas, while a seasoned manager with industry knowledge can provide valuable context. Diversity is like having a team with a variety of skills and experiences.

Equity: In HR, equity goes beyond simply having a diverse workforce. It focuses on creating a fair and just environment where everyone has equal opportunities to succeed and thrive. This means:

- **Removing barriers:** Equity acknowledges that people come from different backgrounds and may have faced different challenges. HR practices should actively address these disparities, for example, by providing unconscious bias training or offering targeted development programs for underrepresented groups.
- **Equal access to resources:** This ensures everyone has the tools and support they need to perform their jobs well. This could include access to mentorship programs, training opportunities, or professional development resources, all distributed fairly based on need and potential, not background or identity.
- **Fair compensation and rewards:** Equity strives for compensation and recognition systems based on performance and contribution, not influenced by factors like race, gender, or other demographics.
- Now, imagine during the brainstorming session, only the most senior manager's ideas are considered. Not exactly fair, right? Equity ensures everyone has a fair shot at being heard and contributing. It's about removing barriers and creating a level playing field where everyone has access to the resources and opportunities they need to succeed.

Inclusion: In HR, inclusion focuses on creating a work environment where everyone feels valued, respected, and empowered to contribute their unique talents and perspectives. It's about fostering a sense of belonging and psychological safety. Here's a breakdown of key aspects:

- **Feeling Welcome:** Employees from all backgrounds should feel comfortable being themselves and expressing their ideas without fear of judgment or exclusion.
- **Psychological Safety:** The environment should encourage open communication and risk-taking without fear of reprisal. This fosters an atmosphere where employees feel safe to learn, grow, and contribute innovative ideas.
- **Valuing Differences:** Inclusion celebrates the diversity of the workforce. It recognizes that different perspectives and experiences are strengths, not challenges. This can be achieved through initiatives like diversity and inclusion councils, team-building activities that promote understanding, and open communication channels.
- **Empowerment and Participation:** Inclusion ensures everyone has a seat at the table. They have access to opportunities for professional development, are encouraged to participate in decision-making processes, and have their voices heard and valued.
- Now, picture a team meeting where everyone feels comfortable sharing their ideas, even if they seem out there. That's inclusion! It's about fostering a welcoming environment where everyone feels valued, respected, and safe to bring their authentic selves to work.

Here's the magic: When DE&I are working together, it's like a well-oiled machine. Different employees, each with their strengths, collaborate seamlessly to achieve a common goal. In a company with strong DE&I, diverse ideas and perspectives lead to innovative solutions, stronger teams, and ultimately, a more successful organization.

So, how can you embrace DE&I in your daily work life?

Challenge your own biases: We all have them, but becoming aware is the first step to creating a more inclusive environment.

Celebrate differences: From employee resource groups to cultural events, create spaces where people can share their unique experiences and perspectives.

Be an advocate for equal opportunity: Speak up if you see someone being excluded or not given a fair chance.

DE&I is a continuous journey. By embracing it, we can create workplaces that are not just diverse, but truly inclusive and empowering for everyone.

CHAPTER EIGHTY-THREE

Importance of DE&I

The importance of Diversity, Equity, and Inclusion (DE&I) in the workplace can't be overstated. It's not just a feel-good initiative; it's a strategic approach that benefits both employees and the organization as a whole. Here's why DE&I matters:

Boosts Innovation and Problem-Solving:

Diverse perspectives: A team with a variety of backgrounds and experiences brings a wider range of ideas to the table. This leads to more creative solutions, better decision-making, and a stronger ability to adapt to changing market conditions.

Understanding a broader audience: A diverse workforce can better understand and connect with a wider range of customers and clients, leading to increased sales and market share.

Enhances Employee Engagement and Retention:

Feeling valued and respected: Employees who feel like they belong and their contributions are valued are more likely to be engaged, productive, and satisfied with their jobs. This translates to lower turnover rates and a more positive work environment.

Attracting top talent: Companies with a strong DE&I reputation are more attractive to talented individuals from diverse backgrounds. This creates a wider pool of qualified candidates to choose from.

Improves Brand Reputation and Social Responsibility:

Positive public image: Companies that champion DE&I are seen as more ethical and socially responsible, which can enhance their brand reputation and attract more customers and investors.

Alignment with societal values: DE&I reflects the increasing diversity of society. By embracing it, companies demonstrate their commitment to fairness and inclusion, aligning themselves with evolving social values.

Here's an additional benefit:

Financial gains: Studies have shown a direct correlation between DE&I practices and financial performance. Companies with diverse workforces tend to be more profitable and have higher shareholder value.

Activity for you:

Imagine you're on a team project at work. Everyone on your team is very similar in terms of background and experiences. Now imagine you're on a different team project with people from various backgrounds, ethnicities, and areas of expertise. How do you think the team dynamics and the final outcome of the project might differ between these two scenarios? Explain your reasoning.

....

....

CHAPTER EIGHTY-FOUR

Dimensions of DE&I

The dimensions of diversity encompass a wide range of factors that contribute to the unique qualities, experiences, and backgrounds of individuals. Here's a breakdown of some key dimensions:

Visible Dimensions:

Race: This refers to a person's physical characteristics associated with ancestry or heritage, such as Black, White, Asian, Indigenous, etc.

Ethnicity: This refers to a person's cultural identity based on shared heritage, language, and traditions, which can overlap with race but is distinct. (e.g., Hispanic, Latinx, Vietnamese)

Gender Identity: This refers to a person's internal sense of being male, female, transgender, genderqueer, or non-binary.

Sexual Orientation: This refers to who a person is attracted to romantically or sexually, such as heterosexual, homosexual, bisexual, asexual, etc.

Age: This refers to a person's chronological age and the associated life experiences and perspectives that come with different age groups.

Non-Visible Dimensions:

Ability: This refers to a person's physical, sensory, or mental abilities. It includes people with disabilities as well as those who are neurodivergent (e.g., dyslexia, ADHD).

Religion: This refers to a person's spiritual or ethical beliefs and practices.

Socioeconomic Status: This refers to a person's education level, income, and social class.

Military Service: This refers to a person's experience serving in the military, which can shape their work ethic and leadership skills.

Personality: This refers to a person's unique combination of psychological traits and preferences.

Language: This refers to a person's native or preferred language, which can impact communication and cultural understanding.

Work Style: This refers to a person's preferred way of working, such as being detail-oriented, collaborative, or independent.

It's important to note that these dimensions are not always siloed. They can intersect and influence each other, creating a unique individual experience. Recognizing these diverse dimensions allows organizations to create inclusive workplaces that value and empower everyone to contribute their best.

Activity for you:

Consider a job advertisement you've seen recently. Does the language used and the requirements listed seem accessible to people from diverse backgrounds (race, gender, age, ability etc.)? Would someone from a different background than the typical candidate feel welcome to apply? Explain your answer.

....

....

CHAPTER EIGHTY-FIVE

Intersectionality at Work

Definition:

Intersectionality is a framework for understanding how different aspects of a person's identity combine to create unique experiences of privilege and disadvantage. These aspects include:

- Gender
- Race
- Ethnicity
- Sexual orientation
- Gender identity
- Disability
- Class
- Age
- And other social categories

Key points to remember:

Not just a sum of parts: Intersectionality emphasizes that a person's experience can't be reduced to a simple addition of their identities. A Black woman's experience will be different from both a white woman's and a Black man's due to the unique ways that race and gender discrimination intersect.

Systems vs. individuals: Intersectionality focuses on the way systems of power (like racism, sexism, ableism) interact to shape experiences, not just individual acts of prejudice.

It's about everyone: Intersectionality recognizes that everyone has multiple identities that create both privilege and disadvantage depending on the situation.

Origin: The term "intersectionality" was coined by legal scholar and activist Kimberlé Crenshaw in 1989 to illustrate how the law failed to address the specific challenges faced by Black women.

Imagine the office is a giant toolbox. A truly diverse toolbox would be filled with all sorts of wrenches, screwdrivers, hammers - a variety of tools for any job. But what if some tools are rusty, dull, or the wrong size for certain hands? That's where intersectionality comes in.

Intersectionality recognizes that people come to work with their own unique set of tools. A young Asian woman might be a brilliant programmer, but unconscious bias based on her age and gender could prevent her from getting promoted. Her skills (the tools) are there, but she might not be given the same opportunities as others (access to the toolbox).

Here's how intersectionality helps build a better work environment:

Identifying blind spots: Say the company has a policy of rewarding employees who stay late. This might benefit someone without childcare responsibilities, but a single parent might have to leave on time. Intersectionality helps recognize these gaps and create policies that work for everyone.

Tailored solutions: Imagine a training program designed specifically for women in leadership. This acknowledges the challenges women might face in a male-dominated field, providing them with the tools they need to succeed.

Understanding the bigger picture: A worker with a disability might need extra time to complete tasks due to physical limitations. Intersectionality encourages looking beyond the immediate issue and finding ways to support that employee's overall success.

Examples:

A company with a diverse team is developing a new product. An employee who uses a wheelchair points out that the current design is inaccessible. Because of intersectionality, the team incorporates accessibility features from the start, creating a better product for everyone.

A company with a large immigrant workforce offers English language classes during work hours. This recognizes that language fluency can be a barrier to advancement and helps integrate these employees more fully into the team.

By considering these intersecting identities, workplaces can ensure everyone has the tools and support they need to thrive. It's about recognizing that a one-size-fits-all approach won't work. Building an inclusive toolbox means ensuring everyone has the right tools in the right size, so they can all contribute their unique skills and talents.

A truly diverse toolbox would be filled with all sorts of wrenches, screwdrivers, hammers - a variety of tools for any job. But what if some tools are rusty, dull, or the wrong size for certain hands? That's where intersectionality comes in.

Intersectionality recognizes that people come to work with their own unique set of tools. A young Asian woman might be a brilliant programmer, but unconscious bias based on her age and gender could prevent her from getting promoted. Her skills (the tools) are there, but she might not be given the same opportunities as others (access to the toolbox).

Here's how intersectionality helps build a better work environment:

Identifying blind spots: Say the company has a policy of rewarding employees who stay late. This might benefit someone without childcare responsibilities, but a single parent might have to leave on time. Intersectionality helps recognize these gaps and create policies that work for everyone.

Tailored solutions: Imagine a training program designed specifically for women in leadership. This acknowledges the challenges women might face in a male-dominated field, providing them with the tools they need to succeed.

Understanding the bigger picture: A worker with a disability might need extra time to complete tasks due to physical limitations. Intersectionality encourages looking beyond the immediate issue and finding ways to support that employee's overall success.

Examples:

A company with a diverse team is developing a new product. An employee who uses a wheelchair points out that the current design is inaccessible. Because of intersectionality, the team incorporates accessibility features from the start, creating a better product for everyone.

A company with a large immigrant workforce offers English language classes during work hours. This recognizes that language fluency can be a barrier to advancement and helps integrate these employees more fully into the team.

By considering these intersecting identities, workplaces can ensure everyone has the tools and support they need to thrive. It's about recognizing that a one-size-fits-all approach won't work. Building an inclusive toolbox means ensuring everyone has the right tools in the right size, so they can all contribute their unique skills and talents.

Activity for you:

Think about a time at work (or school) where you felt you, or someone you know, was treated differently because of more than one aspect of their identity. For example, maybe a young woman was overlooked for a promotion even though she was highly qualified, or maybe someone with a disability wasn't given the resources they needed to succeed. Describe the situation and how the person's background played a role in the experience.

....

....

CHAPTER EIGHTY-SIX

Benefits of a diverse workforce

Let's face it, the office can sometimes feel like a bad rerun of high school cliques. But what if I told you that ditching the "closed circle" vibe and building a truly diverse team could be the secret weapon your company needs?

Hold up, before you glaze over at another HR buzzword, hear me out. Diversity isn't just a feel-good talking point. It's a strategic advantage that can supercharge your creativity, innovation, and ultimately, your bottom line.

Why? Here's the lowdown:

Brainstorming Bonanza: Imagine a room full of people who all went to the same school, had the same hobbies, and ordered the same thing for lunch (boring, right?). Now picture a team with a mix of backgrounds, experiences, and perspectives. This diversity of thought fuels out-of-the-box thinking, leading to groundbreaking ideas and solutions your company might have missed otherwise.

Customer Connection Champions: Let's be honest, the world isn't made up of clones. By having a team that reflects the diversity of your customer base, you gain a deeper understanding of their needs and preferences. Think of it like having a built-in panel of advisors who can help you tailor your products and services for maximum impact.

Problem-solving Powerhouse: Diverse teams bring a wider range of skills and knowledge to the table. When you have people with different approaches tackling a challenge, you're more likely to find creative solutions that wouldn't have emerged from a homogenous group.

Real World Results: Winning with Diversity

Don't just take my word for it. Here are some real-life examples of companies that are winning big thanks to diversity:

The Lego Group: By incorporating more female designers, Lego saw a surge in sales of their "Friends" line, which was previously targeted mainly at boys.

Johnson & Johnson: A study by their own researchers showed that teams with greater diversity in leadership were more likely to deliver superior financial performance.

General Motors: When GM began focusing on diversity in their workforce, they were able to develop a more culturally sensitive car design for the Chinese market, leading to a significant increase in sales.

Building Your Dream Team: How to Get Started

Ready to embrace the power of diversity? Here are some tips:

Broaden your talent pool: Go beyond the usual recruiting channels and actively seek out candidates from diverse backgrounds.

Unconscious Bias Training: We all have biases, but unconscious ones can hold us back. Equip your team with training to recognize and challenge these biases in the hiring process.

Create a Culture of Inclusion: Diversity is just the first step. Make sure everyone feels valued, respected, and empowered to share their unique ideas.

The Takeaway:

Diversity isn't just about political correctness, it's about smart business. By building a team that reflects the richness of the world around us, you'll unlock a treasure trove of creativity, innovation, and problem-solving power. So ditch the cliques, embrace the differences, and watch your company soar!

Activity for you: The Movie Mashup!

This activity helps you understand how different perspectives can create something more interesting and engaging.

Grab some paper and a pen.

Think of two (very different!) movies you've seen. It could be a superhero movie and a historical drama, a rom-com and a sci-fi thriller - the more different, the better!

Imagine a mashup! Now, pretend you're creating a brand new movie that combines these two completely different films.

- **Write down some details:**

- **What's the basic plot of your mashup movie?**
- **How do the characters from each original film interact in your new story?**
- **Does the setting change?**
- **How do the genres of the original films influence your mashup?**

Bonus Challenge! Sketch or write a short scene from your new movie.

Benefits of Diverse Teams:

Think about the mashup movie you created. Would it have been as interesting if you only used characters or ideas from one movie?

Just like in movies, diverse teams with different ideas and backgrounds can create something more creative and engaging by bringing together different perspectives!

....

....

CHAPTER EIGHTY-SEVEN

Unconscious Bias: Making Fair Decisions at Work

Have you ever made a judgment about someone without realizing it? We all do it sometimes. These snap judgements can be influenced by our own experiences and can lead to unfair biases against others.

This is called unconscious bias, and it can happen when we:

Favor someone similar to us: We might subconsciously view someone more positively if they share our background or interests.

Disadvantage someone different: Race, religion, age, or even something as simple as appearance can lead us to underestimate someone's abilities.

These biases can cloud our decisions, leading to unfair outcomes at work, like hiring the wrong person or overlooking someone for a promotion.

The good news? Unconscious bias is something we can all manage. Here's how:

Be aware: The first step is acknowledging that unconscious bias exists.

Cast a wider net: Advertise jobs in diverse places to attract a wider range of candidates.

Teamwork makes the dream work: Use interview panels with diverse perspectives and consider anonymizing applications during the initial screening process.

Slow down: Take your time with decisions, especially those with lasting consequences. Document your thought process to ensure fairness.

By following these tips, we can create a more level playing field for everyone in the workplace.

Remember: Employment law protects people from discrimination based on certain characteristics. Unconscious bias can lead to discriminatory actions, so it's important to be mindful.

Example: A manager might believe men are inherently harder workers. During recruitment, they might favor a male candidate over a demonstrably better qualified female candidate simply because of their gender. This is unconscious bias in action, and it's not fair or legal.

Unconscious Bias: Activity for you

The Name Game:

Grab a piece of paper and write down 10 names (celebrities, historical figures, or fictional characters will work). Make sure the names represent a variety of genders and ethnicities.

Next to each name, write down the first word that pops into your head when you think of that person. Don't overthink it - the first instinct is often the most revealing.

Review your list. Are there any patterns? Do certain names trigger positive words like "strong" or "intelligent," while others lead to negative words like "lazy" or "unqualified"?

What this reveals:

This simple activity can show how names, which can hint at background or ethnicity, can trigger unconscious biases. Even if the positive or negative words aren't entirely true, they can influence how we perceive someone.

Bonus:

Discuss the activity with a friend or family member. Did they have similar biases triggered by the names?

Repeat the activity, but this time focus on professions instead of names. Did the chosen profession influence the words you associated with it?

....

....

CHAPTER EIGHTY-EIGHT

Examples of Unconscious Bias and How to avoid them

Here's a breakdown of 16 common unconscious biases that can creep into the workplace, along with tips for creating a fairer hiring process:

Examples of Unconscious Bias:

Affinity Bias: Favoring people similar to ourselves (background, interests).

Ageism: Negative stereotypes about people based on their age.

Anchor Bias: Relying too heavily on the first piece of information we learn about a candidate.

Attribution Bias: Making assumptions about someone's behavior without considering all the facts.

Authority Bias: Giving more weight to ideas from those in positions of power.

Beauty Bias: Assuming attractive people are more competent.

Confirmation Bias: Seeking information that confirms our existing beliefs about a candidate.

Conformity Bias: Going along with the majority opinion, even if you disagree.

Contrast Effect: Comparing candidates and judging them against each other, rather than on their own merits.

Gender Bias: Preferring one gender over another.

Halo Effect: Letting one positive aspect of a candidate overshadow their other qualities (or lack thereof).

Height Bias: Judging someone based on their height.

Horn Effect: Letting one negative detail about a candidate influence your entire perception.

Name Bias: Favoring candidates with certain names.

Nonverbal Bias: Letting a candidate's body language influence your opinion.

Overconfidence Bias: Believing your judgment is better than it actually is.

How to Avoid Unconscious Bias:

Unconscious Bias Training: Educate yourself and your team on unconscious bias and its effects.

Talent Assessments & Scorecards: Use standardized tools to evaluate candidates objectively.

Diversity Hiring Goals: Set goals to actively seek out and hire qualified candidates from diverse backgrounds.

Different Interview Techniques: Use structured interviews with a set of questions for all candidates.

Diverse and Inclusive Culture: Foster a workplace environment that values different perspectives and experiences.

By being aware of unconscious bias and taking steps to mitigate it, we can create a more level playing field for everyone in the workplace.

CHAPTER EIGHTY-NINE

Case Study: Unconscious Bias at Work

Case Study: Unconscious Bias and the Missed Promotion

The Situation:

Sarah, a highly skilled software engineer at Technovation Inc., had been consistently exceeding expectations for two years. She regularly received positive performance reviews, mentored junior colleagues, and took initiative on complex projects. When a senior software engineer position opened up, Sarah felt confident she was the strongest candidate.

During the interview process, Sarah presented well-developed solutions to technical problems. However, the interview panel, consisting of three senior male engineers, seemed less engaged with her responses compared to the other candidate, David. David had a more outgoing personality and peppered his answers with jokes and anecdotes.

Ultimately, **David was offered the promotion,** despite Sarah's demonstrably stronger technical skills and experience.

The Impact of Unconscious Bias:

Demotivation and Disengagement: Sarah felt undervalued and demotivated. Her hard work and contributions seemed to be overlooked. This could lead to decreased productivity and a higher chance of her leaving the company.

Loss of Talent: Technovation missed the opportunity to promote a highly skilled and dedicated employee. This could hinder their ability to retain top talent and impact their long-term success.

Limited Diversity: Promoting David over Sarah reinforces the existing gender imbalance in Technovation's senior leadership. This could create a culture where women don't feel they have equal opportunities for advancement.

What Should Have Been Done:

Structured Interviews: Technovation should have used a structured interview format with pre-defined questions and scoring rubrics. This would have ensured all candidates received the same evaluation criteria and minimized the influence of personality or personal connections.

Diverse Interview Panels: Including an interviewer with a different background (e.g., a female engineer) could have provided a different perspective and mitigated gender bias.

Focus on Skills and Experience: Interview questions should have focused on the technical skills and experience required for the senior position, not on personality traits.

Moving Forward:

Unconscious Bias Training: Technovation should implement unconscious bias training for all employees, including managers involved in the hiring and promotion process.

Feedback Mechanisms: Creating anonymous feedback channels would allow employees to report any concerns about bias they might experience.

Mentorship Programs: Matching Sarah with a senior leader, male or female, could provide her with career guidance and advocate for her future advancement.

By acknowledging the role of unconscious bias in this case and taking steps to address it, Technovation can create a fairer and more inclusive workplace environment where everyone has the opportunity to reach their full potential.

CHAPTER NINETY

Strategies for Mitigating Unconscious Bias

Taming the Hidden Monster: Strategies for Mitigating Unconscious Bias

Unconscious bias, those automatic judgments we make without even realizing it, can wreak havoc on our decision-making in the workplace. From hiring practices to performance reviews, bias can lead to missed opportunities, unfair treatment, and a stifled work environment. But fear not! Here are some practical strategies to combat this hidden monster:

Shine a Light on Your Biases:

The first step is acknowledging that we all have biases. Take online assessments or attend workshops to understand your own blind spots. Common biases include affinity bias (favoring similar people), confirmation bias (seeking information that confirms existing beliefs), and beauty bias (associating attractiveness with competence).

Embrace Structure:

Structured interview formats with pre-defined questions and scoring rubrics can help mitigate the influence of bias in the hiring process. This ensures all candidates are evaluated on the same criteria and reduces the impact of personality or personal connections. Consider anonymizing resumes during initial screening stages to further minimize bias based on names or backgrounds.

Diversify Your Thinking (and Your Team):

Surround yourself with people from different backgrounds and experiences. Diverse teams bring a wider range of perspectives to the table, fostering creativity and challenging biases. Incorporate diverse interview panels to get a well-rounded picture of each candidate.

Focus on Skills and Experience:

Refine your job descriptions to focus on the specific skills and experience required for the role. Train interviewers to ask behavioral interview questions that delve into past actions and accomplishments, providing a more objective picture of a candidate's capabilities.

Embrace Data and Metrics:

Don't rely solely on gut feelings or "cultural fit." Data and metrics can be powerful tools in mitigating bias. Use data to track hiring outcomes and identify any demographic disparities that might indicate bias.

Create a Culture of Feedback:

Encourage open communication and feedback mechanisms within your organization. This allows employees to voice concerns about bias and fosters a culture of continuous improvement.

Lead by Example:

Leaders play a crucial role in setting the tone for a bias-free workplace. Champion diversity and inclusion initiatives, and hold yourself and others accountable for making fair and objective decisions.

Remember: Mitigating unconscious bias is an ongoing process. By adopting these strategies and fostering a culture of awareness, you can create a more inclusive and equitable workplace where everyone has the opportunity to thrive. After all, a diverse and unbiased team is a recipe for success!

CHAPTER NINETY-ONE

DE&I at each stage of HRM

DE&I in Recruitment

Diversity, Equity, and Inclusion (DE&I) are crucial for building a strong, well-rounded team in any company. Here's how DE&I can be integrated into each stage of the recruitment process:

1. Identifying the Need:

DE&I Focus: Analyze your current team composition. Are there any under-represented groups?

2. Crafting the Job Description:

DE&I Focus: Use inclusive language, focusing on skills and experience needed, not specific demographics (e.g., "strong communication skills" instead of "excellent written English").

3. Sourcing Candidates:

DE&I Focus: Post job openings on diverse platforms beyond the usual job boards. Partner with organizations that focus on under-represented talent pools.

4. Screening Resumes/Applications:

DE&I Focus: Anonymised resumes (if possible) can help reduce bias based on names or backgrounds. Focus on qualifications and relevant keywords.

5. Conducting Interviews:

DE&I Focus: Develop a structured interview format with pre-defined questions for all candidates. Utilize diverse interview panels to gain a wider range of perspectives.

6. Evaluation and Selection:

DE&I Focus: Evaluate all candidates based on pre-defined criteria and interview performance. Use scoring rubrics to ensure consistency.

7. Making the Offer:

DE&I Focus: Ensure salary and benefit offers are competitive and equitable across genders and demographics.

DE&I in Employee Life Cycle

Onboarding:

Pre-Start:

DE&I Focus: Provide new hires with information about your company's DE&I initiatives and commitment to a respectful and inclusive workplace. This could be included in their welcome package or pre-boarding emails.

First Day:

DE&I Focus: Ensure the new hire feels welcome and integrated. Pair them with a diverse buddy or mentor who can answer questions and provide support. Offer a tour of the workplace that highlights your company's commitment to diversity through inclusive artwork, team photos, and resource materials.

First Week:

DE&I Focus: Schedule onboarding sessions with leaders from different departments and backgrounds. This will give the new hire a broader understanding of the company culture and allow them to connect with diverse colleagues.

First Month:

DE&I Focus: Offer opportunities for the new hire to connect with employee resource groups (ERGs) or diversity and inclusion committees. This fosters a sense of belonging and provides a safe space to ask questions and share experiences.

Performance Management:

Goal Setting:

DE&I Focus: Work collaboratively with employees to set clear and objective performance goals that align with their career aspirations and company objectives.

Regular Check-Ins:

DE&I Focus: Conduct regular performance reviews that are free from bias. Utilize a standardized performance review format to ensure consistency across the organization. Offer diverse team members the opportunity to provide feedback during the review process.

Development Opportunities:

DE&I Focus: Identify and address any potential roadblocks that might be hindering an employee's progress, particularly for those from underrepresented groups. Offer access to training and development programs that cater to diverse learning styles and career goals.

Employee Training:

Needs Assessment:

DE&I Focus: Conduct regular surveys or focus groups to identify employee needs and training gaps. Consider the specific needs of diverse employee groups.

Curriculum Development:

DE&I Focus: Develop training programs that cover a range of DE&I topics, from unconscious bias and microaggressions to cultural competency and building inclusive teams. Ensure training materials incorporate diverse perspectives and case studies.

Delivery Strategies:

DE&I Focus: Offer training programs in various formats (e.g., online modules, in-person workshops, interactive sessions) to cater to diverse learning styles and preferences. Consider offering training in multiple languages if your company has a multilingual workforce.

Evaluation and Feedback:

DE&I Focus: Evaluate the effectiveness of your training programs by collecting feedback from participants. This feedback can be used to refine the curriculum and ensure it meets the needs of a diverse workforce.

Development and Retention:

Career Development:

DE&I Focus: Provide access to mentorship programs that pair employees with mentors from diverse backgrounds. Offer opportunities for cross-functional projects that allow employees to expand their skill sets and network with colleagues from different departments.

Succession Planning:

DE&I Focus: Develop a talent pipeline that includes qualified candidates from diverse backgrounds. Utilize diverse interview panels when evaluating candidates for promotions or leadership roles.

Compensation and Benefits:

Pay Equity:

DE&I Focus: Conduct regular pay audits to ensure equal pay for equal work regardless of gender, race, ethnicity, or other demographic factors.

Benefits:

DE&I Focus: Offer benefits that cater to the diverse needs of your workforce. This might include childcare options, flexible work arrangements, and parental leave policies that are inclusive of all family structures.

Separation (Offboarding):

Exit Interviews:

DE&I Focus: Conduct exit interviews with departing employees, focusing on questions related to their experience with DE&I at your company. Use this feedback to identify areas for improvement and ensure a positive offboarding experience for everyone.

Remember: DE&I is an ongoing process that requires continuous commitment from leadership and all employees. By integrating these strategies into every stage of the employee lifecycle, you can create a more equitable and inclusive workplace where everyone feels valued, respected, and empowered to reach their full potential.

CHAPTER NINETY-TWO

DEI: Creating inclusive policies and practices

There are several policies that organizations can implement to incorporate diversity, equity, and inclusion (DEI) principles into their operations. Here are some examples:

Anti-Discrimination Policy: A comprehensive anti-discrimination policy prohibits discrimination based on race, ethnicity, gender, sexual orientation, age, religion, disability, or any other protected characteristic. This policy ensures that all employees are treated fairly and equitably.

Equal Employment Opportunity (EEO) Policy: An EEO policy reaffirms the organization's commitment to providing equal employment opportunities to all individuals regardless of their background. It emphasizes merit-based hiring, promotion, and compensation decisions.

Diversity Recruitment and Hiring Policy: This policy outlines strategies for attracting and hiring diverse talent. It may include initiatives such as targeted outreach to underrepresented groups, diverse candidate sourcing, and the use of blind recruitment techniques to mitigate unconscious bias.

Harassment Prevention Policy: A harassment prevention policy establishes zero tolerance for harassment or bullying in the workplace. It defines prohibited behaviors, outlines reporting procedures, and ensures that complaints are promptly and thoroughly investigated.

Accommodation Policy: An accommodation policy ensures that employees with disabilities or special needs have equal access to job opportunities, facilities, and resources. It outlines procedures for requesting and providing reasonable accommodations.

Flexible Work Arrangements Policy: A flexible work arrangements policy allows employees to balance their work and personal responsibilities more effectively. It may include options such as telecommuting, flexible hours, job sharing, or compressed workweeks to accommodate diverse needs.

Diversity Training and Education Policy: This policy mandates regular training and education on diversity, equity, and inclusion topics for all employees. It ensures that staff members understand the importance of DEI principles and know how to foster an inclusive work environment.

Promotion and Advancement Policy: A promotion and advancement policy ensures that opportunities for career growth are accessible to all employees based on merit and performance. It includes transparent promotion criteria, advancement pathways, and mentorship programs.

Supplier Diversity Policy: A supplier diversity policy promotes the inclusion of minority-owned, women-owned, and other diverse businesses in the organization's supply chain. It sets goals for sourcing from diverse suppliers and encourages the development of diverse vendor relationships.

Employee Resource Groups (ERGs) Policy: An ERG policy supports the formation and operation of employee resource groups or affinity networks. It provides guidelines for establishing ERGs, defines their purpose, and outlines the support and resources available to them.

By implementing these policies, organizations can create a more inclusive and equitable workplace where diversity is celebrated, and all employees have the opportunity to thrive. Additionally, regularly reviewing and updating these policies ensures that they remain relevant and effective in addressing the evolving needs of the workforce.

CHAPTER NINETY-THREE

Psychological Safety & Belonging in the Workplace

Promoting Psychological Safety and Belonging in the Workplace

Creating a workplace environment where employees feel psychologically safe and a sense of belonging is crucial for fostering productivity, creativity, and overall well-being. When individuals feel safe to express their thoughts, ideas, and concerns without fear of judgment or reprisal, they are more likely to engage actively in their work and collaborate effectively with their colleagues. Furthermore, a strong sense of belonging cultivates a supportive atmosphere where individuals feel valued, respected, and included, regardless of their background or identity.

Here are some strategies to promote psychological safety and belonging in the workplace:

Encourage Open Communication: Establishing open channels of communication is fundamental to fostering psychological safety. Encourage employees to share their ideas, opinions, and feedback freely, whether it's during team meetings, brainstorming sessions, or one-on-one discussions with supervisors. Actively listen to their input, validate their perspectives, and demonstrate a willingness to consider diverse viewpoints.

Lead by Example: Leaders play a pivotal role in shaping the organizational culture. Demonstrate authenticity, vulnerability, and empathy in your interactions with employees. Share your own challenges and mistakes openly to create a culture where transparency and honesty are valued. By modeling behaviors that promote psychological safety, leaders can inspire trust and encourage others to do the same.

Provide Constructive Feedback: Feedback should be delivered in a constructive and supportive manner that focuses on improvement rather than criticism. Encourage a growth mindset by framing feedback as an opportunity for learning and development. Emphasize strengths and areas for growth while offering specific guidance on how individuals can enhance their performance. Additionally, be receptive to receiving feedback from employees, as this demonstrates a commitment to continuous improvement.

Cultivate Inclusive Practices: Create an inclusive environment where all employees feel respected, valued, and empowered to contribute their unique perspectives. Foster diversity by embracing differences in background, experience, and thought. Ensure that policies, practices, and decision-making processes are fair and equitable for everyone. Provide opportunities for underrepresented groups to participate in leadership development programs, mentorship initiatives, and career advancement opportunities.

Foster Social Connections: Encourage team-building activities, social events, and networking opportunities that facilitate meaningful connections among employees. Building strong interpersonal relationships fosters a sense of belonging and camaraderie within the workplace. Consider implementing affinity groups or employee resource groups where individuals with shared identities or interests can connect, support each other, and advocate for inclusivity.

Address Conflict Promptly: Conflict is inevitable in any workplace, but how it is managed can significantly impact psychological safety. Encourage open dialogue and constructive conflict resolution strategies to address disagreements and tensions effectively. Provide mediation or conflict resolution training to equip employees with the skills needed to navigate challenging situations respectfully and collaboratively.

Prioritize Well-being: Recognize the importance of employee well-being and prioritize initiatives that promote mental health and work-life balance. Offer resources such as counseling services, mindfulness programs, or flexible work arrangements to support employees' holistic well-being. Create a culture that values self-care, boundaries, and resilience, acknowledging that individuals perform their best when their mental and emotional needs are met.

In conclusion, promoting psychological safety and belonging in the workplace is essential for fostering a culture of trust, collaboration, and inclusivity. By prioritizing open communication, inclusive practices, and supportive relationships, organizations can create environments where employees feel empowered to bring their whole selves to work, driving innovation, productivity, and employee engagement. Building a psychologically safe and inclusive workplace requires ongoing commitment, but the benefits for individuals and the organization as a whole are well worth the investment.

CHAPTER NINETY-FOUR

Addressing DE&I Challenges & Conflicts

Addressing Diversity-Related Challenges and Conflicts in the Workplace

Diversity-related challenges and conflicts can arise in any workplace, especially in environments that strive to promote **diversity, equity, and inclusion (DE&I).** While diversity brings unique perspectives, experiences, and strengths to the table, it can also lead to misunderstandings, biases, and conflicts if not managed effectively. Addressing these challenges and conflicts proactively is essential for creating a supportive and inclusive work environment where all employees feel valued, respected, and empowered to contribute their best.

Here are some strategies for addressing diversity-related challenges and conflicts in the workplace:

Foster Awareness and Education: Many diversity-related challenges stem from unconscious biases, stereotypes, and misconceptions. Foster awareness and education around diversity, equity, and inclusion by providing training programs, workshops, or seminars that raise awareness of implicit biases, promote cultural competence, and encourage empathy and understanding. Educating employees about the value of diversity and the impact of bias can help mitigate conflicts and foster a more inclusive workplace culture.

Encourage Open Dialogue: Create opportunities for open dialogue and honest conversations about diversity-related issues within the workplace. Encourage employees to share their experiences, perspectives, and concerns openly, while also promoting active listening and empathy among colleagues. Establishing a culture of open communication enables employees to address conflicts constructively and collaboratively, rather than allowing them to escalate.

Implement Fair and Equitable Policies: Review and revise organizational policies, practices, and procedures to ensure they are fair, equitable, and inclusive for all employees. Address any systemic barriers or biases that may exist in recruitment, hiring, promotion, performance evaluation, and decision-making processes. Implementing policies that promote diversity, equity, and inclusion sends a clear message that discrimination and bias will not be tolerated in the workplace.

Provide Conflict Resolution Resources: Offer resources and support for resolving diversity-related conflicts effectively and respectfully. This may include providing access to mediation services, conflict resolution training, or diversity and inclusion specialists who can facilitate difficult conversations and help parties find mutually acceptable solutions. By providing employees with the tools and resources they need to address conflicts proactively, organizations can prevent tensions from escalating and promote a culture of collaboration and respect.

Lead by Example: Leaders play a crucial role in addressing diversity-related challenges and conflicts within the workplace. Lead by example by demonstrating a commitment to diversity, equity, and inclusion in your words and actions. Hold yourself and others accountable for promoting respectful behavior, addressing bias, and fostering a culture of belonging. By modeling inclusive leadership behaviors, leaders can inspire trust, build credibility, and drive positive change throughout the organization.

Create Supportive Networks: Establish affinity groups or employee resource groups where individuals with shared identities or experiences can come together to support each other, share resources, and advocate for inclusivity. These networks provide a sense of belonging and community for underrepresented employees, while also serving as valuable allies in promoting diversity and inclusion initiatives within the organization.

Conduct Regular Diversity Assessments: Regularly assess the organizational climate and employee experiences through surveys, focus groups, or interviews to identify areas of improvement and address emerging diversity-related challenges proactively. Collecting feedback from employees allows organizations to gain valuable insights into the effectiveness of their diversity and inclusion efforts and make data-driven decisions to drive positive change.

In conclusion, addressing diversity-related challenges and conflicts in the workplace requires a multifaceted approach that prioritizes awareness, education, open dialogue, equitable policies, conflict resolution resources, inclusive leadership, supportive networks, and regular assessment and feedback. By proactively addressing diversity-related issues and fostering a culture of respect, understanding, and collaboration, organizations can create environments where all employees feel valued, included, and empowered to succeed.

CHAPTER NINETY-FIVE

Handling discrimination, harassment, and microaggressions

Handling Discrimination, Harassment, and Microaggressions in the Workplace

Discrimination, harassment, and microaggressions are detrimental to both individuals and organizations, undermining morale, productivity, and overall well-being. Addressing these harmful behaviors effectively is essential for creating a safe, respectful, and inclusive workplace where all employees can thrive. While prevention is key, it's equally important to have robust mechanisms in place to handle instances of discrimination, harassment, and microaggressions when they occur.

Here are some strategies for handling discrimination, harassment, and microaggressions in the workplace:

Establish Clear Policies and Procedures: Develop comprehensive policies and procedures that explicitly prohibit discrimination, harassment, and microaggressions based on protected characteristics such as race, gender, age, sexual orientation, disability, religion, or nationality. Ensure that all employees are aware of these policies and understand the consequences of engaging in prohibited behavior. Clearly outline the steps for reporting incidents and the investigation process.

Provide Training and Education: Offer regular training sessions to educate employees on what constitutes discrimination, harassment, and microaggressions, as well as their rights and responsibilities in preventing and addressing these behaviors. Training should cover topics such as unconscious bias, bystander intervention, respectful communication, and cultural competence. By raising awareness and promoting understanding, organizations can create a more inclusive and respectful workplace culture.

Encourage Reporting: Create a culture where employees feel comfortable reporting incidents of discrimination, harassment, or microaggressions without fear of retaliation. Establish multiple reporting channels, including anonymous options, and ensure that reports are handled promptly, confidentially, and impartially. Encourage bystander intervention by empowering employees to speak up when they witness inappropriate behavior and providing support for those who come forward.

Conduct Thorough Investigations: Take all reports of discrimination, harassment, or microaggressions seriously and conduct thorough investigations to determine the facts and appropriate course of action. Assign trained investigators who are impartial and objective to handle the investigation process. Interview all parties involved, gather relevant evidence, and document findings in a detailed report. Treat all individuals involved with dignity, respect, and confidentiality throughout the investigation process.

Enforce Consequences: Hold perpetrators of discrimination, harassment, or microaggressions accountable for their actions by enforcing appropriate consequences in accordance with organizational policies and legal requirements. Consequences may include disciplinary action, such as counseling, training, suspension, or termination, depending on the severity and recurrence of the behavior. Send a clear message that discrimination and harassment will not be tolerated in the workplace.

Provide Support for Victims: Offer support and resources for employees who have experienced discrimination, harassment, or microaggressions, including counseling services, employee assistance programs, and legal assistance if necessary. Take proactive measures to address any adverse effects on the victim's well-being, job satisfaction, or career advancement opportunities. Ensure that victims are treated with empathy, sensitivity, and respect throughout the process.

Prevent Recurrence: Take proactive measures to prevent future incidents of discrimination, harassment, or microaggressions by addressing underlying systemic issues and promoting a culture of respect and inclusivity. Conduct regular assessments of the organizational climate, solicit feedback from employees, and make necessary adjustments to policies, practices, and training programs. Foster a culture where diversity is celebrated, differences are valued, and all employees feel safe and respected.

In conclusion, handling discrimination, harassment, and microaggressions in the workplace requires a comprehensive approach that includes establishing clear policies and procedures, providing training and education, encouraging reporting, conducting thorough investigations, enforcing consequences, providing support for victims, and preventing recurrence. By taking proactive steps to address these harmful behaviors, organizations can create a safer, more inclusive, and equitable workplace where all employees can thrive.

Activity for you

Discrimination, harassment, and microaggressions can create a hostile work environment. But what can we do to address them?

Question: You witness a microaggression happening in the workplace. The target is someone from a different background than you. Create a short role-play (written script or skit) demonstrating how you would intervene as an upstander in a respectful and effective way.

Consider these points in your role-play:

- Your safety and the safety of the target.
- Directly addressing the microaggression or speaking to the target privately to offer support.
- Educating the person who made the microaggression in a constructive way (if appropriate).
- Also include: Discuss the potential challenges of intervening and how you would overcome them in your role-play.

....

....

CHAPTER NINETY-SIX

DE&I Best Practices from Corporates

Championing Diversity, Equity, and Inclusion: Best Practices Across Industries

Diversity, Equity, and Inclusion (DE&I) are no longer just buzzwords. They are crucial for fostering innovation, attracting top talent, and building a successful organization. However, implementing effective DE&I strategies requires a nuanced approach that considers the unique needs and challenges of different industries and contexts. Here's a look at best practices across various sectors, along with real-world examples:

DE&I best practices

Tech Industry:

- **Focus on unconscious bias training:** The tech industry has a well-documented gender gap. Companies like Accenture Source: [Accenture Diversity and Inclusion Report: [invalid URL removed]] incorporate unconscious bias training into their onboarding process to mitigate bias in hiring and promotion decisions.
- **Targeted recruitment efforts:** Many tech companies partner with organizations like Girls Who Code Source: [Girls Who Code: https://girlswhocode.com/] to reach out to underrepresented talent pools during the recruitment process.

Healthcare Industry:

- **Culturally competent care:** The healthcare industry needs to ensure all patients receive culturally competent care. Hospitals like Northwell Health Source: [Northwell Health Diversity and Inclusion: [invalid URL removed]] offer language interpreter services and training programs to address cultural sensitivities in patient interactions.

- **Diversity in clinical trials:** Clinical trials often lack diversity, leading to medications that may not be effective for all populations. Organizations like the Alliance for Clinical Trials Equity Source: [Alliance for Clinical Trials Equity: [invalid URL removed]] advocate for more inclusive participation in clinical research.

Manufacturing Industry:

- **Focus on apprenticeship programs:** Manufacturing jobs are often seen as lacking diversity. Companies like Siemens Source: [Siemens USA Diversity and Inclusion: [invalid URL removed]] offer apprenticeship programs that provide opportunities for people from underrepresented groups to enter the skilled trades.
- **Breaking down gender stereotypes:** Manufacturing is often perceived as a male-dominated field. Organizations like the Women in Manufacturing Association Source: [Women in Manufacturing Association: https://www.womeninmanufacturing.org/] work to change stereotypes and encourage women to pursue careers in manufacturing.

Non-Profit Sector:

- **Diverse leadership teams:** Non-profit organizations need to reflect the communities they serve. Boards and leadership teams should be actively seeking out diverse candidates.
- **Inclusive fundraising strategies:** Non-profits often rely on donations from a limited donor pool. Developing fundraising strategies that reach out to new and diverse donors is crucial for long-term sustainability.

Small Businesses:

- **Leverage technology:** Small businesses may not have the resources for large-scale DE&I initiatives. Utilizing online tools and resources for unconscious bias training and creating inclusive job postings can be a cost-effective way to make a difference.
- **Employee Resource Groups (ERGs):** Even small businesses can benefit from ERGs, which provide a space for employees from similar backgrounds to connect and support one another.

These are just a few examples, and the most effective DE&I strategies will vary depending on the specific industry and context. However, by focusing on these core principles and seeking out relevant resources, organizations of all sizes and sectors can take concrete steps towards creating a more diverse, equitable, and inclusive workplace.

Nextgen Hr Reviews

"Meghana's profound understanding of HRM and her skill in captivating trainees are qualities i have come to admire from working closely with her. Her book, with its practical approach and thoroughness, exemplifies these attributes".

Bhavya Shetty, Assistant Manager, Paysquare"

"We had a really good time at training period, Meghana's training was very informative, interactive. As an instructor, she demonstrated a clear understanding of team roles, providing clarity on our responsibilities and boundaries.... Opportunity to discuss the scenarios in our working environment. Thank you"

Arpitha, Payroll Operations, Paysquare"

Training & Development at Paysquare

“*"I attended Recruitment and Talent Acquisition training by NextGen HR. It was a helpful training course. It benefited me a lot. The explanation by Meghana was very good and beautifully articulated. Thank you".*

Sanjay Agnihotri, one of NextGen HR's trainee”

“*"I took the Talent Acquisition course by NextGen HR. The course helped me a lot in my career development".*

Rakshith, Talent Acquisition Specialist ”

“*"One of the best HR Course Academy (NextGen HR) and one of the best trainer (meghana ma'am)I have ever met,*
Firstly I would like to thank meghana ma'am, who was big supporter to me for always solving my queries, and for always encouraging me to learn more and work Hard,
You're positive attitude has really kept me going iam very grateful for your support ma'am. So far, this HR course has been very informative and the content is well organised and focused on pratical situations too, Gained knowledge from basic to advanced level of Recruitment,payroll Management, CTC, salary Negotiation, Gained knowledge about how to implement in pratical ways, I'm glad to have been taught by meghana ma'am
I would recommend if anyone would like to join HR Course please go ahead without thinking twice".

Chaitra. V., HR Associate ”

“*"I really appreciate the NextGen HR accademy who really made very easily way to understand all the about HR Generalist. It will definitely help to grow my career".*

Saroj Prasad, HR Beginner”

“*"The explanation by Meghana is too good"*

Monica Acharya, HR Professional”

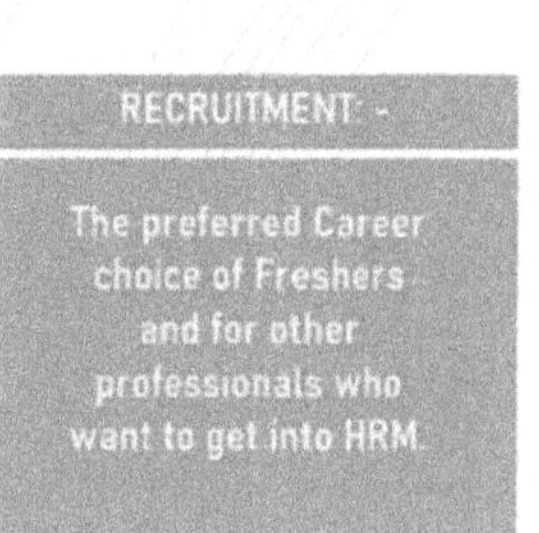

Online Training Programs by NextGen HR

“*"Thank you for putting this together, the break down in each segment made learning easier".*

Adeniyi kanyinsola, HR Associate, Nigeria”

“*"It helped me to gain knowledge and skills in payroll and compensation benefits".*

Vaishnavi Karwanje, Mumbai”

“*"Yes. Meghana did a very excellent and thought provoking job in this course"*

Elvis, Nigeria”

“*"I got it whatever I want. Well explained and it's met my expectations. Love this course".*

Sonali Joshi , Indore”

“*"Its a great course and I encourage every practioner and Manager to take this course".*

Richard Ronalds Sena Agbo, Accra, Ghana”

“*"Thanks for such a wonderful course, expecting more such courses in future. Its been really a great experience throughout the course which covered every module".*

Uday Kumar, Bangalore”

“*"Thanks for sharing knowledge and more power."*

Junex Marcha, Guisguis, Sta. Cruz, Zambales”

“*"NextGen HR best academy to learn. Exceeded my expectations."*

Anna, Cyprus”

“*"Nice course. Learnt about Salary Negotiation in detail."*

Sam Hooper, New Zealand”

“*"Hi, I have 1 Year and 9 months of experience as an HR Recruiter. This course is very useful for me for the future goal".*

Shruti Shekhar”

RECRUITMENT PROCESS

1. **Gather Manpower Requirements to Identify Vacancy.**
2. **Prepare Job Description and Job Specification**
3. **Post Job/Announce Job: Internal / External Sources**
4. **Managing the Candidate Responses**
5. **Review Applications**
6. **Initial Candidate Screening (Telephone/VC)**
7. **Personal Interview, Tests, and Decision Making.**

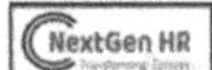

Online Training Programs

“*"That was incredibly clear and insightful! I gained so much from learning about HR fundamentals."*

Sajisha T”

“*"It was an amazing experience. Thank you for giving us immense knowledge on the topics. Your teaching is clear and I am able to understand every topic clearly".*

Esther”

“*Hi, this is the best course I've ever . You can learn all the HRM from attracting a talent till the exit of an employee in a detailed manner with clear examples".*

Niwas Jack”

“*"The course was really amazing. step by step process about employee life cycle management is well explaned. It was clear understanding about the process".*

Naveen Kumar”

“*"The course is a good match for me, it help to access ones knowledge and understanding of lessons with the aid of exercise and assignment. It is easy to understand. God bless my instructor Nextgen hr. Amazing, beyond expectation".*

Esther Seun-Jesu David”

Key Take-aways From Course

We thank you for learning with us. Congratulations, you have now completed the book. This is a time to not only celebrate your accomplishment but also to reflect on the valuable insights and knowledge you've gained.

Learning is a continuous journey. We encourage you to not stop learning. If you wish to go a step higher and learn from NextGen HR's blended learning system, do visit www.nextgenhr.co.in for complete details on our Online Certification Programs which includes most of the topics covered in this book.

Our programs are career oriented and industry-endorsed. NextGen HR has trained 15000+ working HR & payroll professionals, HRM beginners and aspirants. Many of our students have got their first job, promotion to next level and also got better job offers upon completion of our courses.

Now take a moment to reflect on these and do share with us on *nextgenhr.training@gmail.com*

Taking Stock: Your Journey of Growth with The Ultimate HR Generalist Handbook

Seeds Sown: New Learnings

1. What are the key takeaways from this course that were entirely new to you?
2. Perhaps you discovered a new concept, approach, or skill that resonated deeply.
3. Note down these "aha moments" that will shape your future endeavors.

....

Familiar Ground: Building on Existing Knowledge

1. Were there any topics in the course that you already had some familiarity with?
2. How did this course experience deepen your understanding or offer a fresh perspective on those existing ideas?
3. Reflect on how these newly acquired insights connect to your prior knowledge.

....

Blooms and Thorns: Favorite Aspects and Areas for Improvement

- What aspects of the course did you find most engaging or helpful?
- Was it the writing style, the activities, the specific topics covered?
- Pinpoint these elements that enhanced your learning experience.
- On the other hand, were there any sections that you found challenging or could be improved?
- Perhaps you craved more depth on a particular topic or a different format for presenting information. Please do share your constructive feedback to help us improvise the book.

....

Your Growth Journey

- How has this course contributed to your overall personal or professional development goals?
- Did it equip you with new tools or strategies to tackle challenges or navigate situations differently?

....

Planting the Seeds for the Future

- How do you plan to integrate the learnings from this course into your life moving forward?
- Are there specific actions you can take to put this knowledge into practice?

....

We hope to hear from you soon. Please do rate and review your book purchase as well. Thank you.

Best Regards and All the best,

Meghana B N

NextGen HR

Share your learning experience to: nextgenhr.training@gmail.com

www.ingramcontent.com/pod-product-compliance
Ingram Content Group UK Ltd.
Pitfield, Milton Keynes, MK11 3LW, UK
UKHW061132310726
14090UKWH00035B/793

9 798893 224207